브라운편입

편입영어,
이 종 현으로 통한다!

이것이 독해다

이종현 저

Part 2 복합유형 총정리

도서출판 상학당

There is only one thing that makes
a dream impossible to achieve - the fear of failure

- Paulo Coelho -

꿈을 불가능으로 만드는 데에는 단 한가지 요소가 존재한다.
실패에 대한 두려움이다.

이 종 현

(전) 평촌 학원가 학원 고3 대표강사

(현) 브라운 편입 영어 대표강사

PREFACE 머리말

학생들이 편입영어를 공부하다 보면 독해 부분에서 막힌 기분이 들 때가 많습니다. 영어 구문을 공부해도 무슨 말인지 해석을 못하고 문제를 못 푸는 경우도 허다합니다. 이 이유를 살펴보면 대부분의 경우 문제는 영어 독해력입니다. 이 책은 그런 학생들을 위해 진짜 독해력을 키우기 위한 책입니다.

영어 문장들이 모여 영어 독해 지문을 형성하게 됩니다. 그럼 이 지문들은 일정한 구조를 가지게 됩니다. 이를 글의 구조라고 합니다. 학생들이 가장 먼저 익혀야 하는 것은 바로 이러한 글의 구조입니다. 글의 구조를 알아야 다음에 어떤 내용이 나올지를 정확하게 추론하면서 독해를 할 수 있고 필요한 부분과 필요하지 않은 부분을 나누어서 글을 바라볼 수 있게 됩니다.

그리고 그 이후 학생들에게 필요한 것은 유형별 독해 풀이법입니다. 실제로 편입시험엔 여러 유형의 문제들이 출제가 됩니다. 각각의 유형들을 정확하게 풀이하기 위한 연습이 필요합니다. 모든 유형엔 접근법이라는 것이 있고 이 접근법대로 풀 수 있다면 답을 못 찍는 독해 문제는 없어질 것입니다.

모든 독해 문제의 정답은 지문 속에 있습니다. 이 책을 통해 여러분들이 문제 풀이법을 정확하게 익혀서 어떤 독해 문제를 만나도 정확하게 답을 찍고 편입에 성공하기를 소망합니다.

차례

Unit 1

순서 배열 유형

주제 문제를 풀 땐 말 그대로 핵심 논리 하나를 명확하게 잡으면 된다. 그 중에 가장 중요한 것은 결과다. 특히 첫 문장의 논리를 잡았을 때 결과 중심으로 주제를 이해하는 연습이다.

가령, 첫 문장이 "AI 때문에 인간은 발전해왔다."로 시작하는 글이면, 이걸 본 순간 우리가 해야 하는 생각은 "아 '이 글 주제는 인간이 발전할 수 있었던 이유'가 될 수 있겠구나."라는 생각을 하고 다음을 가는 것이다. 지금부터 인간이 발전하면서 생긴 결과가 뒤에 또 나오거나, 문제점 반박이 나오지 않는 이상 이 글의 결과는 바뀌지 않는다. 그러니 마지막까지 그런 포인트를 잡지 못했다면 그냥 첫 문장이 주제가 되는 것이고, 그럴 땐 선지로 가기 전에 일단 내가 잡은 결과가 선지에 써 있는 것부터 답을 찍겠다고 생각하면 된다. 그리고 답을 못 찍겠으면 원인을 중심으로 있는 선지를 찍으면 된다.

여기서 주의할 점은 인과관계 반박은 기본적으로 결과가 바뀌지 않는 글이다. 이 점을 꼭 기억하자.

● 순서 배열 유형을 푸는 방법

결국 글을 한 줄 논리로 연결해주는 것이 중요하다.

그러기 위해서 우리는 그 한 줄 논리의 중간에서 논리가 바뀌는 포인트, 즉 글이 둘로 나뉠 수 있는 포인트를 잡아내는 것이 중요하다.

예를 들어

글이 a → b → c로 전개되어 가는 것이라면

b → c가 시작되는 부분을 잡아내고, c 얘기면 이 뒤로 보내고, c 얘기가 아니면 앞으로 보내는 식으로 문제를 풀 수 있다.

그러니 제일 먼저 뭐가 올지에 대해 생각할 것이 아닌, 중간에 오는 것으로 중심을 잡고 나머지를 해결한다는 생각이 좋다.

● 기억하면 좋은 둘로 나누는 포인트

1) 인과관계의 부사가 있는 문장(Therefore, Thus, As a result, As a consequence, Hence 등)
2) 부사절 ~, 주절 ~
   분사구문 ~, 주절 ~
3) 의문문의 표현(앞 내용 요약)
4) 모든, 항상 등이 들어간 부분
5) S be more than A, S Vt more than A
   S be based on more than A 등이 들어간 부분
6) 전치사 these events/benefits 등의 표현

핵심은 한 줄 논리로 연결하는 것이다. 그러니 어설프게 어떤 것이 오는게 더 좋을지 고민하지 말고 한 줄로 연결할 수 있는 방향만 생각하자.

예시 문제

1. If we lived on a planet where nothing ever changed, there would be little to do. There would be nothing to figure out. ⓐ And if we lived in an unpredictable world, where things changed in random or very complex ways, we would not be able to figure things out. ⓑ Again, there would be no such thing as science. ⓒ But we live in an in-between universe, where things change, but according to patterns, rules, or, as we call them, laws of nature. ⓓ There would be no impetus for science. If I throw a stick up in the air, it always falls down. If the sun sets in the west, it always rises again the next morning in the east. And so it becomes possible to figure things out. We can do science, and with it we can improve our lives.

※ Which of the following is the best order?

① ⓐ - ⓒ - ⓓ - ⓑ
② ⓐ - ⓓ - ⓒ - ⓑ
③ ⓓ - ⓐ - ⓑ - ⓒ
④ ⓓ - ⓒ - ⓐ - ⓑ

2. Within the set of gestures that accompany speech, we can distinguish between those that echo the content of the spoken message and those that indicate something being referred to. Iconics are gestures that seem to be a reflection of the meaning of what is said, as when we trace a square in the air with a finger while saying, "I'm looking for a small box." By itself, an iconic gesture doesn't 'mean' the same as what is said, but it may add 'meaning., For example, a woman was moving her forearm up and down, with a closed hand, as if holding a weapon, while she was saying, "I chased the dog again." The communicated message, including the weapon, was accomplished through speech and gesture combined. Another common group of gestures can be described as deictics.

(A) In this case, the gesture and the speech combine to accomplish successful reference to something that only exists in shared memory rather than in the current physical space.

(B) The term deictic means 'pointing' and we often use gestures to point to things or people while talking.

(C) We can also use the same gesture and the same table (with a cake no longer on it) when we later say, "That cake was delicious."

(D) We can use deictics in the current context, as when we use a hand to indicate a table (with a cake on it) and ask someone, "Would you like some cake?"

※ Which is the proper order of the sentences (A) – (D)?

① (A) – (C) – (D) – (B)
② (B) – (D) – (C) – (A)
③ (C) – (A) – (D) – (B)
④ (D) – (A) – (B) – (C)

3. Choose the most logical order of the following sentences.

(A) All readers of Charlotte Perkins Gilman's work know that she tells the same stories over and over again. (B) In Gilman's fiction the use of the analogue is more than the mere repetition of particular plots or themes. (C) For example, it is especially effective when she is dealing with the relationship between the individual and the social health. (D) This feature of her writing I would like to describe as the writing of the analogue. (E) It is crucial to any understanding of the way in which she organized and expressed both her art and her ideology.

① (A) - (C) - (E) - (B) - (D)
② (A) - (C) - (D) - (E) - (B)
③ (A) - (E) - (C) - (D) - (B)
④ (A) - (D) - (B) - (E) - (C)
⑤ (A) - (D) - (E) - (B) - (C)

4. The ancient Greeks pursued mathematics and astronomy for their own sake. They did not study them out of their wish to be accountants or season predictors. Their sole desire was to gain a better understanding of the world. We read Shakespeare's Hamlet and Walt Whitman's poetry. Their lines strike us as beautiful as a comet across the sky — so much so that we are compelled to recite all the famous verses.

(A) But I find there is something praiseworthy about the Greeks. They were not ashamed to be eccentric when their curiosity demanded it. They always valued the intrinsic interest of knowledge over its material benefit. There was no practical reason for their scrutiny of mathematical knowledge, or even knowledge of how we should live. They suggest that useless knowledge is essential in making civilisation possible, by cultivating what is desirable in life.

(B) How then does the study of stars and other useless knowledge make civilisation possible? The study of stars suggests that there is something inherently elegant and wonderful in the night sky other than city lights. The splendour of the stars, whose light originated perhaps millions of years ago, confronts us with a natural work of art. Yet the study of stars doesn't only allow us to appreciate the beauty of nature, it also produces in us a contemplative habit of mind.

(C) Snap back to reality, and what use are those verses? Does remembering a beautifully-written line of Shakespeare's get us a brand new Mercedes? Does it help to highlight the ills of capitalism, or get us to the top of the social hierarchy? I'm afraid not. Knowledge, as I have been told, is merely a tool for providing us with a good career. Therefore I must bow to the necessities of practical knowledge, and neglect the arts and humanities in their uselessness.

City life is fast, and makes people nervous. The day of a businessman is dense with meetings. He seldom has the time to engage in serenity and scrutinise himself and everything that happens around him. By looking at the stars, he discovers the beauty he previously neglected. As the stars stand still and look upon him, he is in awe of their remote beauty and able to obtain the peace of mind essential for meditation. Through the study of them, the pleasure we derive from appreciating the world becomes fuller and richer. It enhances our sensitivity and purifies our soul, civilising us.

윗 글의 단락을 논리적 흐름에 맞게 순서대로 배열한 것으로 가장 적합한 것을 고르시오.

① (A) — (B) — (C)
② (A) — (C) — (B)
③ (B) — (A) — (C)
④ (C) — (A) — (B)

5. Many people have trouble starting their cars on a cold winter morning. In a cold car, the engine turns over more slowly, and it sometimes does not turn over at all. Car owners may blame their cold engines, but the real problem is a cold battery, which powers the starter motor. This motor is generally connected to its circuit by using a battery.

(A) Increasing the number of electrons moving increases the current and so increases the amount of power available to the motor.

(B) When a motor is hooked up in a circuit with a battery, electrons move through the circuit, creating a current.

(C) Likewise, decreasing the number of electrons moving will decrease the amount of power available.

① (A) – (B) – (C)	② (A) – (C) – (B)
③ (B) – (A) – (C)	④ (B) – (C) – (A)

6. A number of diseases are due to faulty genes. The goal of gene therapy is to insert the correct genes into the cells of a patient in order to remedy the disorder. Some initial treatments have been successful. However, gene therapy does have some drawbacks.

(A) For one, the treatments must be given repeatedly.
(B) Despite these obstacles, scientists believe that gene therapy offers the potential for medical treatments to be tailored for individual patients.
(C) In addition, there is a chance the body's immune system will respond negatively and reject the treatment, causing the patient to die.

More recent efforts have been successful in restoring sight to patients with retinal disease.

① (A) – (B) – (C)	② (A) – (C) – (B)
③ (B) – (C) – (A)	④ (B) – (A) – (C)

7. December is here : store fronts are festooned with holiday decorations, the cold is setting in, and another year is reaching its close. December has marked the end of the year and the beginning of winter since the ancient Romans established their first calendar. As its etymology indicates, December is formed from the Latin root decem– "ten," though December is our twelfth month.

(A) This is because the ancient Roman calendar had only ten months in the year, which began in March. Eventually January and February were added to the end of the year after December, though by the time the Julian calendar was established in 45 B.C.

(B) The strange numbering discrepancy is also present for the months of September, October, and November, which mean "seven," "eight," and "nine," even though they are our ninth, tenth, and eleventh months, respectively.

(C) January and February appeared at the beginning of the year, bumping all of the original months back by two, and leaving the names as they were originally assigned.

① [A] – [B] – [C]
② [A] – [C] – [B]
③ [B] – [A] – [C]
④ [B] – [C] – [A]
⑤ [C] – [B] – [A]

8. In a series of experimental studies with young children, feeding practices commonly employed by parents were shown to accidentally encourage behaviors counter to their intentions.

(A) In American society, high-fat and sweet food items are used almost exclusively in positive child contexts as rewards, thus further reinforcing the preference for these foods.

(B) On the other hand, if children are given both sweet and non-sweet foods as rewards for encouraged behavior, the preference for those foods is enhanced.

(C) For example, limiting access to tasty foods promotes children's preference for and intake of these "forbidden foods." Forcing or pressuring children to eat certain foods decreases the preference for those foods. Rewarding children for eating a disliked food resulted in a decline in the preference for that food.

① (A) - (C) - (B) ② (B) - (A) - (C) ③ (B) - (C) - (A)
④ (C) - (A) - (B) ⑤ (C) - (B) - (A)

9. Believing in what you desire to be true and then seeking evidence to justify it doesn't seem to be the best approach to everyday situations. For instance, if you're at the races, it is rational to bet on the horse you think is fastest, but it doesn't make sense to believe a horse is fastest because you bet on it.

(A) In both these instances, the research shows, it is the latter choice that people are likely to make. The "causal arrow" in human thought processes consistently tends to point backward, not forward.

(B) Similarly, it makes sense to choose a job you believe is appealing, but it's irrational to believe a job is appealing because you've accepted the offer.

(C) Still, even though in each case the latter approach doesn't make rational sense, it is the irrational reasoning that would probably make you happier. And the mind generally seems to work toward happiness.

① (A) - (C) - (B) ② (B) - (A) - (C) ③ (B) - (C) - (A)
④ (C) - (A) - (B) ⑤ (C) - (B) - (A)

10. Labeling people according to our first impressions is an inevitable part of the perception process. These labels are a way of making interpretations. “She seems cheerful.” “He seems sincere.” “They sound awfully conceited.”

(A) Suppose, for instance, you mention the name of your new neighbor to a friend. “Oh, I know him,” your friend replies. “He seems nice at first, but it’s all an act.” Perhaps, this appraisal is off - base.

(B) If they’re accurate, impressions like these can be useful ways of deciding how to respond best to people in the future. Problems arise, however, when the labels we attach are inaccurate, because after we form an opinion of someone, we tend to hang on to it and make any conflicting information fit our image.

(C) Whether the judgment is accurate or not, after you accept your friend’s evaluation, it will probably influence the way you respond to the neighbor. You’ll look for examples of the insincerity you’ve heard about — and you’ll probably find them.

① (A) - (C) - (B)
② (B) - (A) - (C)
③ (B) - (C) - (A)
④ (C) - (A) - (B)
⑤ (C) - (B) - (A)

11. Naturally, people eat many different kinds of meals and choose them with the intention of communicating the right message to the right audience.

(A) Equally, a meal of roast beef offered to a vegetarian might be construed as a calculated insult. As with all language, there can be miscommunication. Despite this, an outsider observing or commenting on an eating event can usually decode the intended message without too much difficulty.

(B) One would not reheat half-eaten leftovers when trying to impress a potential lover, just as one would not spend a fortune on extravagant ingredients for a hurried everyday meal eaten in solitude. Every meal has, in a sense, its own coded message.

(C) This is not to say, however, that it is always readily perceived or interpreted correctly by others. What may be intended as cozy informality to someone preparing a meal might be interpreted as laziness by an invited guest.

① (A) - (C) - (B)
② (B) - (A) - (C)
③ (B) - (C) - (A)
④ (C) - (A) - (B)
⑤ (C) - (B) - (A)

12. In Mediterranean countries, ancient shipwrecks have long been treated like any other archaeological site. Regardless of its origin, an ancient shipwreck belongs to the nation in whose territorial waters it lies.

(A) Because in the last century so many antiquities were taken from these countries to foreign museums and collections, this approach developed as a safeguard.

(B) To disturb it in any way, a foreign or national archaeologist must have the proper credentials to obtain official permission from the archaeological service of the government of that nation.

(C) Thus, there has been less treasure hunting in the Mediterranean than in many places, although illegal stealing of antiquities does occur under the Mediterranean seas as on surrounding lands.

① (A) - (C) - (B) ② (B) - (A) - (C) ③ (B) - (C) - (A)
④ (C) - (A) - (B) ⑤ (C) - (B) - (A)

13. How one behaves at any point in adulthood is strongly influenced by one's past experiences and the issues one is facing. These life-cycle factors must be taken into consideration in evaluating adults' behaviors. For instance, a middle-aged woman who chooses to go back to school might not have an adjustment disorder; she may simply want to develop a new aspect of herself.

(A) Similarly, an older man who provides vague answers to personal questions may not be resistant; he may simply be reflecting his generation's tendency not to disclose one's inner self to a stranger.

(B) Some might interpret her decision as an inability to deal with her current life situation when that is not true at all; instead, she has a rational evaluation of her life and realizes, for example, that she needs a degree to advance in her profession.

(C) Most important, the meaning of particular symptoms may change with age. For example, problems with waking up early in the morning may indicate depression in a young adult but may merely be a result of normal aging in an older adult.

① (A) - (C) - (B) ② (B) - (A) - (C) ③ (B) - (C) - (A)
④ (C) - (A) - (B) ⑤ (C) - (B) - (A)

14. In the early 1980s, when personal computers were first made available, software publishers were worried that hackers might copy what they considered to be their intellectual property (that is, the core code of their programs).

(A) This way, if the core code was stolen and adapted for another application, the undocumented feature would also be incorporated into the new program. And that would constitute proof of the theft.

(B) The practice really took off later in the 1980s when programmers were not always given official credit for their work. To prove their involvement, they'd bury a little something in the code, just to prove they were there in the beginning.

(C) It was quite simple to access the core code of a program, and the laws against it weren't all that clear at the time. So little undocumented features were added before applications were released.

① (A) - (C) - (B)
② (B) - (A) - (C)
③ (B) - (C) - (A)
④ (C) - (A) - (B)
⑤ (C) - (B) - (A)

15. It's well known that good verbal communication is the foundation of any successful relationship, be it personal or professional. It's important to recognize, though, that it's our nonverbal cues that speak the loudest when we communicate.

(A) These messages don't stop when you stop speaking either. Even when you're silent, you're still communicating nonverbally. Oftentimes, what comes out of our mouths and what we communicate through our body language are two totally different things.

(B) When we interact with others, we continuously give and receive such wordless signals. All of our nonverbal behaviors — the gestures we make, the way we sit, how fast or how loud we talk, how close we stand, how much eye contact we make — send strong messages.

(C) When faced with these mixed signals, a listener has to choose whether to believe your verbal or nonverbal message, and, in most cases, the listener is going to choose the nonverbal because it's a natural, unconscious language that broadcasts our true feelings and intentions in any given moment.

① (A) - (C) - (B)
② (B) - (A) - (C)
③ (B) - (C) - (A)
④ (C) - (A) - (B)
⑤ (C) - (B) - (A)

16. Sleep, rather than rest, and 'unconsciousness' (when the term can be used), are certainly to be found in insects.

(A) For example, at night the bee sleeps for about 6-8 hours, when it will often have 'droopy' antennae, and be fairly unresponsive to other bees bumping into it. Although most insects have very good eyes, there are no eyelids, and so we cannot tell from their eyes whether they are asleep.

(B) When the jar stops moving they settle down and are even less responsive than normal to further, gentle shaking of the jar. It is as if their sleep has become deeper in compensation for its loss.

(C) However, as antennae are just as important as eyes, and probably more so, droopy antennae certainly indicate that the animal is not in contact with reality and is not just resting. Bees, for example, can easily be deprived of sleep by keeping them in continuously moving jars, so that the insects have to fly about all the time.

① (A) - (B) - (C)
② (A) - (C) - (B)
③ (B) - (C) - (A)
④ (C) - (A) - (B)
⑤ (C) - (B) - (A)

17. An interesting question related to processing fluency in organizations concerns how organizations gauge their employees' and customers' opinions. Consider the following example.

(A) Will the vocal employee's frequent requests bias the manager's sense of how the rest of the people in the organization feel about the policy? Research by Weaver, Garcia, Schwartz, and Miller suggests the answer is yes.

(B) A manager consistently gets requests from one employee that a company policy be changed. From those requests, the manager must decide how the other people in the organization feel about the issue in question.

(C) In a series of six experiments, they demonstrated that people have a tendency to infer that a familiar opinion is a prevalent one, even if the perceived familiarity is the result of one particularly vocal group member.

① (A) - (C) - (B)
② (B) - (A) - (C)
③ (B) - (C) - (A)
④ (C) - (A) - (B)
⑤ (C) - (B) - (A)

18. One warm spring day, a tennis coach was working with a student on the art of serving the ball. While the student tossed and hit the ball over and over again, the coach directed his attention toward each part of the student's motion and swing.

(A) Yet remarkably, the coach never once checked to see where the ball landed after the student's serve. Instead, the coach focused his feedback exclusively on ways to improve each part of the student's service stroke.

(B) The coach was confident that once the student learned each of the relevant skills, the student would be able to combine them so that the ball would consistently reach the target area.

(C) The coach never criticized the student for his mistakes, but instead gave feedback after each hit about the position of the racquet, the height of the ball toss, the angle of the racquet as it hit the ball, and the student's motion during the racquet follow-through. In tennis, the ball needs to land in a service square to count as a successful hit.

① (A) - (B) - (C)
② (A) - (C) - (B)
③ (B) - (A) - (C)
④ (C) - (A) - (B)
⑤ (C) - (B) - (A)

19. In the past couple of decades, we've seen changes in tax policy, increased overseas competition, unchecked government waste, and Wall Street thievery. But when we look at the data and research, we realize that none of these are the primary driver of growing inequality.

(A) For example, in Sweden, Finland, and Germany, income inequality has actually risen more rapidly over the past twenty to thirty years than in the United States.

(B) Because these countries started with less inequality in their income distributions, they continued to be less unequal than the United States, but the underlying trend is similar worldwide across surprisingly different institutions, government policies, and cultures.

(C) Instead, the main driver is exponential, digital, and combinatorial change in the technology that underlies our economic system. This conclusion is strengthened by the fact that similar trends are visible in most advanced countries.

① (A) - (C) - (B)
② (B) - (A) - (C)
③ (B) - (C) - (A)
④ (C) - (A) - (B)
⑤ (C) - (B) - (A)

20.

(A) Anyone who has ever stayed out in the rain too long or soaked for hours in a tub knows their hands and feet can become wrinkled. Conventional wisdom suggests it is little more than the skin absorbing water.

(B) Now a paper in the journal Brain, Behavior and Evolution offers evidence that wet wrinkles serve a purpose. Similar to the tread on a tire, they improve traction. In the study, an evolutionary neurobiologist and his co-authors examined 28 fingers wrinkled by water.

(C) They found that they all had a pattern of wrinkles that split like the branches of a tree. This branching pattern allows water to drain away from the fingertips, allowing for more skin contact and better grip.

(D) But a number of questions have puzzled scientists. Why do "wet wrinkles" appear only on the hands and feet? And why are the most prominent wrinkles at the ends of the digits?

① (B) - (A) - (C) - (D)
② (C) - (B) - (D) - (A)
③ (A) - (C) - (D) - (B)
④ (A) - (D) - (B) - (C)
⑤ (D) - (C) - (B) - (A)

21. Quite frequently, we make mistakes in our observations. For example, what was your instructor wearing on the first day of class? If you have to guess, it's because most of our daily observations are casual and semiconscious.

(A) Moreover, they add a degree of precision well beyond the capacity of the unassisted human senses. Suppose, for example, that you'd taken color photographs of your instructor that day.

(B) If you'd gone to the first class with a conscious plan to observe and record what your instructor was wearing, you'd be far more likely to be accurate. In many cases, both simple and complex measurement devices help guard against inaccurate observations.

(C) In contrast to casual human inquiry, scientific observation methods like this one constitute a conscious activity. They require you to focus all of your attention on a given subject.

① (A) - (C) - (B)
② (B) - (A) - (C)
③ (B) - (C) - (A)
④ (C) - (A) - (B)
⑤ (C) - (B) - (A)

22.

(A) But we already know the dangers of assuming cause and effect — just because she ate the watermelon before recovery does not mean that it caused her recovery. Remember, too, that only survivors speak: perhaps 50 other people died of cancer after trying the 'miracle watermelon cure.'

(B) Anecdotal evidence is often the most difficult advice to resist because it is based on someone else's personal experience, which can sound extremely convincing and compelling. If your next-door neighbor recovered from cancer after a watermelon diet, that can sound very persuasive.

(C) Anecdotal reports can give an unbalanced perspective. Now, if there had been a randomized controlled trial showing that patients who ate watermelon survived twice as long, that would have been a different story.

(D) You cannot infer a general rule from a single experience — especially someone else's.

① (A) - (C) - (B) - (D)
② (D) - (B) - (A) - (C)
③ (B) - (D) - (C) - (A)
④ (C) - (A) - (D) - (B)
⑤ (C) - (B) - (A) - (D)

23. There is no doubt that mountainous areas with low valleys among them tend to have higher species richness than surrounding areas of flat land.

(A) A similar diversity of species composition with elevation is found in the Siskiyou Mountains of Oregon, and in fact on almost any set of high mountains, simply because there is a wide range of climates there.

(B) For example, in the Santa Catalina Mountains of Arizona, many different plant species occur in the same mountains but at distinct altitudes, each species at its own climatic optimum.

(C) This is partly because there are more different environments, each with its own characteristic set of species. For one thing, there are different climate zones on a mountain, but only one climate in a flat lowland area.

① (A) - (C) - (B)	② (B) - (A) - (C)	③ (B) - (C) - (A)
④ (C) - (A) - (B)	⑤ (C) - (B) - (A)	

24. With the fall of communism at the end of the 1980s, a particular view became increasingly dominant around the world : a democratic approach to government and a market approach to economics. As promoters of democracy, we are heartened by the decline of totalitarian regimes and the success of democracy.

(A) We understand the positive role that markets can play, for instance, in competition among publications or pharmaceutical companies. And like many others, we have personally benefited from a flexible and relatively laissezfaire economic system.

(B) As Winston Churchill rightly observed, democracy may be an imperfect form of government, but all the others are worse. We have no fundamental problem with the operations of the market in economic spheres.

(C) But not all spheres of life are best run on a market model. Major professional spheres — medicine, science, education, art — ought not to function in the same way as commercial enterprises do.

① (A) - (C) - (B)	② (B) - (A) - (C)	③ (B) - (C) - (A)
④ (C) - (A) - (B)	⑤ (C) - (B) - (A)	

25. Adam Smith recommended the establishment of universal public schooling, largely at government expense, so that even the poor could acquire the essential skills of reading, writing, and arithmetic.

(A) Instead, he offered a plan to make it more accessible and more practical. He suggested offering support to encourage parents to have their children educated.

(B) This suggestion went against the prevailing wisdom of the dominant classes in Britain, who feared it would discourage deference. However, Smith did not advocate making schooling compulsory.

(C) Such incentives were necessary because, as Smith knew, the spread of manufacture supported by the division of labor, by making it possible for children to be employed at income-generating tasks, led many parents to send even very young children out to work.

① (A) - (B) - (C) ② (B) - (A) - (C) ③ (B) - (C) - (A)
④ (C) - (A) - (B) ⑤ (C) - (B) - (A)

26. When you watch a theatrical production, you engage in something called the "willing suspension of disbelief." That is, your conscious mind fully understands that the events being portrayed were written by a playwright and may never have truly taken place at all.

(A) But if, on the other hand, the actors have become complacent and the action is boring, you will not be able to fully suspend your disbelief, and you will have the uncomfortable awareness of watching actors who are merely reciting memorized lines.

(B) If the actors are succeeding at their job, you may, for a time, actually believe that what is taking place before you is real and that the events and interactions you are seeing are only just now taking place for the first time.

(C) Yet you willingly suspend your disbelief of the action onstage so that you may be drawn into the production and experience the story with all of your emotions.

① (A) - (C) - (B) ② (B) - (A) - (C) ③ (B) - (C) - (A)
④ (C) - (A) - (B) ⑤ (C) - (B) - (A)

27. When an animal is injured the first thing it will do, if it is able, is get back on its feet.

(A) Just labeling this as denial misses the deeper truth. The organism, animal or human, is trying not only to look fine in order to avoid attack, but trying to be fine.

(B) Despite the fact that this action will probably cause further pain, the instinct to get up drives the animal because the alternative, taking no action to get up, invites predators who will kill and eat the defenseless one.

(C) Emotionally, we do the same thing. Often a person who has just suffered an injury or a devastating shock or loss will respond, "Fine" when asked, "How are you doing?"

① (A) - (B) - (C)	② (A) - (C) - (B)	③ (B) - (A) - (C)
④ (B) - (C) - (A)	⑤ (C) - (A) - (B)	

28. Our traditions encourage us to think of justice as an issue of equal opportunities for every individual to pursue whatever he or she desires. Equal opportunities are guaranteed by fair laws and political procedures — laws and procedures applied in the same way to all people.

(A) Thus, there could be great differences in the income given to people in different occupations in a just society so long as everyone had an equal chance of obtaining a well-paid job.

(B) But this way of thinking about justice does not in itself offer a vision of what the distribution of goods in a society would end up looking like if individuals had an equal chance to pursue their dreams.

(C) But if, as is now becoming painfully apparent, there are more qualified applicants than openings for the interesting jobs, is equal opportunity sufficient to ensure justice? What of the socially disadvantaged for whom a fair race is beyond reach since they are left well short of the starting line?

① (A) - (C) - (B)	② (B) - (A) - (C)	③ (B) - (C) - (A)
④ (C) - (A) - (B)	⑤ (C) - (B) - (A)	

29. Most medieval storytellers and illustrators were not zoologists, nor did they pretend to be.

(A) So, a fire-breathing dragon perfectly suited their needs. No reader had ever met with one, but the mere idea that such an encounter might be possible was sufficiently frightening — and there was no way to prove that it could not happen.

(B) On the other hand, writers could not exaggerate the dangers posed by familiar animals — not even especially fierce ones such as bears and wolves — simply because they were familiar and the audience was used to living with them.

(C) Their goal was either to entertain their readers or to provide them with religious and moral instruction. They knew that people love to be amazed and frightened.

① (A) - (C) - (B)　② (B) - (A) - (C)　③ (B) - (C) - (A)
④ (C) - (A) - (B)　⑤ (C) - (B) - (A)

30. According to one traditional definition, aesthetics is the branch of philosophy that deals with beauty, especially beauty in the arts. Examining the pleasing features of the Mona Lisa or a snowcapped mountain, for instance, would fall under aesthetics.

(A) This work is widely admired but not for being beautiful. So a better definition of aesthetics would be that it is the branch of philosophy that studies the ways things please people when experienced.

(B) That definition seems too narrow, however, since works of art and natural objects may attract us with features other than their beauty. Instead of evoking admiration of beauty, artists may evoke puzzlement, shock, and even disgust.

(C) Consider Picasso's Guernica, a huge (11-ft.×25.6ft.) painting in black, white, and grey that he created in response to the slaughter of Spanish civilians by German and Italian warplanes during the Spanish Civil War. Images of dying soldiers and people screaming dominate the canvas.

① (A) - (C) - (B)　② (B) - (A) - (C)　③ (B) - (C) - (A)
④ (C) - (A) - (B)　⑤ (C) - (B) - (A)

31. You want your toddler to grow up with all the smarts he was born with, don't you? In order to activate those smarts, a child must be active.

(A) In that context, I'm afraid, television simply fails to live up. Television produces an electronic environment that depresses exploration and experi-mentation. For proof of what I'm talking about, simply take up station and watch a child watch television.

(B) See the blank expression? See the listless hands? See the lack of any creative, constructive behavior? You're seeing a child wasting time, and time is all the human mind has with which to develop its gifts.

(C) The more opportunities to experiment he has, the smarter he will become. My Formula for a Smart Kid consists of what I call the "Six E's of Excellence": Expose the child to Environments and Experiences that Encourage Exploration and Experimentation.

① (A) - (B) - (C) ② (B) - (A) - (C) ③ (B) - (C) - (A)
④ (C) - (A) - (B) ⑤ (C) - (B) - (A)

32. Some people make few intentional changes in life. Sure, over time they may get fatter, gather lines, and go gray.

(A) They train for marathons, quit smoking, switch fields, write plays, take up the guitar, or learn to tango even if they never danced before in their lives. What is the difference between these two groups of people?

(B) But they wear their hair the same way, buy the same brand of shoes, eat the same breakfast, and stick to routines for no reason other than the ease of a comfortable, predictable life. Yet as both research and real life show, many others do make important changes.

(C) It's their perspective. People who change do not question whether change is possible or look for reasons they cannot change. They simply decide on a change they want and do what is necessary to accomplish it. Changing, which always stems from a firm decision, becomes job number one.

① (A) - (C) - (B) ② (B) - (A) - (C) ③ (B) - (C) - (A)
④ (C) - (A) - (B) ⑤ (C) - (B) - (A)

33.

(A) That is, the reader is the writer's "customer" and one whose business or approval is one we need to seek. The more you know about your reader, the greater the chances you will meet his or her needs and expectations.

(B) Why? You were never asked what you were seeking, how much you could spend, or if the computer would be used for business or pleasure or your child's homework assignments.

(C) In brief, the salesperson never considered or asked about your needs and preferences. Just as it would come as no surprise to learn the salesperson who was indifferent to a potential customer's needs was soon out of a job, the same holds true for writers who ignore their readers.

(D) If you walk into a store looking for a new computer and the first salesperson you meet immediately points to a group of computers and says, "Any of those are good," and then walks away, there is a good chance you will walk away, too, and with good reason.

① (A) - (C) - (D) - (B)
② (D) - (B) - (A) - (C)
③ (D) - (B) - (C) - (A)
④ (C) - (A) - (B) - (D)
⑤ (C) - (D) - (B) - (A)

34. Cultural characteristics are not only passed from parents to children, but may be passed on from any one individual to another by word of mouth or by writing.

(A) Like those infectious diseases, cultural habits such as pop music preferences and clothing fashions may spread very quickly nowadays, especially through the media of radio and television.

(B) So some cultural changes may be adopted quite quickly by a whole population. Transmission of culture is rather like transmission of an infection. Flu and colds spread very quickly, especially with the large amount of contact that people now have with each other.

(C) However, other deep-rooted cultural characteristics of races and racial subgroups are much more difficult to change. These are the cultural patterns that are so resistant to alteration that they have the appearance of being inherent.

① (A) - (C) - (B)
② (B) - (A) - (C)
③ (B) - (C) - (A)
④ (C) - (A) - (B)
⑤ (C) - (B) - (A)

35.

(A) The psychological effects of warm and cool hues seem to be used effectively by the coaches of the Notre Dame football team. The locker rooms used for half-time breaks were reportedly painted to take advantage of the emotional impact of certain hues.

(B) The home-team room was painted a bright red, which kept team members excited or even angered. The visiting-team room was painted a blue-green, which had a calming effect on the team members. The success of this application of color can be noted in the records set by Notre Dame football teams.

(C) The temperature was maintained at the same level, but the walls were painted a warm coral. The employees stopped complaining about the temperature and reported they were quite comfortable.

(D) The impact of color has been studied for decades. For example, in a factory, the temperature was maintained at 72˚F and the walls were painted a cool blue-green. The employees complained of the cold.

① (D) - (A) - (C) - (B)
② (B) - (A) - (D) - (C)
③ (B) - (C) - (A) - (D)
④ (D) - (C) - (A) - (B)
⑤ (C) - (D) - (B) - (A)

36. We've all heard the phrase "the family that plays together, stays together." The wisdom in this phrase is that social play builds ties between people that are lasting and consequential.

(A) In crying out, the danger-spotting squirrel draws attention to itself, which may well attract the predator. Scientists used to think that animals would risk their lives like this only for kin with whom they shared common genes.

(B) This wisdom holds outside the human family circle as well. For example, when one ground squirrel sees a predator in the distance, it will sound an alarm call that alerts other squirrels to run for cover. It's a risky move.

(C) New evidence suggests, however, that squirrels also sound alarm calls for former playmates, not genetically related. These squirrels developed a social resource while playing—and these buddies will put their lives on the line to save their playmates.

① (A) - (C) - (B)
② (B) - (A) - (C)
③ (B) - (C) - (A)
④ (C) - (A) - (B)
⑤ (C) - (B) - (A)

37.

(A) Avoidance training, however, doesn't always work in our favor. For instance, a child who has been repeatedly criticized for poor performance on math may learn to dodge difficult math problems in order to avoid further punishment.

(B) Unfortunately, because of this avoidance, the child fails to develop his math skills and therefore improve the capabilities he has, and so a vicious cycle has set in. The avoidance must be unlearned through some positive experiences with math in order for this cycle to be broken.

(C) Psychologists call this avoidance training because the person is learning to avoid the possibility of a punishing consequence. Avoidance training is responsible for many everyday behaviors. It has taught you to carry an umbrella when it looks like rain to avoid the punishment of getting wet, and to keep your hand away from a hot iron to avoid the punishment of a burn.

(D) Sometimes, after punishment has been administered a few times, it needn't be continued, because the mere threat of punishment is enough to induce the desired behavior.

① (A) - (C) - (B) - (D)
② (B) - (A) - (D) - (C)
③ (B) - (D) - (C) - (A)
④ (D) - (C) - (A) - (B)
⑤ (C) - (B) - (A) - (D)

38.

(A) Studies suggest that you would not. In fact, people are more attracted to individuals who are consistently negative than to people who initially behave positively and then switch to negative behavior.

(B) The reason is this: people who start out being nice get our hopes up, so the letdown we experience when we discover that they are not nice makes it worse than if they had acted badly from the start.

(C) This effect reflects what happens to attraction when a person's behavior moves from positive to negative or from negative to positive. For example, if someone seemed very nice to you early in the interaction, but then began to act like a fool, would you be more attracted to that person than if that person were a fool from the start?

(D) The timing of positive versus negative behavior seems to influence attraction. Several studies have identified what has been called the loss-gain effect.

① (A) - (C) - (D) - (B)
② (B) - (A) - (C) - (D)
③ (D) - (B) - (C) - (A)
④ (D) - (C) - (A) - (B)
⑤ (C) - (D) - (B) - (A)

39. Food plays a large part in how much you enjoy the outdoors. The possibilities are endless, so you can constantly vary your diet.

(A) They walk only a few miles each day and may use the same campsite for several nights. Survival eaters eat some dry cereal for breakfast, and are up and walking within minutes of waking.

(B) Wilderness dining has two extremes: gourmet eaters and survival eaters. The first like to make camp at lunchtime so they have several hours to set up field ovens; they bake cakes and bread and cook multi-course dinners.

(C) They walk dozens of miles every day; lunch is a series of cold snacks eaten on the move. Dinner consists of a freeze-dried meal, "cooked" by pouring hot water into the package.

① (A) - (C) - (B)
② (B) - (A) - (C)
③ (B) - (C) - (A)
④ (C) - (A) - (B)
⑤ (C) - (B) - (A)

40. Since group performance in problem solving is superior to even the individual work of the most expert group members, it should not be surprising that students learn better when they cooperate. However, there is one issue that needs further consideration.

(A) In addition to that benefit, helping lower-ability students often pulls higher-ability students to a more sophisticated understanding of the material. The cliche that teachers learn as much as their pupils is certainly true.

(B) Not quite. Knowledge, happily, is not a zero-sum product. Higher-ability students can reinforce their own knowledge by teaching those with lower ability.

(C) Specifically, the technique of having students help one another raises the question of whether students with lower ability are being helped at the expense of those with higher ability. Is this true?

① (A) - (C) - (B)
② (B) - (A) - (C)
③ (B) - (C) - (A)
④ (C) - (A) - (B)
⑤ (C) - (B) - (A)

41. Mom and Dad went to dinner at a nice restaurant. On that first night to myself, Dad entrusted me with his movie projector and all the reels of film.

(A) Then I can play the film backward and watch the cat fly down to the floor and see all the splashes of ice cream slurp themselves back into the dish. I made Simon jump in and out several times before I watched the rest of the film.

(B) He said I could do everything myself that night. So I set up the screen at one end of the living room. I turned on the projector, turned off the light, put the bowl of popcorn in my lap, and settled in to watch the film labeled HATTIE-1951.

(C) It's one of my favorites because my third birthday party is on it and I can watch our old cat Simon jump up on the dining room table and land in a dish of ice cream.

① (A) - (C) - (B)
② (B) - (A) - (C)
③ (B) - (C) - (A)
④ (C) - (A) - (B)
⑤ (C) - (B) - (A)

42. Most of the words we use and the meanings we think about are a combination of simpler ideas.

(A) Some of them are specialized for sitting at certain high places, like bar stools. If you learned about a culture in which a certain type of chair was used only for the purpose of sitting while waiting for a bus, you might think this is odd but would have no difficulty understanding it.

(B) Consider a chair. Before you can have an idea of a chair, you need to understand that there exist in the world certain functional objects. Some of these objects support human activity, in this case, sitting.

(C) The combination of the concepts chair and waiting for bus allows you to create the new complex concept chair used while waiting for bus. But the basic concept of chair is built out of the simpler ideas that we take for granted: object, furniture, sitting.

① (A) - (C) - (B)
② (B) - (A) - (C)
③ (B) - (C) - (A)
④ (C) - (A) - (B)
⑤ (C) - (B) - (A)

43. A former resident of Canton, Ohio, was trying to describe her image of the city to her classmates. She found they had no image of this mid-sized city. She described Canton as a city with major manufacturing facilities and a downtown revitalization program.

(A) That fact suddenly crystallized the concept of Canton. If Canton is destroyed, the nation might fall. That's an image that gave meaning and fullness to what it meant to live in Canton.

(B) Her explanation moved the city from the position of no image to that of a negative image. The class concluded that Canton is a typical, boring, industrialized city.

(C) Then she suddenly recalled an experience: "I remember hearing from a teacher that during World War II Canton was a major U.S. target of the Germans." Imagine, right after the cities of Chicago, New York, and Los Angeles, appears the name of Canton.

① (A) - (C) - (B)
② (B) - (A) - (C)
③ (B) - (C) - (A)
④ (C) - (A) - (B)
⑤ (C) - (B) - (A)

Unit 2

문장 삽입 유형

문장 삽입 유형을 푸는 방법

1. 제시문의 논리를 잡아내는 것이 중요하다. 그리고 우리는 제시문을 대할 때, 제시문부터 새로운 논리가 시작되는 부분일 수 있다고 생각하면 된다. 왜냐하면 제시문으로 나왔다는 것부터가 이 문장이 빠지면 지문의 연결이 어색해지기 때문일 것이기 때문이다.

   보통 제시문에 있는 결과가 제시문에서 시작하게 된다. 그러니 제시문의 결과를 보고 아 여기부터 이 결과에 대한 얘기가 시작될 수 있겠다는 생각을 하면 된다.

2. 이제 지문으로 들어가서 각 선지 다음 문장들을 보며 내가 생각한 결과가 처음 나오는 부분을 찾는다. 만약 처음 그 결과가 나오는 문장이 있다면 그 앞에 있는 선지에 답을 찍으면 되는 것이 가장 기본적인 문장 삽입을 푸는 방법이다. 이를 새로운 소재가 시작되는 점이라고 한다.

3. 만약 이렇게 되지 않는다면, 제시문이 어떤 논리가 끝나는 점이라고 보면 된다. 첫 문장의 논리가 시작하고, 중간에 한 줄로 논리를 요약한 후 다음 논리로 진행될 때가 있는데, 바로 제시문이 그 역할을 하는 것이다. 따라서 시작점으로 안된다면 끝점이라고 생각하고 답을 찍으면 된다.

4. 이 두 방식의 핵심은 어떤 선지로 답을 찍든, 선지를 기준으로 선지 앞 문장과 선지 뒷 문장은 논리가 달라야 한다는 것이다. 끝점이 되었든 시작점이 되었든 정답 선지를 기준으로 문장 안의 논리는 달라질 것이다. 따라서 이 부분에 답을 찍겠다고 생각하고 있으면 된다.

5. 만약 판단이 잘 안된다면 선지들 중 선지 바로 다음 문장에 연결사가 있는 선지, 그리고 바로 다음 문장에 지시사/대명사가 있는 선지를 골라주면 된다. 시작점이라고 생각한다면 여기가 답이 될 확률이 아주 높은 것은 분명하다.

예시 문제

1. 글의 흐름으로 보아, 주어진 문장이 들어가기에 가장 적절한 곳은?

In the 11th century, the Chinese government began issuing these receipts which became the world's first paper money.

Coins were very convenient to use, but they were heavy. (①) In 10th century China, iron coins had square holes in the middle, and string was used to tie them together in heavy bundles of one hundred. (②) People began leaving these bundles with merchants in exchange for receipts. (③) The receipts could be used over time to purchase goods from the merchants. (④) The money would be worthless if the government did not guarantee its value. (⑤) Paper currency has no value if the people do not have confidence in its worth.

2. Choose the best place for the sentence given in the box.

Michelangelo attended dissections to perfect his understanding of surface form, while Leonardo opened the body to see and discover for himself our physical mechanisms.

Artists are thought to have begun drawing from the nude during the Italian Renaissance. In this period, the junior workshop apprentices posed as part of their duties. Drawings were usually made from the male nude to avoid offending the church. (①) Look closely at Renaissance drawings of the female body and you will see that most are actually young men with minor adjustments. (②) During this time, artists also tried to define ideal proportions in the body; Leonardo drew a man within a circle and square, while Durer took his research further —— he sought perfection in the infinitesimal measurement of the body and produced four volumes of illustrated explanation. (③) Renaissance artists studying anatomy from dissection were decades ahead of their medical counterparts. (④) Leonardo even believed he had located the soul in the pituitary fossa beneath the brain and behind the eyes, giving physical foundation to the theory that the eyes are the windows of the soul.

3. 아래의 문장이 들어갈 위치로 가장 적합한 곳을 고르시오.

The two types of memory entail different biological processes.

In the late 1890s two German psychologists, Georg Miiller and Alfons Pilzecker, found out that it takes an hour or so for memories to become fixed, or “consolidated”, in the brain. Subsequent studies confirmed the existence of short-term and long-term forms of memory and provided further evidence of the importance of the consolidation phase during which the former are turned into the latter. In the 1960s, University of Pennsylvania neurologist Louis Flexner made a particularly intriguing discovery. After injecting mice with an antibiotic drug that prevented their cells from producing proteins, he found that the animals were unable to form long-term memories but could continue to store short-term ones. The implication was clear: long-term memories are not just stronger forms of short-term memories. ⓐ Storing long-term memories requires the synthesis of new proteins. Storing short-term memories does not. More recent research turned to the issue of the physical workings of both short-term and long-term memory. ⓑ The results demonstrated that the more times an experience is repeated, the longer the memory of the experience lasts. Repetition encourages consolidation. Particularly, when researchers examined the physiological effects of repetition on neuronal signals, they discovered something amazing. ⓒ Not only did the concentration of neurotransmitters in synapses change, altering the strength of the existing connections between neurons, but the neurons grew entirely new synaptic terminals. The formation of long-term memories, in other words, involves not only biochemical changes but anatomical ones. ⓓ That explains why memory consolidation requires new proteins. Proteins play an essential role in producing structural changes in cells.

① ⓐ
② ⓑ
③ ⓒ
④ ⓓ

4. 아래의 문장이 들어갈 위치로 가장 적합한 곳을 고르시오.

Or encourage him to entertain an even more forgiving listener.

To truly enjoy reading, it needs to become second nature. ⓐ "Children should read both silently and aloud," says Judy Cheatham. ⓑ That's where a child's fluency — the ability to read smoothly and expressively — comes in, says Dr. Cheatham. ⓒ Since kids gain fluency by practicing familiar text, don't worry if your child chooses the same book over and over again. ⓓ If your kid is anxious about reading aloud to you, let him read to himself or into a recording device and then play it back for himself or a younger sibling. ⓔ A study from the University of California, Davis showed that second-graders who read aloud to the family dog improved reading skills by 12 percent over ten weeks.

① ⓐ
② ⓑ
③ ⓒ
④ ⓓ
⑤ ⓔ

5. 아래의 문장이 들어갈 위치로 가장 적합한 곳을 고르시오.

And yet, though much changed, Old English did in fact survive.

It was the invasion of the Norman French that changed everything. The defeat of King Harold at the Battle of Hastings in 1066 resulted in the installation of a dynasty of French kings on the throne in London (the first, the Hastings victor William I, actually spending very little time in England). ⓐ And for the next 300 years the French held sway over almost all areas of English power, governance, and culture. ⓑ Norman French became the language of England's administration and in time settled as the country's politer forms of intercourse. ⓒ Old English came briefly to be despised, regarded haughtily as the language of the peasant and the pleb. ⓓ After a century-and-a-half of linguistic mystery when no one is certain quite what happened to the language, Old English miraculously lived on, transmuted itself into what is now called Middle English, adopted thousands of new loanwords from the French and became stronger by doing so. ⓔ Finally it emerged, fully established, to be displayed to greatest advantage for all time in the writings of that most impressive of the early figures of English literature, Geoffrey Chaucer.

① ⓐ
② ⓑ
③ ⓒ
④ ⓓ
⑤ ⓔ

6. 아래의 문장이 들어갈 위치로 가장 적합한 곳을 고르시오.

Instead, Athena persuades them to join the city, giving them a place of honor beneath the earth, in recognition of their importance for those same legal institutions and the future health of the city.

At the end of Aeschylus' Oresteia, two transformations take place in the archaic world of the characters. In the famous transformation, Athena introduces legal institutions to replace and terminate the seemingly endless cycle of blood vengeance. ⓐ Setting up a court with established procedures of reasoned argument and the weighing of evidence, an independent third-party judge, and a jury selected from the citizen body of Athens, she announces that blood guilt will now be settled by law, rather than by the Furies, ancient goddesses of revenge. ⓑ But the Furies are not simply dismissed. ⓒ Typically this move of Athena's is understood to be a recognition that the legal system must incorporate the dark vindictive passions and honor them. ⓓ Thus the great Hellenist Hugh Lloyd-Jones concludes, "Far from wishing to abolish the prerogatives of the Erinyes, Athena is anxious to conserve them."

① ⓐ
② ⓑ
③ ⓒ
④ ⓓ

7. 아래의 문장이 들어갈 위치로 가장 적합한 곳을 고르시오.

But again, that belief was not supported by the data in the study.

There is a common belief that many Americans get fat because they eat too many carbohydrates. ⓐ The idea is that a high-carbohydrate, low-fat diet leads to weight gain, higher insulin and blood glucose levels, and more diabetes, even if the calories are the same as in a higher-fat diet. That did not happen in the study. Others have said the opposite: that low-fat diets enable people to lose weight naturally. ⓑ As for heart disease risk factors, the only one affected was LDL cholesterol, which increases heart disease risk. ⓒ The levels were slightly higher in women eating the higher-fat diet, but not high enough to make a noticeable difference in their risk of heart disease. ⓓ Although all the study participants were women, the results should also apply to men.

① ⓐ
② ⓑ
③ ⓒ
④ ⓓ

8. **Choose the most appropriate position for the following sentence in the passage below.**

However, though the science and methodology of meteorological methods have improved, there are still large gaps in the understanding of atmospheric and weather-related activity.

Modern forecasting methods are fairly accurate when it comes to short-range predications, but the longer the forecast, the more chances there are that the forecasts are going to be incorrect. ⓐ The current metho d of mathematically calculating weather conditions confine s accurate predictions to about five days in advance due to the chaotic nature of the weather. ⓑ Meteorologists combine the results of the computational data collection methods with the actual atmospheric conditions occurring in th e present. ⓒ Current information concerning the temperature, dew point, and winds at various levels is gathered throughout the day all around the world to provide clues that are compared to computer models based on past conditions to come up with probable weather patterns. ⓓ As a result, an experienced meteorologist who has seen a great variety of weather conditions and is knowledgeable about the changes and shifts that they are likely to make stands nearly as good of a chance at accurately predicting future weather conditions as a computer-generated model does.

① ⓐ
② ⓑ
③ ⓒ
④ ⓓ

9. 글의 흐름으로 보아 주어진 문장이 들어가기에 가장 적절한 곳은?

보기

Recordings at theaters around the world show that the pattern transcends different cultural habits and that different crowds all follow one universal curve showing how the sound rises over several seconds.

When the curtain closes at any stage theater, the audience bursts into applause. (①) It's usually a few clappers who hesitantly start on their own, and then others join in. (②) Applause is a funny thing in which each person tries to give credit to the performers, but also tries to blend into the crowd; you don't want to clap before everyone else, or to go on after others have stopped. (③) In fact, if you study it, you'll discover there is a pronounced pattern in the way an audience goes from silence to full volume of applause. (④) Even more remarkably, this curve is absolutely identical to a curve known from physics that describes how a group of atoms or molecules collectively go from one kind of behavior to another, rapidly and abruptly, because what one does depends very strongly on what others nearby do.

10. 주어진 문장이 들어갈 위치로 가장 적절한 것은?

보기

On the front pages were large black-and-white photographs of the death and destruction in Guernica.

One sunny morning in 1937, the small village of Guernica in northern Spain was crowded with people enjoying market day. (①) Suddenly, something terrible happened. German military planes appeared overhead, dropping bombs on the village below. Many people and animals were instantly injured or killed. The democratically elected government of Spain was fighting in a civil war against a military leader named Francisco Franco. (②) It was Franco who had asked Germany to bomb Guernica. At that time, Pablo Picasso, a well-known artist from Spain, was living in Paris. A few days after the attack, Picasso saw the newspapers. (③) The sufferings of these people from his country affected Picasso deeply. Picasso became a political activist for Spain during the Spanish Civil War. He decided to create a painting about the bombing of Guernica to exhibit at the World's Fair in Paris that year. (④) He knew that many people would come to the fair. He hoped the painting would make visitors think, talk, and be inspired to do something to help Spain.

11. 주어진 문장이 들어갈 위치로 가장 적절한 곳은?

보 기

He dismally fails the first two, but redeems himself in the concluding whale episode, where he does indeed demonstrate courage, honesty, and unselfishness.

Disney's work draws heavily from fairy tales, myths, and folklore, which are profuse in archetypal elements. (①) Pinocchio is a good example of how these elements can be emphasized rather than submerged beneath a surface realism. (②) Early in the film, the boy/puppet Pinocchio is told that in order to be a "real boy," he must show that he is "brave, truthful, and unselfish." (③) The three principal episodes of the movie represent ritualistic trials, testing the youth's moral fortitude. (④) As such, like most of Disney's works, the values in Pinocchio are traditional and conservative, an affirmation of the sanctity of the family unit, the importance of a Higher Power in guiding our destinies, and the need to play by society's rules.

12. 글의 흐름으로 보아, 주어진 문장이 들어가기에 가장 적절한 곳은?

보 기

However, elevated levels and/or long term exposure to air pollution can lead to more serious symptoms and conditions affecting human health.

A variety of air pollutants have known or suspected harmful effects on human health and the environment. In most areas of Europe, these pollutants are principally the products of combustion from space heating, power generation or from motor vehicle traffic. (①) Pollutants from these sources may not only prove a problem in the immediate vicinity of these sources but can travel long distances. (②) Generally if you are young and in a good state of health, moderate air pollution levels are unlikely to have any serious short term effects. (③) This mainly affects the respiratory and inflammatory systems, but can also lead to more serious conditions such as heart disease and cancer. (④) People with lung or heart conditions may be more susceptible to the effects of air pollution.

13. 주어진 문장이 들어갈 위치로 가장 적절한 곳은?

보 기

Teaching is also one of the few jobs where you can say you are making a significant and positive impact on the world around you.

The rewards that come from teaching are numerous. (①) One of those is the emotional connections you make with your students. (②) You are constantly engaging with them on a personal level, inspiring them to strive to do the best they can and providing support when they run into problems. (③) Watching them grow from the experience and ultimately seeing them succeed because of your tuition and guidance is a feeling without comparison. (④) While other jobs may leave a more obvious mark, few can say that over the course of their career they have helped countless young people fulfill their potential and become the adults they are today.

14. 다음 문장이 들어갈 위치로 가장 적절한 것은?

보 기

We can in consequence establish relations with almost all sorts of them.

Reptiles and fish may no doubt be found in swarms and shoals; they have been hatched in quantities and similar conditions have kept them together. In the case of social and gregarious mammals, the association arises not simply from a community of external forces but is sustained by an inner impulse. They are not merely like one another and so found in the same places at the same times; they like one another and so they keep together. This difference between the reptile world and the world of our human minds is one our sympathies seem unable to pass. (①) We cannot conceive in ourselves the swift uncomplicated urgency of a reptile's instinctive motives, its appetites, fears and hates. (②) We cannot understand them in their simplicity because all our motives are complicated; ours are balances and resultants and not simply urgencies. (③) But the mammals and birds have self-restraint and consideration for other individuals, a social appeal, a self-control that is, at its lower level, after our own fashion. (④) When they suffer they utter cries and make movements that rouse our feelings. We can make pets of them with a mutual recognition. They can be tamed to self- restraint towards us, domesticated and taught.

15. 다음 주어진 문장이 들어가기에 가장 적절한 곳은?

보기

If the numbers continue to rise at the same rates, tobacco and a number of smoking-related diseases will be the world's biggest killer in just 15 years.

According to the World Health Organization(WHO), the world's biggest killer in 2030 will be something that is preventable, but voluntary. (①) Today, the WHO says that tobacco is the second major cause of death in the world, responsible for killing one in ten adults world wide. (②) Developing countries are the most susceptible because eighty-four percent of all smokers currently live in middle to low income countries, where tobacco use has been increasing since 1970. (③) Though many governments have taken measures to ban public smoking and educate young potential smokers of health hazards, until tobacco products are entirely prohibited, it will ultimately be up to the individual to choose to take the risk or not. (④)

16. 다음 보기 안의 문장이 들어가기 가장 적절한 곳은?

> **보 기**
>
> Yet even in families, the mother and children may feel their home to be backstage when Father is not home, and onstage when he is.

Report-talk, or what I am calling public speaking, does not arise only in the literally public situation of formal speeches delivered to a listening audience. The more people there are in a conversation, the less well you know them, and the more status differences among them, the more a conversation is like public speaking or report-talk. (①) The fewer the people, the more intimately you know them, and the more equal their status, the more it is like private speaking or rapport-talk. (②) Furthermore, women feel a situation is more public —— in the sense that they have to be on good behavior —— if there are men present, except perhaps for family members. (③) Many children are instructed to be on good behavior when Daddy is home. (④) This may be because he is not home often, or because Mother — or Father —— doesn't want the children to disturb him when he is.

17. 글의 흐름으로 보아 주어진 문장이 들어가기에 가장 적절한 곳은?

보 기

He might instead reply by saying, "it is clear that the questioner has not read the works of Nietzsche carefully."

One might think that intelligent, articulate individuals would feel no need to insult other people, but they do. (①) They disguise this need by carefully couching the language they use in their insults. (②) Suppose, for example, that after a man presents a paper on the works of Nietzsche at an academic conference, someone in the audience asks a question that reveals what looks like a critical flaw in the presenter's argument. (③) In this case, the presenter is unlikely to call the questioner a big dummy. (④) The academics in the audience will immediately recognize that the speaker has just called the questioner a big dummy but has done so with style and elegance.

18. 다음 주어진 문장이 들어갈 위치로 가장 적절한 곳은?

보 기

However, if they are too lenient, they can have major discipline problems.

Creating an environment in which students feel accepted, secure, and free to explore is crucial to learning, but classroom discipline issues also need to be addressed. The teacher needs to create clear boundaries for permissible behavior, while maintaining a relaxed, open environment for learning to take place. (①) Teachers with easy-going personalities are often good at creating a positive learning environment. (②) Young students are always testing to see how much they can get away with, and a teacher trying too hard to be friendly and accommodating will soon find the class completely out of control. (③) Teachers with strict personalities and teaching styles usually have better classroom discipline, but going too far with rules can have negative effects. (④) When students make mistakes, overly strict responses following the letter of the law may create a tense atmosphere which inhibits participation, especially if the teacher embarrasses the student in front of his or her peers.

19. 다음 주어진 문장이 들어갈 위치로 가장 적절한 것은?

보 기

But sometimes, MacNeill says, you have to help customers along because they do not always voice their complaints directly to the company.

Better understanding of customer needs can lead to increased sales and a larger market share. (①) Chris Craft's Vice President and General Manager, Bob MacNeill, is a believer. (②) He has had first-hand experience watching his company improve its products by listening to customer complaints. (③) Some boat owners report that they do not express dissatisfaction because they are not sure what to ask for, or they fear being perceived as a nuisance by the boat dealer. (④) Other boat owners lack confidence in the dealers' knowledge about the boats they sell or think that everyone has these problems. (⑤) So Bob MacNeill encourages his dealers to go out and interact with boat owners when they are on their boats to actively ask for complaints.

20. 다음 주어진 문장이 들어갈 위치로 가장 적절한 것은?

보 기

For example, there is the myth that older consumers are fixed on certain products and are unwilling to try new alternative products.

It is estimated that people age fifty and older spend about 48 percent of consumer dollars. (①) They buy about 48 percent of all luxury cars, and they are responsible for about 80 percent of luxury travel. (②) They even buy about 25 percent of all toys annually (there are about fifty-five million grandparents age fifty years and older in the United States). (③) Nevertheless, marketing and merchandising programs commonly treat these customers as if they are much older. (④) Therefore, why should advertising of a new product be directed at older consumers? (⑤) In fact, a survey of five hundred people over age fifty in shopping malls revealed that about 80 percent of them were quite willing to try new products.

21. 다음 주어진 문장이 들어갈 위치로 가장 적절한 것은?

보 기

It often requires great cleverness to conceive of measures that tap into what people are thinking without altering their thinking, called reactivity.

Researchers in psychology follow the scientific method to perform studies that help explain and may predict human behavior. (①) This is a much more challenging task than studying snails or sound waves. (②) It often requires compromises, such as testing behavior within laboratories rather than natural settings, and asking those readily available (such as introduction to psychology students) to participate rather than collecting data from a true cross-section of the population. (③) Simply knowing they are being observed may cause people to behave differently (such as more politely!). (④) People may give answers that they feel are more socially desirable than their true feelings. (⑤) But for all of these difficulties for psychology, the payoff of the scientific method is that the findings are replicable; that is, if you run the same study again following the same procedures, you will be very likely to get the same results.

22. 다음 주어진 문장이 들어갈 위치로 가장 적절한 것은?

보 기

The major shortcoming of the traditional dictionary is that there is limited space available to give only a sampling of how words are used.

Our 21st century technologies, such as the World Wide Web, have profound implications for the way we define the words in our language. (①) In pre-Internet times, the hard copy dictionary always served as the final authority for what a word means and how it is used. (②) The authors of dictionaries (lexicographers) traditionally have arrived at their definitions by carefully analyzing as many examples as possible of how a particular word is used. (③) While some complex words found in any standard desk dictionary can have as many as nine or ten possible uses, even these definitions fail to cover all possible usages. (④) According to lexicographer Erin McKean, a recent study showed that in a set of randomly chosen passages from modern fiction, 13 percent of the nouns, verbs, and adjectives were used in ways not found in large desk dictionaries. (⑤) There are, in other words, many more contemporary usages that never make it into a standard dictionary because of the limitations of physical space.

23. 다음 주어진 문장이 들어갈 위치로 가장 적절한 것은?

보기

Somehow, the students in the room were liberated from the moral constraints of behaving honestly.

Students at the University of North Carolina participated in an experiment some years ago. The students had five minutes to complete as many of twenty maths problems as they could. (①) Each of the students completed the experiment in the same small room, but the room was brightly lit with twelve lightbulbs for some of them, and more dimly lit with only four bulbs for others. (②) After five minutes had elapsed, the students told the experimenter how many problems they had answered correctly. (③) Students in the bright room were reasonably honest, reporting that they felt they were being watched in the room. (④) Meanwhile, those in the dimly lit room inflated their scores by roughly 50 percent, reporting that they felt their identity was not revealed in the room. (⑤) The researchers attributed the result to the illusion that the darkness preserved their anonymity.

24. 다음 주어진 문장이 들어갈 위치로 가장 적절한 것은?

> **보기**
>
> It describes in fascinating detail the vaporization at the impact point, the earthquakes, the fires, and the debris that caused a worldwide period of intense heat followed by darkness and freezing temperatures.

Trade books can provide the space to bring a subject to life with interesting observations and details, presenting the reader with a richer understanding of the topic. (①) Because textbooks must cover such a large number of topics, they are unable to develop a single idea with any depth. (②) Therefore, textbooks offer a broad and consequently shallower view of subjects that does not allow for the kind of compelling presentation available in trade books. (③) For example, one passage in the textbook simply mentions that asteroids can hit the Earth. (④) The trade book, however, chronicles the event of an asteroid's entry into atmosphere, its collision with the planet, and the blasting of a crater 25 miles deep and 100 miles across. (⑤) It is difficult to provide readers this kind of detail and insight in the limited space allowed by a textbook.

25. 다음 주어진 문장이 들어갈 위치로 가장 적절한 것은?

보 기

However, not all people's moral values, achievement motivation or communication styles are the same.

One aspect of diversity in psychology lies in the wide range of people that psychologists study and serve. This change is significant because most psychologists once assumed that all people were very much alike and that whatever principles emerged from research or treatment efforts with one group would apply to everyone, everywhere. (①) They were partly right, because people around the world are alike in many ways. (②) They tend to live in groups, have religious beliefs and create rules, music, dances and games. (③) The principles of nerve cell activity or reactions to heat or a sour taste are the same in men and women everywhere, as is their recognition of a smile. (④) These and many other aspects of behaviour and mental processes are affected by sociocultural factors, including people's gender, ethnicity, social class and the culture in which they grow up. (⑤) These variables create many significant differences in behaviour and mental processes, especially from one culture to another.

26. 다음 주어진 문장이 들어갈 위치로 가장 적절한 것은?

보기

This degree of similarity is so close that some scientists have proposed it might be possible to perform crossbreeding and make a hybrid species.

Evolution is much like a big highway that species travel down. Changes in direction are fairly gradual, since too sharp a turn will cause the quickly traveling vehicles (or evolving species) to fly off the road into extinction. (①) At the biological level, this idea of a highway shows up in the form of continuous slow change, with a lot of similarity between various animal species, especially at the genetic level. (②) It might be surprising, or even disturbing, for some people to learn that recent findings in modern biochemistry suggest that humans are not so genetically unique as we might have thought. (③) DNA analysis suggests that at the molecular and genetic levels, humans and chimpanzees are at least 98 percent identical. (④) Of course, presumably moral and ethical considerations would forbid such a genetic experiment, but this possibility does illustrate how similar human beings are to other primates. (⑤) Even an animal as apparently distant from humans as our pet dog is still quite similar to us.

27. 다음 주어진 문장이 들어갈 위치로 가장 적절한 것은?

보 기

The problem with this solution is that the benefits of using these sites are also lost.

There are a number of ways in which technology can be used to protect social network users from disclosure or privacy threats or violations. (①) More drastic technical solutions involve disabling or banning social media/social networking. (②) For example, some schools and workplaces place explicit restrictions or in some cases a complete ban on social networking sites and they are disabled at the IT level so that students or employees cannot access these sites. (③) Additionally, while this may prevent use of these sites during school or work hours, it has no impact on what is done after hours. (④) The context collapse that occurs in an online environment blurs the line between people's professional and personal lives such that online information exchanges that occur outside of school or work hours impact people's lives at school or work. (⑤) Therefore, employing these strategies is not necessarily effective in minimizing the potential risks overall.

28. 다음 주어진 문장이 들어갈 위치로 가장 적절한 것은?

보 기

There was also a gender division of labor within the hunter-gatherer culture.

As the hominid groups progressed through time, so did the development of the hunter-gatherer culture. At first glance, this culture appears to be very simple, but it was and still is quite complex; there are still groups of indigenous people across the globe that continue with this way of life. First and foremost, it was based on the simple family unit, which expanded into ties of kinship between families. (①) Those ties of kinship eventually combined to create larger connected groups called clans. (②) Clans became interconnected and developed into tribes. (③) The tribes existed through hunting and gathering and in the process created a sophisticated social and political organization that included political leaders (the chief) and religious figures (the priest). (④) Males dominated hunting, war, and heavy labor because of their natural upper-body strength. (⑤) Women became the gatherers and preparers of food, and also tended to the children of the tribe.

29. 다음 주어진 문장이 들어갈 위치로 가장 적절한 것은?

보 기

Communication problems help to explain why the empires of early modern Europe, Russia excepted, were seaborne empires.

Communication by sea was usually swifter than communication over land. (①) In Mexico, for example, the Spaniards had to construct what they called 'royal roads', like the famous 'silver road' from the mines in Zacatecas to Mexico City. (②) The names of these roads survive in modern California and New Mexico. (③) In Eastern Europe, where the population was less dense and cities smaller and fewer than in the West, communication was correspondingly slower. (④) In the Russian Empire in the age of Catherine the Great, for example, it might take 18 months for an imperial order sent from St. Petersburg to reach Kamchatka in Siberia, and another 18 months for the reply to be received in the capital. (⑤) They included the Portuguese, Spanish, Dutch, French and British intercontinental empires, and also the Swedish Empire in Europe, constructed around the Baltic Sea.

30. 다음 주어진 문장이 들어갈 위치로 가장 적절한 것은?

보기

This approach forces us to examine the interconnections between local economic, social, and environmental goals.

There is a growing interest in promoting social, economic, and environmental sustainability at the local level. (①) This concept is taken from the environmental literature but has much broader meaning in the context of community development. (②) Efforts to promote community sustainability focus on local policies that contribute to the long-term survival of the social, economic, and environmental base of the locality. (③) Sustainability is often considered an outcome of community development, but we view it as a guiding principle throughout the process of community development practice. (④) This interaction is often referred to as the triple bottom line. (⑤) Practices that promote economic development, for example, need to ensure the sustainability of the environment and provide opportunities for marginalized residents in the community.

31. 다음 주어진 문장이 들어갈 위치로 가장 적절한 것은?

보 기

According to the above, a season-to-season or year-to-year effect, such as extremely wet or extremely dry conditions, can be described as a climatic variation if it is within the expected variations of the normal climate.

Climate is the total sum of the weather experienced over a long enough time period for the pattern to be established. (①) Traditionally, the period for determining the 'normal climate' is 30 years. (②) Thus, the climate is an ensemble average of climate states, together with some measure of its variability over a specific period of time. (③) Differences between such climate states of the same kind over monthly, seasonal or annual time scales are referred to as climatic variations, including changes of the average or of the variability. (④) Climate change, however, is a shift of the normal climate according to some factor, which may be known, lasting for many years. (⑤) The gradually melting of sea ice, however, as a result of warming may finally be interpreted as a climate change.

32. 다음 주어진 문장이 들어갈 위치로 가장 적절한 것은?

보 기

But they were a sign of our universe's astonishing capacity to build complex objects from simple building blocks.

In the first minutes of its existence, the universe cooled so rapidly that it was impossible to manufacture elements heavier or more complex than hydrogen, helium, and (in minute amounts) lithium. (①) In the heat and chaos of the early universe, nothing more complex could survive. (②) From a chemical point of view, the early universe was very simple, far too simple to create complex objects such as our earth or the living organisms that inhabit it. (③) The first stars and galaxies were constructed from little more than hydrogen and helium. (④) Once created, stars laid the foundations for even more complex entities, including living organisms, because in their fiery cores they practiced an alchemy that turned hydrogen and helium into all the other elements. (⑤)

33. 다음 주어진 문장이 들어갈 위치로 가장 적절한 것은?

보기

Instead, he recognized the zigzag pattern separating the light and dark areas of the moon.

It's not just that a certain kind of original person seeks out exposure to the arts. (①) The arts also serve in turn as a powerful source of creative insight. (②) When Galileo made his astonishing discovery of mountains on the moon, his telescope didn't actually have enough magnifying power to support that finding. (③) Other astronomers were looking through similar telescopes, but only Galileo was able to appreciate the implications of the dark and light regions. (④) He had the necessary depth of experience in physics and astronomy, but also breadth of experience in painting and drawing. (⑤) Thanks to artistic training in a technique called chiaroscuro, which focuses on representations of light and shade, Galileo was able to detect mountains which others were not able to detect.

34. 다음 주어진 문장이 들어갈 위치로 가장 적절한 것은?

보기

That might have suggested it was the presence of danger that determined whether they used magic or not, but that explanation didn't match with other observations.

When the anthropologist Bronislaw Malinowski observed the daily lives of native people living on the Trobriand Islands of the South Pacific, he realized that while the islanders used magic rituals abundantly, they saved them only for certain activities. (①) When they went after the plentiful fish in a sheltered lagoon, for instance, they didn't use magic, but when they fished in the open sea, they did. (②) The islanders used magic to keep insects from destroying their crops, for example, but they didn't in gardening generally. (③) Malinowski realized that what made the difference was control. (④) When the islanders felt their own work and skill would determine success or failure, they did not turn to magic. (⑤) When the outcome involved luck or other factors they couldn't control, they did.

35. 다음 주어진 문장이 들어갈 위치로 가장 적절한 것은?

보기

Although their original food customs may have been nutritionally adequate, their new environment may lead them to alter their eating habits.

When people move from one country to another or from one area to another, their economic status may change. (①) They will be exposed to new foods and new food customs. (②) For instance, if milk was a staple food in their diet prior to moving and is unusually expensive in the new environment, milk may be given up for a cheaper, nutritionally inferior beverage such as soda, coffee, or tea. (③) Candy, possibly a luxury in their former environment, may be inexpensive and widespread in their new environment. (④) As a result, a family might increase consumption of soda or candy and limit purchases of more nutritious foods. (⑤) Someone who is not familiar with the nutritive values of foods can easily make such mistakes when shopping.

36. 다음 주어진 문장이 들어갈 위치로 가장 적절한 것은?

보기

To ensure that every research project has these protections, investigators must submit their proposed studies for formal review by a local panel of experts and community representatives prior to any data collection.

Choosing a good research design requires more than just selecting a particular method. (①) Researchers must determine whether the methods they plan on using are ethical. (②) That is, when designing a research study, investigators must do so in a way that does not violate the rights of people who participate. (③) Only with the approval of this panel can scientists begin their study. (④) If the review panel doesn't approve of some aspects of the proposed study, the researcher must revise those aspects and present them again for the panel's approval. (⑤) Likewise, each time a component of a study is altered, the review panel must be informed and give its approval.

37. 다음 주어진 문장이 들어갈 위치로 가장 적절한 것은?

보 기

Obvious examples would be the use of uniforms to communicate a particular social role and the modern white wedding dress Western cultures use to mark this rite of passage.

Obviously, clothes protect against the elements. However, textiles and clothing also have other roles that surpass merely just protecting the body. Dress and textiles alike are used as a means of nonverbal communication. (①) Both types of clothing communicate important information nonverbally to the onlooker. (②) The female wearing the white dress is soon to be wed and change her status and role in society. (③) The person in the uniform has some specialized function in society, such as police officer, nurse, or soldier. (④) Therefore, it can be said that clothing visually communicates information regarding group membership and functions as an identity marker. (⑤) One can dress down or up to display wealth, education, or social standing, depending on the message the wearer would like onlookers to receive.

38, 다음 주어진 문장이 들어갈 위치로 가장 적절한 것은?

보기

Once science has taken off, however, its link to technology becomes much tighter.

From our modern point of view, it is natural to see an important and necessary connection between science and technology. (①) However, technology did not have to await the specific discoveries, concepts, and mathematical equations of the past five hundred years. (②) Indeed, that is precisely why in many respects the China of 1500 seemed more advanced than its European or Middle Eastern counterparts. (③) One can create perfectly functional (even exquisite) clocks, gunpowder, compasses, or medical treatments without convincing scientific theories or well-controlled experiments. (④) It is barely imaginable that we could have nuclear power plants, supersonic airplanes, computers, lasers or a medley of effective medical and surgical interventions in the absence of the sciences of our epoch. (⑤) Those societies that lack science must either remain deprived of technological innovations or simply copy them from societies that have developed them.

39. 다음 주어진 문장이 들어갈 위치로 가장 적절한 것은?

보기

With the pervasiveness of television, increased mobility, growing cultural diversity, and the proliferation of single-parent families, however, role models are often influenced by forces outside the home.

Owing to the sociological changes of the past forty years, we no longer cling to particular notions of the male and female role in American society. (①) Yet that does not mean that all stereotypes have been eradicated. (②) It means, rather, that the number of stereotypes has multiplied. (③) Prior to the days of widespread media influence, a person's idea of what a husband or wife should do and how he or she should behave was influenced primarily by one's own parents. (④) Whatever influences you've been exposed to, chances are your spouse perceives marital roles somewhat differently than you do. (⑤) An openness to examining and changing stereotypes is necessary in order to express love more effectively.

40. 다음 주어진 문장이 들어갈 위치로 가장 적절한 것은?

> **보 기**
>
> Making them free maximizes these societal benefits.

There should be a sizable increase in public goods such as public transportation, public parks, and public museums and libraries in America. And they should be free of charge to users. (①) Such public goods improve the quality of life of those who cannot afford the equivalent private goods — their own cars, manicured gardens, art collections, and books, for example. (②) In this way, public goods somewhat offset the effect of stagnant or declining wages. (③) Public goods typically have less of an impact on scarce resources and the environment than their private equivalents, and they create jobs and add to overall demand in the economy. (④) For instance, an expanded system of free public transportation, including high-speed rail, would significantly decrease traffic congestion — estimated to cost Americans more than $85 billion a year in wasted hours and gas — and reduce carbon emissions. (⑤) The benefits far outweigh the costs.

41. 다음 주어진 문장이 들어갈 위치로 가장 적절한 것은?

> **보기**
>
> After a few years, however, the soil is compacted and needs breaking up, and weeds have proliferated.

One of the reasons that farming spreads quickly once it has begun is that the first few crops are both more productive and more easily grown than later crops, so farmers are always eager to move on to uncultivated land. (①) If you burn down a forest, you are left with fertile soil. (②) All you need to do is dig a small hole in the ground, plant a seed, and wait for it to grow. (③) If you now let the ground rest to allow the fertility to build up again, the tough roots of weeds need to be removed to make a good seedbed — and for that you need a plough and an ox to pull it. (④) But an ox must be fed, so you need pasture as well as cultivable land. (⑤) It's no surprise that shifting agriculture remains so popular with many tribal people in forests to this day.

42. 다음 주어진 문장이 들어갈 위치로 가장 적절한 것은?

> **보기**
>
> But when you peel back the layers, the truth is that they, too, struggle with fear and self-doubt.

To be an original, you need to take radical risks. This belief is embedded so deeply in our cultural psyche that we rarely even stop to think about it. (①) However, I want to disprove the myth that originality requires extreme risk taking and persuade you that originals are actually far more ordinary than we realize. (②) In every domain, from business and politics to science and art, the people who move the world forward with original ideas are rarely paragons of conviction and commitment. (③) As they question traditions and challenge the status quo, they may appear bold and self-assured on the surface. (④) We view them as self-starters, but their efforts are often fueled and sometimes forced by others. (⑤) And as much as they seem to crave risk, they really prefer to avoid it.

43. 다음 주어진 문장이 들어갈 위치로 가장 적절한 것은?

보 기

For example, after marinating raw meat in a dish, don't put the meat back in the same dish after cooking it.

Meat, poultry, and fish demand special handling because they often harbor high levels of bacteria. (①) Additionally, they provide a moist, nutritious environment — ideal for microbial growth. (②) Wash anything that has been in contact with such foods to prevent cross-contamination. (③) Wash it in hot, soapy water before reusing it; otherwise, the bacteria inevitably remaining in the dish from the raw meat can contaminate and grow in the cooked product or other food — a classic example of cross-contamination. (④) Likewise, wash a cutting board (and your hands) after, say, skinning chicken on it. (⑤) If you don't, and you use the contaminated board to cut up raw vegetables for a salad, the vegetables can be contaminated by bacteria from the poultry.

Unit 3

무관한 문장 유형

Unit 3 무관한 문장 유형

무관한 문장 유형은 문장 삽입 유형과 거의 비슷하다고 볼 수 있다. 문장 삽입이 문장을 끼워 넣는 유형이라면 무관한 문장은 문장을 제거하는 유형이다. 두 유형 모두 논리가 갑자기 바뀐 점이 답이 된다는 점에서 똑같다고 볼 수 있다.

1. 일단 첫 문장의 논리를 잡아내는 것이 중요하다. 이게 선지 판단의 기준이 될 것이다.

2. 각 선지 문장들이 나왔을 때 첫 문장과 비교해서 결과의 결과에 해당하는 문장인지, 반박에 해당하는 문장인지, 논리 추가에 해당하는 문장인지를 본다. 셋 중 하나에 해당한다면 그 밑줄 문장은 그냥 글의 주제가 바뀌는 부분이 될 수도 있지만, 그 문장이 무관한 문장이 될 수도 있는 것이다. 이런 경우가 아니라면 아예 터무니 없는 소재가 써 있을수도 있다.

3. 정답의 후보가 되는 문장을 정했을 때 이제 그 문장을 기준으로 밑줄 문장 앞 문장에서 밑줄 뒷 문장으로 이어지는 것이 있는지를 확인한다. 만약 밑줄 문장을 사이에 두고 밑줄 앞 문장에서 밑줄 뒷 문장으로 이어지는게 있다면 그 밑줄 문장은 정답이 된다. 마지막에 답인지 아닌지를 정할 때 반드시 확인해야 할 부분이다.

ex

나는 착하다.
그런데, 난 게으르다.
그 착함 때문에 자꾸 내가 손해 보는 일을 하게 된다.

밑줄 문장을 기준으로 밑줄 앞의 착함이 밑줄 뒷 문장으로 이어지므로 '그런데,'가 들어간 밑줄 문장은 무관한 문장이 되는 것이다.

예시 문제

[1-2] 다음 글에서 전체 흐름과 관계 없는 문장을 고르시오.

1. It is time for a deeper probe in a different setting, entered at a different angle, to a greater depth, and exploring a deeper causation. Why have the creative arts so dominated the human mind, everywhere and throughout history? We will not find the answer in the finest art galleries and symphony halls. ① The innovations of jazz and rock, arising more directly from human experience, will probably give us a better idea of where to excavate. ② Nevertheless, Hollywood composers began experimenting in the vocabularies of jazz and the structuring model of rock. ③ Because the creative arts entail a universal, genetic trait, the answer to the question lies in evolutionary biology. ④ Bear in mind that Homo sapiens has been around about 100,000 years but literate culture has existed for less than a tenth of that time. ⑤ So the mystery of why there are universal creative arts comes down to the question of what human beings were doing during the first nine-tenths of their existence.

2. To keep from breaking glass, all movement near and on the glass must be parallel (don't put any pressure on the glass when scraping), and always use a pull-type scraper. ① That way if you slip, all the force is away from the glass and it won't break. ② To remove glazing points, hook the sharp edge of the pull-type scraper into their soft metal points and pull them out along with the putty. ③ The glass manufacture corporations have begun to move their factories to some of East Asian countries to reduce the production cost. ④ Double-check to make sure all of the glazing points are removed, and that old putty beside and under the edge of the glass is loose. ⑤ If not, you need another round of heat.

3. The Internet of Things(IoT) can revolutionize the business and consumer landscape by bridging digital and material worlds. ① Any industry reliant on making, moving or selling objects that were previously not connected to the internet stands to benefit. ② Many industries, however, do not have the infrastructure with 5G broadband connection that can mobilize their IoT. ③ The specific benefits IoT can bring to a business depend on how the technology is used. ④ For example, sensors can be used to reduce waste by optimizing lighting or heating based on occupancy levels, or reduce spoilage of products in transit by monitoring temperatures. ⑤ IoT can also generate revenue and increase productivity, such as acoustic offshore oilfield sensors that analyze activity through pipelines to maximize output and help identify new resource pools.

4. Students of criminology, as well as the average citizen, are often unaware that criminalization of drugs is a twentieth-century American creation. Earlier, what we now construe as "drugs" were not dealt with differently than the vast array of other substances that arguably hold some potential for damaging (or enhancing) health. ① What we now think of as "hard drugs" were once readily available as medicines and even food additives. ② Coca-Cola once lived up to the advertisement jingle dubbing it the "real thing" by including cocaine as a stimulating ingredient, later replaced by caffeine. ③ The past 40 years have witnessed a "drug war" based on the idea that law enforcement should aggressively seek to eliminate specified drugs. ④ Our contemporary view of drugs was launched when Congress passed the Harrison Act in 1914, effectively criminalizing the sale and possession of opiates. ⑤ Legislation criminalizing marijuana was in place in 16 states by 1930, and in all states by 1937.

5. America is not actually a “melting pot” in the sense that people from different backgrounds somehow all become the same. America has always included a great diversity of ideas, attitudes, and behaviors. ① For example, the constitutional separation of church and state, a fundamental principle present since early days in the United States, guarantees that people of all religion have the same freedoms and rights for worship and religious behavior. ② People of diverse religious backgrounds are not expected to “melt” together into one religion. ③ Conflicts simply occur among people, whether of the same or different background. ④ Other laws guarantee the equal rights of all people regardless of skin color, gender, and age. ⑤ The United States does not even have an official national language—and many government and other publications in various geographical areas are offered in a variety of languages as well. In short, America as a nation has always recognized the realities and benefits of diversity.

6. No one questions that machines displace individual workers from certain jobs and that in the short run this often creates difficult problems. ① For example, the use of diesel engines and electric power by railroads has made obsolete the position of fireman—the employee who shoveled coal into the locomotive boiler that produced the steam for the train's steam engine—but because of union support, railroads had to fill this position for many years after steam power ceased being used by trains. ② However, such problems are temporary. ③ Ultimately, advances in machine technology tend to reduce costs and prices or to hold them down, and by enabling people to buy more goods, they create new employment opportunities. ④ Machines reduce the need for human skills. ⑤ If some industries employ fewer workers, others employ more. At the same time, new products are introduced and new industries are established.

7. 다음 글에서 전체 흐름과 관계 없는 문장은?

Many animals cooperate effectively, and a few even give loans. The most famous lenders in nature are vampire bats. These bats congregate in their thousands inside caves and every night fly out to look for prey. When they find a sleeping bird or careless mammal, they make a small incision in its skin, and suck its blood. ① But not all vampire bats find a victim every night. ② In order to cope with the uncertainty of their life, the vampires loan blood to each other. ③ Vampires, however, don't give loans in order to alleviate their evolutionary pressure. ④ A vampire that fails to find prey will come home and ask a more fortunate friend to regurgitate some stolen blood. ⑤ Vampires remember very well to whom they loaned blood, so at a later date if the friend returns home hungry, he will approach his debtor, who will reciprocate the favour.

8. As a rule, physicians should not be considered altruistic when acting in their patients' best interests because they do not have the choices in acting that we ordinarily associate with altruism. Doctors have professional duties to patients that they cannot discharge as a matter of choice. To be sure, becoming a doctor and thereby entering into a professional relationship with patients is an optional act. ① Once a doctor enters into this relationship, however, he or she cannot choose obligations. ② A doctor can choose not to treat a particular patient in a particular situation if doing so would compromise personal and professional integrity. ③ Thus there arises a potential conflict for a physician who sees patients as individuals needing therapeutic treatments. ④ But the doctor must ensure that the patient's care is transferred to another physician. ⑤ Once one becomes a physician, one promises to promote the best medical interests of one's patients. This is not optional, but obligatory.

9. Unlike other climate issues, the science of sea level rise is fairly simple. ① Ocean levels are increasing mostly because of what heat does to water, in all its various states. ② To combat the rise in ocean levels, it is of utmost importance to understand the molecular structure of water. ③ As global temperature rises, most of the extra heat in the atmosphere — about 90 percent — sinks into the ocean. ④ As the water warms, it expands like mercury in a thermometer. ⑤ This thermal expansion accounts for one-third of sea level rise. The other two-thirds comes from melting mountain glaciers and ice sheets in Greenland and Antarctica.

10. Pasta's ethnic roots have been long debated. ① Many theories have been put forward, some notably far-fetched. ② An enduring myth, based on the writings of the 13th-century explorer Marco Polo, that pasta was brought to Italy from China, rose from a misinterpretation of a famous passage in Polo's Travels. ③ In it, Polo mentions a tree from which something like pasta was made. ④ It was probably the sago palm, which produces a starchy food that resembles, but is not pasta. ⑤ This tree, native to Asia, provided undeniable evidence that Pasta originated in China.

11. Another difference in the concept of justice lies in various societies' ideas of what laws are. In the West, people consider "laws" quite different from "customs." There is also a great contrast between "sins" (breaking religious laws) and "crimes" (breaking laws of the government). ① In many non-Western cultures, however, there is little separation of customs, laws, and religious beliefs; in other cultures, these three may be quite separate from one another, but still very much different from those in the West. ② For these reasons, an action may be considered a crime in one country but be socially acceptable in others. ③ For instance, although a thief is viewed as a criminal in much of the world, in a small village where there is considerable communal living and sharing of objects, the word thief may have little meaning. ④ In small villages, everyone, in a sense, becomes a judge; in such societies, social disapproval of people's activities can serve both as powerful punishment for and as strong deterrent to crime. ⑤ Someone who has taken something without asking is simply considered an impolite person.

12. On the face of it, industrialized agriculture promised to be a most welcome solution to the timeless problem of world hunger. ① But some so-called solutions, as writer and farmer Wendell Berry observed, led to ramifying sets of new problems. ② And during the past several decades, it has become increasingly clear that industrial agriculture has indeed created a host of new problems impacting the health of people and the planet. ③ So corporations and governments, recognizing the opportunity presented by the new technologies, fostered the rapid spread of industrialized agriculture. ④ The use of fertilizers and pesticides, for example, has led to higher rates of cancer and the contamination of soil, streams, and groundwater. ⑤ Monoculture farming has led to the loss of biodiversity, undermining the productivity and stability of ecosystems.

13. From the artfully styled grain bowls to the popular slow-simmered bone broth, the message is clear: The beauty-and-wellness set has become obsessed with nutrition. ① Today, eating virtuously isn't just a means to stay trim; it's a crucial step in fortifying the body for an increasingly fit, and busy, life. ② But in this multitasking age, where lunch comes with a side of email, everyone's got a lot on their plate except, too often, a square meal. ③ This lack of proper nutrition from local foods is only worsened by a sedentary lifestyle. ④ Answering the call across the country is a wave of enterprising young chefs and tech pioneers who are marrying wholesome meals with door-to-door convenience. ⑤ If last year was dominated by the juice cleanse, this is shaping up to be the year of the designer meal delivery.

14. To conclusively set new safety standards for CT radiation, researchers are beginning to directly investigate the number of cancers among people who have received CT scans. ① About a dozen such studies from different countries will be published in the next few years. ② In the meantime, some researchers have started testing whether good images can be produced with radiation doses lower than those generated in typical CT scans. ③ Radiologists at Mass General Hospital have an unusual way of conducting such investigations. ④ A single CT scan subjects the human body to between 150 and 1,100 times the radiation of a conventional X-ray. ⑤ In that way, they scan bodies many times without worrying about making people sick and perform an autopsy to check whether the scan has correctly identified a medical problem. Rather than recruiting living, breathing human volunteers for their studies, they work with cadavers.

15. Foreign language learners may perform different speech acts than native speakers in the same contexts, or, alternatively, they may elect not to perform any speech act at all. The best examples of this come from authentic conversations and role-plays where speakers have some flexibility in determining what they will say or do. In academic advising sessions, native speakers and learners favor different speech acts. ① Native speakers produce more suggestions than learners per advising session, whereas learners produce more rejections per advising session than native speakers do. ② In addition, the absence of the speech act of advice was salient for academic advisers. ③ The two speech acts of suggestion and rejection seem to serve the same function, that of control. ④ Native speakers exert control over their course schedules by making suggestions; in contrast, the learners do so through rejections, by blocking the suggestions of the advisers. ⑤ Although both groups of students participate in determining what courses they ultimately take, the resulting feeling of harmony in the interview is perceived by the advisers to be noticeably different.

16. Thanks to advances in cell cultivation, researchers are closer than ever to growing real, edible meat in labs. Beyond the ethics of raising some 9 billion animals to be killed for food each year in the U.S., factory farms produce vast amounts of waste. ① Scientists are working to come up with efficient ways to recycle this waste. ② The 2 trillion pounds of animal waste pollutes the air and water. ③ Besides the pollution problem, the global demand for meat is expected to grow 60% by 2050, and the amount of farmland and grain needed to feed those chickens, pigs, and cows may be unsustainable. ④ But producing in vitro meat — muscle tissue that is cultured from animal cells and grown in a laboratory — has none of those hang-ups. ⑤ In fact, it's mouthwateringly efficient compared with existing methods of meat production, using 45% less energy and 99% less land.

17. An infant's lack of sparkling dialogue may obscure the fact that we are all born with an ability to communicate. ① A capacity for language exists in our tiny, screaming bodies in the delivery room, along with our eyes, ears, arms, legs, and vital organs. ② The capacity must be stimulated — we need to hear people talk in order to form words — but we are born eager to speak. ③ The newborn baby is patiently waiting for answers to questions: "What will I call the objects that surround me? How will I form positive and negative sentences? How can I express feelings about objects and people?" ④ Only when the baby is able to clearly articulate such questions, do the parents initiate communication. ⑤ The child's brain instinctively searches for answers to these questions and then, like a sponge, soaks them up.

18. Some of the men working nearby would watch me and laugh. ① Two or three of the older men took the trouble to teach me the right way to shovel. "You're doing it wrong," one man scolded. ② Beginning around seven each morning, I would feel my body resist the first thrust of the shovel. "Don't make your back do so much work," he instructed. ③ I stood impatiently listening, vaguely watching, then noticed his work-thickened fingers clutching the shovel. I was annoyed and wanted to tell him that I enjoyed shoveling the wrong way. I was about to, but, as it turned out, I didn't say a thing. ④ Rather it was at that moment I realized that I was fooling myself if I expected a few weeks of labor to gain me admission to the world of laborer. I would not learn in three months what my parents had meant by "real work." For me the sensations of exertion and fatigue could be savored. ⑤ For my parents, working at comparable jobs when they were my age, such sensations were to be feared. Fatigue took a different toll on their bodies and minds.

19. "What is your blood type?" is an unusual question from the Western point of view. From the Korean and Japanese perspective, such a question is quite normal. ① People of these cultures believe that specific personality traits are related to blood type. ② These days, however, more and more Westerners are buying into the idea of a connection between these two seemingly distinct features. ③ This belief is very similar to Western notions of astrology and signs of the zodiac. ④ Most Westerners are surprised by such a question because they are unaware of the concept of a relationship between blood type and personality. ⑤ In fact, many Westerners do not even know their own blood type.

Unit 4

어휘 유형

어휘 유형은 선택형, 밑줄형 두 가지 유형으로 나뉘게 된다. 선택형은 두 어휘 중 문맥상 적절한 어휘를 고르는 유형이고, 밑줄형은 밑줄 친 어휘 중에 문맥상 적절하지 않게 쓰인 어휘를 찾는 유형이다.

선택형이든 밑줄형이든 접근 방식은 빈칸 문제와 크게 다르지 않다. 그러니 빈칸 문제가 여러 개 있다고 생각하고 빈칸처럼 풀어주면 된다. 그렇다면

1) 근거를 찾는 방향을 정해야 한다. 밑줄/선택지 앞 부분에서 근거를 찾을지, 아니면 뒤에서 찾을지를 정해야 한다. 기본은 뒤에서 찾는 것이고 뒤로 갈 수 없겠다고 판단할 때 앞에서 판단한다.

2) 방향을 정했으면 어떤 것을 찾을지 정해야 한다. 이걸 정하려면 선택지/밑줄이 원인 자리에 있는지 결과 자리에 있는지를 보는 것이다. 원인 자리에 있다면 결과에 해당하는 것을 찾는 것이고, 결과 자리에 있다면 원인 자리에 있는 단어를 찾아서 근거를 잡는다.

3) 근거를 잡았으면 확실하게 생각해야 하는 것은 바로 반대 어휘이다. 선택지에서 두 어휘 중 적절한 것을 고르는 문제라면 선택지로 있는 두 어휘는 의미상 '반대의 뜻이겠다' 라고 생각하고 접근하면 되고, 밑줄형을 풀 땐 내가 잡은 근거와 반대 어휘로 써 둔 밑줄 선지를 찾는 것이다.

예시 문제

1~3. Politics cannot be suppressed, whichever policy process is employed and however sensitive and respectful of differences it might be. In other words, there is no end to politics. It is wrong to think that proper institutions, knowledge, methods of consultation, or participatory mechanisms can make disagreement go away. Theories of all sorts Ⓐ <u>promote</u> the view that there are ways by which disagreement can be processed or managed so as to make it disappear. The assumption behind those theories is that disagreement is wrong and consensus is the Ⓑ <u>desirable</u> state of things. In fact, consensus Ⓒ <u>often</u> comes without some forms of subtle coercion and the absence of fear in expressing a disagreement is a source of genuine freedom. Debates cause disagreements to evolve, often for the better, but a positively evolving debate does not have to equal a reduction in disagreement. The ________ of disagreement should never be made into a goal in political deliberation. A defense is required against any suggestion that political disagreement is not the Ⓓ <u>normal</u> state of things.

1. Which of the underlined words is NOT appropriate?

① Ⓐ　　② Ⓑ
③ Ⓒ　　④ Ⓓ

2. Which is the most appropriate for the blank?

① suppression
② acknowledgement
③ refinement
④ boost

3. According to the passage, what is true?

① It is important to cultivate the skills of debate in political situation.
② people sometimes should withdraw their ideas to reach an agreement.
③ Allowing differences is the fundamental requirement of democratic societies.
④ Politicians try to negotiate with opposite parties to execute effective policies.

4~5. One of the most important characteristics of the new murder mystery was the new demands it placed on readers, requiring that they play an active role in shaping the narrative and assigning guilt for the crime. Whereas execution sermons had required only that readers accept on clerical authority their official version of an uncontestable truth, the new legal narratives effectively treated readers as Ⓐ recipients who must cast a vote for conviction or acquittal.

The anonymous reader who wrote in the margin of a convicted murderer's printed self-exculpation, "This statement is universally regarded as a lie from beginning to end," was responding to this expectation of his role as reader. But murder mysteries required that readers do more than just vote. They made readers actively shape the narrative, sifting through evidence, piecing the fragments together, tracking, detecting, probing, "unveiling" — effectively taking on themselves the responsibility for crafting the master narrative of the event after Ⓑ the withdrawal of the Providential Narrator.

To this end, the murder mystery narrative pulled readers into the Ⓒ investigation of the crime, offering visual illustrations of key evidence, and graphic illustrations of scenes of the crime — both architectural facades and interior scenes, maps aimed at assisting the readers in Ⓓ reconstructing the crime in three-dimensional space, and architectural floor plans that paid special attention to the murderer's mode of access(the rear window, the unlocked door), sometimes tracking his path with a dotted line, increasingly noting the precise location of the victim's body.

4. 위 글의 요지로서 가장 적합한 것을 고르시오.

① The readers of modern society want to know the conclusion of the mystery in advance.
② The new murder mystery has not been attractive to most readers.
③ The readers of the new murder mystery should be agile to catch the narrative.
④ The new modern mystery tends to distract the reader's interest with its narrative.

5. 위 글에서 논지의 흐름상 가장 적합하지 것을 고르시오.

① Ⓐ　　② Ⓑ
③ Ⓒ　　④ Ⓓ

6-7. 다음 글을 읽고 물음에 답하시오.

It's troubling news that gene therapy researchers have long anticipated: A hemophilia patient injected with a virus carrying a therapeutic gene in a clinical trial has developed a liver tumor. The U.S. Food and Drug Administration (FDA) has halted the associated clinical trials, and uniQure, the Dutch firm behind the studies, is now investigating whether the virus itself caused the cancer. Gene therapy experts say Ⓐ <u>that's unlikely</u>. The patient had underlying conditions that predisposed him to liver cancer. Still, scientists say it's crucial to rule out any role for adeno-associated virus (AAV), the viral delivery system, or vector, that is used in hundreds of other gene therapy trials. "Everyone will want to know what happened," says physician-scientist David Lillicrap, a hemophilia researcher who was not involved with the uniQure study.

Gene therapy for various forms of the blood-clotting disorder hemophilia has been one of the field's latest success stories. UniQure's hemophilia B treatment appears to be among the treatments working, with 52 of 54 patients no longer needing injections of factor IX after 6 months in its latest study. But in recent days, uniQure revealed that an abdominal ultrasound done as part of its ongoing safety monitoring of trial participants found a liver mass in a patient treated in October 2019, prompting FDA to Ⓑ <u>impose a hold</u> on the company's three hemophilia trials. The news sent uniQure stock plunging, along with shares of other companies working on AAV gene therapy.

Still, there's reason to believe the virus Ⓒ <u>caused</u> the cancer. The patient was older, uniQure notes, and he had a liver disease that raises cancer risk. He also became infected with the hepatitis B and C viruses more than 25 years ago. Chronic infections of these viruses are linked to 80% of cases of hepatocellular carcinoma, the type of liver cancer found in the trial participant. But FDA and others are concerned because AAV vectors have produced cancer in mouse studies. The AAV-delivered DNA normally forms a free-floating loop in the cell's nucleus. But studies in newborn mice have shown AAV can sometimes integrate its cargo into the recipient's chromosomes and cause liver cancer. And last year, researchers reported that several dogs treated with AAV for hemophilia A had foreign DNA in chromosome locations that apparently triggered rapid cell growth. But this was years after the dogs got the therapy, and the animals Ⓓ <u>did not develop</u> tumors. Because the uniQuere patient received the gene therapy relatively recently, it's "inconceivable" that the AAV was the primary cause of the cancer, Lillicrap says. Still, he adds, if the patient already had a slow-growing liver tumor from his hepatitis infections, the AAV could have inserted into his liver cells, DNA in a way that spurred faster growth.

6. 위 글에서 논지의 흐름상 가장 적합하지 않은 것을 고르시오.

① Ⓐ
② Ⓑ
③ Ⓒ
④ Ⓓ

7. 위 글의 요지로 가장 적합한 것을 고르시오.

① Liver tumor in gene therapy recipient raises concerns about the virus widely used in treatment.
② In gene therapy, there are a variety of viruses which can cause cancer.
③ Chronic infections of viruses may determine the type of liver cancer in gene therapy recipients.
④ It is critical to analyze the cellular samples of tumor before starting gene therapy.

8. 문맥상 낱말의 쓰임이 적절하지 않은 것은?

Depression is the textbook modern psychiatric disease: It is a biological disorder with genetic, neurochemical, and hormonal facets giving rise to mental "illness," and it is a disorder profoundly Ⓐ <u>sensitive</u> to an environment that produces feelings of helplessness. Major depression is heartbreakingly common, afflicting about 15 percent of the people in the developed world at one point or another during their lifetimes. And it is becoming Ⓑ <u>more</u> common: The rates of depression in Western countries have Ⓒ <u>gradually fallen</u> during the last fifty years. While some might question this finding as potentially Ⓓ <u>spurious</u> — since depressed people today are more likely to seek medical help than in past times, and health care professionals are more likely to diagnose depression than were doctors in the 1950s — these studies are among the most rigorous epidemiological studies ever done in psychiatry and carefully controlled to account for such confounds. The rate of depression is indeed ever Ⓔ <u>increasing</u>.

① Ⓐ ② Ⓑ ③ Ⓒ
④ Ⓓ ⑤ Ⓔ

9~10. One way to avoid contributing to overhyping a story would be to say nothing. However, that is not a realistic option for scientists who feel a strong sense of responsibility to inform the public and policymakers and/or to offer suggestions. Speaking with members of the media has (a) advantages in getting a message out and perhaps receiving favorable recognition, but it runs the risk of misinterpretations, the need for repeated clarifications, and entanglement in never-ending controversy. Hence, the decision of whether to speak with the media tends to be highly individualized. Decades ago, it was (b) unusual for Earth scientists to have results that were of interest to the media, and consequently few media contacts were expected or encouraged. In the 1970s, the few scientists who spoke frequently with the media were often (c) criticized by their fellow scientists for having done so. The situation now is quite different, as many scientists feel a responsibility to speak out because of the importance of global warming and related issues, and many reporters share these feelings. In addition, many scientists are finding that they (d) enjoy the media attention and the public recognition that comes with it. At the same time, other scientists continue to resist speaking with reporters, thereby preserving more time for their science and (e) running the risk of being misquoted and the other unpleasantries associated with media coverage.

9. 윗 글의 제목으로 가장 적절한 것은?

① The Troubling Relationship Between Scientists and the Media.
② A Scientist's Choice : To Be Exposed to the Media or Not?
③ Scientists! Be Cautious When Talking to the Media.
④ The Dilemma over Scientific Truth and Media Attention.
⑤ Who Are Responsible for Climate Issues, Scientists or the Media?

10. 밑줄 친 (a)~(e) 중에서 문맥상 낱말의 쓰임이 적절하지 않은 것은?

① (a) ② (b) ③ (c)
④ (d) ⑤ (e)

11~12. We trust our common sense largely because we are prone to *naive realism*: the belief that we see the world precisely as it is. We assume that 'seeing is believing' and trust our intuitive perceptions of the world and ourselves. In daily life, naive realism often serves us well. If you are driving down a one-lane road and see a tractor-trailer moving uncontrollably towards you at 120 kilometres per hour, it is a wise idea to get out of the way. Much of the time, we *should* (a) trust our perceptions. Yet appearances can sometimes be deceptive. The Earth seems flat. The sun seems to revolve around the Earth. Yet in both cases, our intuitions are (b) wrong. Sometimes, what appears to be obvious can mislead us when it comes to evaluating ourselves and others. Our common sense tells us that our memories (c) accurately capture virtually everything we have seen, although scientific research demonstrates otherwise. Our common sense also assures us that people who do not share our political views are biased, but that we are (d) objective. Yet psychological research demonstrates that we are all susceptible to evaluating political issues in a biased fashion. So our tendencies to believe appearances can lead us to draw (e) reliable conclusions about human nature. In many cases, 'believing is seeing' rather than the reverse: our beliefs shape our perceptions of the world.

11. 윗 글의 제목으로 가장 적절한 것은?

① How Did Science Prove That the Earth Is Round?
② Comparison of Common Sense and Scientific Interpretation.
③ Seeing Is Believing : Using Intuition to Make Better Decisions.
④ Beyond Naive Realism : Is Our Perception of Reality Trustworthy?
⑤ When It Comes to Taking Risks, It's Dangerous to Trust Your Instincts.

12. 밑줄 친 (a)~(e) 중에서 문맥상 낱말의 쓰임이 적절하지 않은 것은?

① (a) ② (b) ③ (c)
④ (d) ⑤ (e)

13~14. Some people claim that gratitude is just about thinking nice thoughts and expecting good things — and ignores the negativity, pain, and suffering in life. Well, they're (a) wrong. Consider our definition of gratitude, as a specific way of thinking about receiving a benefit and giving credit to others besides yourself for that benefit. In fact, gratitude can be very difficult, because it (b) requires that you recognize your dependence on others, and that's not always positive. You have to humble yourself, in the sense that you have to become a good receiver of others' support and generosity. That can be very hard — most people are (c) better givers than receivers.

What's more, feelings of gratitude can sometimes stir up related feelings of indebtedness and obligation, which doesn't sound like positive thinking at all: *If I am grateful for something you provided to me, I have to take care of that thing — I might even have to reciprocate at some appropriate time in the future.* That type of indebtedness or obligation can be perceived very negatively — it can cause people real (d) comfort, as Jill Suttie explores in her essay "How to Say Thanks Without Feeling Indebted."

The data bear this out. When people are grateful, they aren't necessarily free of negative emotions — we don't find that they necessarily have less anxiety or less tension or less unhappiness. Practicing gratitude magnifies positive feelings more than it (e) reduces negative feelings. If gratitude were just positive thinking, or a form of denial, you'd experience no negative thoughts or feelings when you're keeping a gratitude journal, for instance. But, in fact, people do.

13. 윗 글의 제목으로 가장 적절한 것은?

① True Gratitude : Something Different from Debt.
② Does the Gratitude of Others Truly Satisfy You?
③ Gratitude : Not an Absolute Form of Positive Thinking.
④ The More Gratitude You Have, the More Benefits You Gain.
⑤ Practice Gratitude to Please People Who Are Meaningful to You.

14. 밑줄 친 (a)~(e) 중에서 문맥상 낱말의 쓰임이 적절하지 않은 것은?

① (a) ② (b) ③ (c)
④ (d) ⑤ (e)

15~16. In all social systems, it is true that people's behavior is influenced by social rules and they are extraordinarily adaptable. One natural experiment involving baboons is instructive. A study in 2004 examined how a troop of baboons dominated by large and aggressive males changed after all those dominant males caught a disease and died. With only smaller, gentler males remaining, the culture of that troop underwent a (a) <u>dramatic</u> shift, moving from a social structure characterized by widespread bullying and fighting to one with much more peaceful grooming. Conflict was still there, of course, but it tended to be resolved with peaceful methods, and the fighting that did happen was more between (b) <u>equally</u> matched baboons, instead of a big one picking on a small one. Remarkably, the culture of that troop persisted even after all those original males had died off and were replaced by others coming in from outside. The new males were acculturated to the group norms, and learned to behave less (c) <u>generously</u>.

Obviously, humans are not baboons. But it seems highly possible that this is basically (d) <u>similar</u> to why different human societies can have much different behavioral norms — consider premodern tribes who worshiped their ancestors and shared food in common, medieval peasants who accepted the divine right of kings and performed free labor for feudal lords, and people today who believe in democracy and corporate employment contracts. Human societies have much more complexity and choice than baboon societies, but the point is that behavioral norms are to a great degree the (e) <u>product</u> of culture and learning, not the other way around.

15. 윗 글의 제목으로 가장 적절한 것은?

① Power of Social Pressure in Decision Making.
② The Fluidity of Human Behavior : Socially Constructed.
③ Learn Different Cultures and Broaden Your Perspective!
④ Survival of the Friendliest : A Universal Feature of All Societies.
⑤ A Blind Spot of the Baboon Experiment : Animal Rights Protection.

16. 밑줄 친 (a)~(e) 중에서 문맥상 낱말의 쓰임이 적절하지 않은 것은?

① (a) ② (b) ③ (c)
④ (d) ⑤ (e)

17~18. Not surprisingly, usage of unsafely designed and insecurely implemented software presents some risks. After distributed software reaches user sites, installation and administration of system and application software, when improperly performed, may adversely affect performance and proper functioning of such software. Due to the complexity as well as due to inadequate documentation of these systems, users (a) <u>hardly</u> understand effects of their attempts to "properly" use such systems. Consequently, users (b) <u>disregard</u> "trial and error" methods in learning to work with new features, rather than trying methodologically to understand which functions may have which effects, and which precautions should be taken to avoid unwished side-effects. This somewhat "explorative" way to use systems rather often leads to a (c) <u>risky</u> attitude with potentially harmful effects, e.g. by clicking on unknown attachments without due care.

Software manufacturers often argue that failure of software is mainly caused by (d) <u>improper</u> actions of users. But in many — if not most — cases, the human-computer interface (e.g. the display of functions and operations on the screen, or the handling of input devices such as mouse and keyboard) is inadequately designed and users are not properly supported by help functions (which when existing in many cases are so complex that users are further misled). While users are primarily interested in doing their work, one must admit that they rather often tend to (e) <u>forget</u> about any precaution and even sometimes bypass security measures when thinking that their work performance is reduced.

17. 윗 글의 제목으로 가장 적절한 것은?

① What Are the Real Causes of Software Failures?
② How to Avoid Unsuccessful Software Implementation.
③ Cyber Security : The Digital Dilemma for Manufacturers.
④ What Can We Expect from New Software Developments?
⑤ Social Responsibility Impacts on Software Development Processes.

18. 밑줄 친 (a)~(e) 중에서 문맥상 낱말의 쓰임이 적절하지 않은 것은?

① (a) ② (b) ③ (c)
④ (d) ⑤ (e)

19~20. In the 1930s, the English psychologist Sir Frederic Bartlett proposed that we gradually build up our knowledge of the world from events we experience, and that these experiences are then clustered in organized mental structures he called "schemata." In turn, these schemata (or "schemas") are used to help us understand new experiences and form frameworks in which to remember them. One potential (a) <u>downside</u> of this arrangement is that it is relatively difficult for us to understand and remember information and events that do not fit our current schemata. One of Bartlett's classic demonstrations was to present an unusual North American folktale to an English university student to learn and recall. The student's written recall differed from the (b) <u>original</u> by being shorter and omitting a number of details. This first student's written recall was then given to a second student to learn and recall with the result that more unusual details were dropped out of his reproduction, but other details were added, apparently to make the story (c) <u>more</u> coherent and comprehensible to English ears. This procedure was repeated until a series of ten students had learned the previous reproduction and produced their own versions. By the end of the series, the reproductions were much shorter, the supernatural details in the original had been (d) <u>lost</u> , and the whole tale was closer to the experience of English university students in the 1930s. This demonstration thus illustrates the constructive nature of remembering, and the effects of beliefs and attitudes on recollection and understanding. Gossip serves as a commonplace example that is (e) <u>counter</u> to Bartlett's findings, with a story progressively changing as it travels across tellings. To return to metaphors for a moment, human memory is *not* like a tape recorder!

19. 윗 글의 제목으로 가장 적절한 것은?

① How Prior Knowledge Impacts Memory.
② How Gossip Affects Personal Relationships.
③ The Need for New Experiences for Storytelling.
④ What You Should Do to Improve Your Memory.
⑤ Why Your Experience Matters in Making Up a Story.

20. 밑줄 친 (a)~(e) 중에서 문맥상 낱말의 쓰임이 적절하지 않은 것은?

① (a) ② (b) ③ (c)
④ (d) ⑤ (e)

21~22. In Singapore, due to road pricing, one can always expect to be able to achieve a speed of 40 miles per hour on the road. While the rich are more likely to afford this, buses can also achieve these speeds, and with the economies of scale of a bus this (a) <u>lowers</u> the per-person trip price for achieving this speed. The full cost of commuting includes not only the out-of-pocket expenditure on gasoline, parking, and road use fees but the value of the lost time. If a commute takes thirty minutes rather than fifteen minutes because of traffic congestion, then the commuter has lost fifteen minutes. Economists have adopted the rule of thumb of (b) <u>valuing</u> such lost time by half of the person's hourly wage. For example, if I earn $80 an hour and I lose fifteen minutes stuck in traffic, then this costs me $10 in lost time (.25 × 80 × .5).

To (c) <u>conserve</u> on such lost time due to congestion, cities such as Stockholm, London, and Singapore have adopted road pricing. Drivers in such cities move at higher speeds and save time but must pay more money out of pocket to travel at peak use times. One explanation for why so few cities have adopted road pricing focuses on behavioral economics: people are used to the roads being free. To an economist, this is a (d) <u>puzzling</u> explanation because congested roads cost us valuable time. This time cost means that free roads are not free to use. A second explanation for the (e) <u>agreement</u> to road pricing is that many poor people drive and they prefer to pay for their commute using their time rather than paying a road use fee.

21. 윗 글의 제목으로 가장 적절한 것은?

① Road Pricing : Is Time More Valuable than Money?
② Varying Compensations for Lost Time on the Road.
③ Too Much Administration to Implement Road Pricing.
④ Analysis of the Underlying Causes of Road Congestion.
⑤ Efforts to Reduce Commute Times : Fighting a Losing Battle.

22. 밑줄 친 (a)~(e) 중에서 문맥상 낱말의 쓰임이 적절하지 않은 것은?

① (a) ② (b) ③ (c)
④ (d) ⑤ (e)

23~24. When it comes to the common belief fallacy in your own life, remember that scientists are always trying to reach better conclusions, and that is something you don't do as an individual, at least not by default, and by extension it is something your institutions are not so (a) <u>great</u> at either. You don't seek out what science calls the null hypothesis. That is, when you believe in something, you rarely seek out evidence to the contrary to see how it matches up with your assumptions. That's the (b) <u>source</u> of urban legends, folklore, superstitions, and all the rest. Having doubts is not your strong suit. Corporations and other institutions rarely set aside a division tasked with paying attention to the faults of the agency. Unlike in science, most human undertakings (c) <u>include</u> a special department devoted to looking for the worst in the operation — not just a complaint department, but a department that asks if the organization is on the right path. Every human effort should systematically pause and ask if it is currently mistaken. To (d) <u>beat</u> your brain, you need that department constantly operating in your cranium. You would do well to borrow from the lessons of the scientific method and apply them in your personal life. In the background, while you sew and golf and browse cat videos, science is fighting against your (e) <u>stupidity</u>. No other human enterprise is fighting as hard, or at least not fighting and winning.

23. 윗 글의 제목으로 가장 적절한 것은?

① Common Beliefs Complement Science.
② Science Is Not a Value-Neutral Discipline.
③ Common Sense Keeps Your Daily Life Smooth.
④ Which Is More Powerful : Intuition or Scientific Evidence?
⑤ Apply Science to Your Life to Avoid Common Misconceptions.

24. 밑줄 친 (a)~(e) 중에서 문맥상 낱말의 쓰임이 적절하지 않은 것은?

① (a) ② (b) ③ (c)
④ (d) ⑤ (e)

25~26. Following the dramatic arc of sporting contests and athletic careers allows us to witness the efforts of athletes to live good human lives — to (a) <u>pursue</u> excellence, victory, fame, and fortune and also to deal with failure and loss. And while the drama of a play or novel is the scripted drama of the author's creation, the drama of sport is that of real people who must live with the consequences of their decisions. This is one reason why I (b) <u>support</u> the idea that sports should be sharply separated from "real life." When we watch sports, we are not watching characters. The actor who plays Romeo doesn't die at the end of the performance; he gets to leave the character's plight behind when he goes home. By contrast, injuries that players suffer in the pursuit of their goals are not (c) <u>rehearsed</u>, and the quarterback of the losing team does not get to divest himself of the game's result. If these features of sports do not necessarily make sports an encouragement to ethical reflection that is (d) <u>superior</u> to drama or literature, I think they at least show that sports are not inferior in this regard. At a minimum, I want to insist that if it makes sense to regard the plays of Shakespeare as legitimate sources for our own thinking about the nature of the good life, then there is no reason to think that sports are (e) <u>less capable</u> of igniting such reflective capacities.

25. 윗 글의 제목으로 가장 적절한 것은?

① Efforts to Deal with Declining Viewership of Sports.
② Watching Sports : A Way to Reflect on What the Good Life Is.
③ Being a Sports Fan : Not Recommended for Your Mental Health.
④ More Than Just a Game : How Sports Can Advance Social Justice.
⑤ Reflective Practice : Does It Help Athletes Improve Their Performance?

26. 밑줄 친 (a)~(e) 중에서 문맥상 낱말의 쓰임이 적절하지 않은 것은?

① (a) ② (b) ③ (c)
④ (d) ⑤ (e)

27~28. Ownership of the media gives control over the nature of the information distributed. Proponents of public ownership of the media argue that because information is a public good — that is, once it has been supplied to some consumers it is hard to keep it away from others who have not paid for it — private owners tend to provide (a) <u>less</u> information than would be socially desirable. They also argue that with private ownership the media industry runs the risk of representing the views of only a (b) <u>narrow</u> group in society, and state ownership of the media is necessary to expose the public to desirable cultural or educational themes or values.

Opponents of public ownership argue that government control of the media can be used to manipulate people and (c) <u>distort</u> the information supplied in the incumbent government's favor. Moreover, experience shows that government-owned enterprises are less likely to be responsive to consumer demand. Finally, government-owned media are not subject to competition, thus giving rise to the danger of both poor-quality production and (d) <u>inefficiencies</u>. A recent article on the British Broadcasting Corporation (BBC) claims that government ownership makes it (e) <u>easier</u> than it would otherwise be for other media companies to grow. The article claims that the large amounts of tax revenue that are given to the BBC give it an advantage relative to private companies. It also contends that as a private company, the BBC would be more dynamic, and therefore better able to compete with global media firms.

27. 윗 글의 제목으로 가장 적절한 것은?

① The Dilemma Between Media Freedom and Public Interest.
② The Effects of Public Funding on Private Media Companies.
③ Major Challenges That Independent Media Ownership Faces.
④ Conflicting Views on the Ownership and Control of the Media.
⑤ Benefits and Risks of Public-Private Partnerships of the Media.

28. 밑줄 친 (a)~(e) 중에서 문맥상 낱말의 쓰임이 적절하지 않은 것은?

① (a) ② (b) ③ (c)
④ (d) ⑤ (e)

※ [29-30] (A), (B), (C)에 들어갈 말로 가장 적절한 것을 고르시오.

29. The realization that the universe consists of atoms and void and nothing else, that the world was not made for us by a providential creator, that we are not the center of the universe, that our emotional lives are no more (A) distinct/indistinct than our physical lives from those of all other creatures, that our souls are as material and as mortal as our bodies — all these things are not the cause for (B) despair/hope. On the contrary, grasping the way things really are is the crucial step toward the possibility of happiness. It is possible for human beings to live happy lives, but not because they think that they are the center of the universe. Unappeasable desire and the fear of death are the principal (C) paths/obstacles to human happiness, but they can be surmounted through the exercise of reason.

	(A)		(B)		(C)
①	distinct	-	despair	-	paths
②	distinct	-	despair	-	obstacles
③	distinct	-	hope	-	obstacles
④	indistinct	-	hope	-	obstacles
⑤	indistinct	-	despair	-	paths

30. Music therapy as an explicit set of practices first developed in the West during the twentieth century — especially during the First World War, when doctors and nurses witnessed the effect that music had on the psychological, physiological, cognitive and emotional states of the wounded. The first major academic study of music's (A) aesthetic/medicinal properties was published in 1948, partly as a response to the continued use of music therapy in military hospitals and in factories during the Second World War. Music therapy is now (B) rarely/widely used for those with mental and/or physical disabilities or illnesses. One of its most significant functions is to relax patients who are preparing for, undergoing or recovering from surgery, notably dental, burns and coronary treatments. It is now well attested that music with slow, steady tempos, legato passages, gentle rhythms, predictable change, and simple sustained melodies is (C) detrimental/conducive to relaxation.

	(A)	(B)	(C)
①	aesthetic	- rarely	- detrimental
②	aesthetic	- widely	- detrimental
③	medicinal	- widely	- detrimental
④	medicinal	- widely	- conducive
⑤	medicinal	- rarely	- conducive

※ [31-32] (A), (B), (C)에 들어갈 말로 가장 적절한 것을 고르시오.

31. Many of us take broadband Internet for granted, but nearly 1 in 5 Americans lacks access to it, says the Federal Communications Commission (FCC). In rural areas, telecom companies balk at the cost of wiring far-flung homes, while low-income families can find the fees (A) <u>prohibitive/affordable</u>. Closing the broadband gap is about more than being able to stream the latest TV dramas. High-speed Internet is a critical tool of modern life, (B) <u>constraining/enabling</u> kids to learn digitally and adults to work via the cloud. The FCC recently approved a small broadband subsidy, but the real solution may lie in (C) <u>increased/decreased</u> competition for a notoriously consolidated industry.

	(A)		(B)		(C)
①	prohibitive	-	enabling	-	increased
②	prohibitive	-	enabling	-	decreased
③	prohibitive	-	constraining	-	decreased
④	affordable	-	constraining	-	increased
⑤	affordable	-	enabling	-	decreased

32. As evolutionary scholar Henry Plotkin says, gaining knowledge of the world across countless generations of organisms, evolution conserves knowledge selectively relative to criteria of need, and that collective knowledge is then held within the gene pool of species. Such collective knowledge is doled out to individuals, who come into the world with (A) innate/acquired ideas and predispositions to learn only certain things in specific ways. In other words, whether you're hunting on the savannah or choosing between millions of videos on YouTube, your brain is programmed to (B) adopt/ignore almost everything and home in only on what is most important or interesting. Otherwise, you'd be pointing your spear at every tree and rock or, just as annoyingly, you'd be lost in an infinite trail of video links, hoping in vain to find something worthwhile. With an understanding of the (C) discriminating/integrating nature of our genes, we can begin to construct the basis for stories that grab our attention and stay in our memory.

	(A)	(B)	(C)
①	acquired	- ignore	- integrating
②	acquired	- ignore	- discriminating
③	innate	- ignore	- discriminating
④	innate	- adopt	- integrating
⑤	innate	- adopt	- discriminating

Unit 5

빈칸 연결사 유형

연결사 문제 총정리

※ 빈출 연결사 정리

1 논리 유지

1) 재진술 : 같은 소재 같은 내용
In other words, that is (to say), so to speak
to put it (in) another way, namely
in brief, in short, in summary, to sum up, in a nutshell
in sum
* 재진술/반박 둘 다 가능한 연결사 : in fact, in reality, as a matter of fact, indeed, actually

2) 인과관계 : 결과의 결과, 원인의 원인
therefore, thus, accordingly, in conclusion, consequently, so, hence, as a result, as a consequence, eventually, naturally, predictably

예외 : 앞 문장이 결과, 뒷 문장이 원인이 되는 것 : To this end

3) 예시 : 소재는 달라지고(인물/집단), 같은 논리 그대로
for example, for instance, likewise, similarly, in the same way, by the same token, equally, in a similar fashion, also

4) 강조 : A → B but AX → BX
However, But, Yet, in/by contrast, on the other hand, conversely, meanwhile, in the meantime
cf) on the one hand(뒤에 on the other hand 또는 But, However가 있어야 가능)

2 논리 추가 : 원인 그대로 결과 추가, 결과 그대로 원인 추가

also, besides, moreover, furthermore, what is more, still more, in addition
at the same time, simultaneously, concurrently

3 논리 반박

- only 반박으로만 역할 : still, even so, nevertheless, nonetheless, regardless, surprisingly, interestingly, unpredictably
- 반박/강조 가능한 것 : however, but, yet in/by contrast, on the other hand, conversely, unfortunately, fortunately, meanwhile, in the meantime, all the while, by the way
- 재진술, 반박이 가능한 것 : in fact, in reality, as a matter of fact, indeed, actually

4 기타 연결사

not A but B같은 관계를 만들어주는 연결사(앞 문장이 부정문 or 해석상 부정문)
; Instead, Rather, On the contrary, If anything

앞에 있는 걸 하지 않았을 때의 결과
: otherwise

Ironically, Paradoxically(역설적으로) : A → B and BX
이렇게 나오는 것이 역설이다.

예시 문제

1. Gettysburg is considered by most historians to be a turning point in the American Civil War. Before Gettysburg, Confederate forces under General Robert E. Lee had defeated their Union counterparts — sometimes by considerable margins — in a string of major battles. In this engagement, Ⓐ_____, the Confederate army was defeated and driven back. Even more important than their material losses, though, was the Confederacy's loss of momentum. Union forces took the initiative, finally defeating the Confederacy less than two years later. By invading Union territory, the Confederate leadership had sought to shatter the Union's will to continue the war and to convince European nations to recognize the Confederacy as an independent nation. Ⓑ_____, the Union's willingness to fight was strengthened and the Confederacy squandered its last chance for foreign support.

1. 빈칸에 들어갈 가장 알맞은 것을 고르시오.

① however - Instead
② however - In addition
③ moreover - Instead
④ moreover - In addition

2~3. Researchers have a hard time measuring how common bullying is because Ⓐ_______. Is bullying only verbal, or does there have to be a physical act? If you hear a schoolyard taunt that you know how to brush off, were you bullied or just annoyed? Does it have to be repeated behavior to count as bullying, or can it happen just once? Does it have to disrupt a whole class, or can it affect only one or two kids? None of this is clear to those who study and make laws to prevent bullying. Most state laws differ on the precise motivations and consequences required for a harassing event to count as bullying. If one 12-year-old boy taunts another, most state laws wouldn't call it bullying unless there is both demonstrable harm — the victim is injured(at least psychologically) — and demonstrable intent. Ⓑ_______, for a bully to be a bully, he can't have just been any insensitive kid. He had to want to hurt his classmate.

2. Which is most appropriate for the blank Ⓐ?

① there are so many kinds of bullying pattern
② it is not possible to check all the schools in the US
③ there's no single definition
④ it is not common among college kids
⑤ there's no way to understand the human mind

3. Which is most appropriate for the blank Ⓑ?

① In other words
② On the contrary
③ On the other hand
④ By contrast
⑤ By all means

4. In the seven-year battle since 2001 to set Afghanistan back on its feet after more than two decades at war, the country's historical sites have been ignored. Its ancient heritage has fallen victim to an epidemic of pillaging on par with the depredations of Genghis Khan's army that in 1220 left the city of Balkh in ruins. Unauthorized excavation on the scale of organized crime is carried out by professional gangs supported by local warlords and even government officials, with ties to the international black market in antiquities. While estimates of this illicit trade vary widely, government authorities put it at as high as $4 billion, roughly on par with the country's drug trade. This hurts historians and archaeologists who are just starting to understand the country's important role in the development of Central Asian civilization. The mid-20th century blossoming of archaeological research in Afghanistan uncovered treasures of unimaginable value. Those findings also ignited gold fever in the country, inspiring hundreds of freelance "archaeologists" to dig for treasures of their own, with a black market value that far exceeded a farmer's annual earnings. Then, starting in 1979, war uprooted the fragile government protections and thousands of priceless artifacts were spirited out of the country. But it was the fall of the Taliban in December 2001, and the subsequent power vacuum, that unleashed the most devastating rape of Afghanistan's heritage to date. ____________ poverty and war are what kept these sites safe. In times of conflict, civilians were afraid to leave home, and the fear of land mines kept many from digging. Now that a nationwide campaign to clear the mines is bearing fruit, looters are returning to sites that have been untouched for years, and are even discovering new ones.

4. Which of the following is most appropriate for the blank?

① Consequently
② Still
③ Ironically
④ By contrast
⑤ Predictably

5. How do banks make money? As financial intermediaries, they earn enough to support their activities by the difference between the interest rate paid to savers and the interest rate charged on loans. When customers make deposits in a savings account, they earn interest on the principal. ________, when customers take out loans, they pay interest on the principal. By charging the borrower a slightly higher interest rate than that which is given to the depositor, a bank is able to cover its expenses.

5. Which of the following is most appropriate for the blank?

① Similarly
② After all
③ Moreover
④ Nevertheless
⑤ Most of all

6. Young people are a fundamental asset of our economies and societies. According to Eurostat, there are over 94 million young people aged between 15 and 29 years in Europe, of whom over 60 million are aged 15-24 years and over 33 million are aged 25-29 years. This amounts to an incredible resource for society. However, if countries want to fully exploit the potential of young people, they need to be productively employed and integrated into society. At present, most EU Member States are facing the growing challenge of absorbing and integrating young people into education systems and labour markets. While our societies are not fully benefiting from the youth dividend, disengagement from the labour market also has serious consequences for individual young people. Ⓐ________, youth employment remains a key to sustainable economic and social development, especially in a context of a changing demography and ageing population. With young people having paid the highest price during the global economic crisis, there is a renewed sense of urgency to integrate them into the labour market and the education system. Successfully tackling this issue is not only a question of meeting young people's aspirations for a better life, but also a necessity for enhancing the well-being of societies in general.

6. Which expression best fits Ⓐ?

① Surprisingly
② For this reason
③ To this end
④ Regardless
⑤ At one extreme

7. There's a common notion that losing your temper must be bad for your heart. In a study carried out at the University of North Carolina in 2000, 13,000 patients were given questionnaires in which they rated their own tendency to get angry, and were followed up a few years later. Although their blood pressure was apparently normal, those who had said they frequently get angry were three times more likely to have had heart attacks in the intervening years than the others, even when factors like smoking, diabetes and weight had been taken into account. Ⓐ________, Mark McDermott from the University of East London found that people who expressed their anger suffered more from heart disease than those who held back from shouting.

7. Which expression best fits Ⓐ?

① On the other hand
② By the way
③ Instead
④ In short
⑤ Likewise

8. The average time between an attacker breaching a network and its owner noticing the intrusion is 205 days. Like most statistics touted by the cyber-security industry, such as the supposed annual $575 billion global cost of 90 million cyber-attacks, it is little more than a guesstimate. Ⓐ________, there is no doubt that criminals and pranksters are thriving by attacking computers and networks, and that businesses offering answers are charging fat fees.

8. Which best fits into the blank Ⓐ?

① Indeed
② However
③ Therefore
④ Accidentally

9. The migrant question is a more serious threat to Europe's future than anything in recent memory, because it can't be resolved by a promise from a central bank or an infusion of someone else's cash. This is a question of Europe's identity — and whether it means as much to European voters as it did a generation ago. Ⓐ________, the refugees will keep coming, and it will become harder for governments to make sacrifices to welcome them.

9. Which best fits into the blank Ⓐ?

① All the while
② On the one hand
③ In conclusion
④ On the other hand
⑤ By the way

10. Praying for the Virgin Mary's intercession and being devoted to her are a global phenomenon. As a universal symbol of maternal love, as well as of suffering and sacrifice, Mary is often the touchstone of our longing for meaning, a more accessible link to the supernatural than formal church teachings. Her mantle offers both security and protection. Pope Francis, when once asked what Mary meant to him, answered, "She is my mama."

Her reported appearances, visions experienced often by very poor children living in remote or conflict-wracked areas, have intensified her mystery and aura. And when the children can't be shaken from their stories—especially if the accounts are accompanied by inexplicable "signs" such as spinning suns or gushing springs--her wonder grows.

Mary is everywhere: Marigolds are named for her. Hail Mary passes save football games. The image in Mexico of Our Lady of Guadalupe is one of the most reproduced female likenesses ever. Mary draws millions each year to shrines such as Fatima in Portugal and Knock in Ireland, sustaining religious tourism estimated to be worth billions of dollars a year and providing thousands of jobs. She inspired the creation of many great works of art and architecture as well as poetry, liturgy, and music. Muslims as well as Christians consider her to be holy above all women, and her name "Maryam" appears more often in the Koran than "Mary" does in the Bible.

Ⓐ________ clues about her life are elusive. Scholars of Mary must take what they can from Hebrew Scriptures, first-century Mediterranean texts, the New Testament, and archaeological digs. Ⓑ________ so little is known of Mary from Scripture, "You can project on her whatever cultural values you have," says Amy-Jill Levine, a professor of New Testament and Jewish Studies at Vanderbilt University. "She can be the grieving mother, the young virgin, the goddess figure. Just as Jesus is the ideal man, Mary is the ideal woman."

10. Which of the following best fits in Ⓐ and Ⓑ?

① Yet — Because
② Since — Still
③ However — Still
④ As — Since

정답 및 해설

Unit 1. 순서 배열 유형

Unit 2. 문장 삽입 유형

Unit 3. 무관한 문장 유형

Unit 4. 어휘 유형

Unit 5. 빈칸 연결사 유형

정답 및 해설

Unit 1. 순서 배열 유형

1.③ 우리가 아무것도 변하지 않는 행성에 살았다면 할 일이 거의 없었을 것입니다. 알아낼 수 있는 것은 아무것도 없었을 것입니다. ⓐ 그리고 만약 우리가 상황이 무작위나 매우 복잡한 방식으로 변하는 예측할 수 없는 세계에 살았다면, 우리는 상황을 파악할 수 없었을 것입니다. ⓑ 다시 말하지만, 과학이란 존재하지 않을 것입니다. ⓒ 하지만 우리는 사물이 변화하는 중간 우주에 살고 있지만 패턴, 규칙, 또는 우리가 자연의 법칙이라고 부르는 것에 따라 살고 있습니다. ⓓ 과학에 대한 추진력은 없을 것입니다. 내가 막대기를 공중에 던지면 항상 아래로 떨어집니다. 해가 서쪽에 지면 다음 날 아침 동쪽에서 항상 다시 떠오릅니다. 그래서 상황을 파악하는 것이 가능해집니다. 우리는 과학을 할 수 있으며, 과학을 통해 우리의 삶을 개선할 수 있습니다.

이종현T의 독해 Point!

글의 중심은 ⓒ의 "but" 전환문이다.
그 앞에는 두 개의 비현실 세계에 대한 가정(ⓓ, ⓐ)이 대조적으로 나열되고, 그 후 과학의 가능성을 말하며 마무리된다.
한 줄 논리를 만들기 위해 ⓒ를 중심으로 전후를 배열한 것이 핵심 전략이다.

2.② 연설에 수반되는 제스처 세트 내에서 우리는 음성 메시지의 내용을 반영하는 제스처와 언급되는 메시지를 나타내는 제스처를 구분할 수 있습니다. 아이코닉은 손가락으로 "작은 상자를 찾고 있어요"라고 말하면서 공중의 사각형을 추적하는 것처럼 말하는 것의 의미를 반영하는 것처럼 보이는 제스처입니다. 상징적인 제스처 자체가 말하는 것과 '의미'가 같은 것은 아니지만 '의미'를 더할 수 있습니다. 예를 들어 한 여성이 "나는 다시 개를 쫓았다"고 말하는 동안 마치 무기를 든 것처럼 손을 감은 채 팔뚝을 위아래로 움직이고 있었습니다. 무기를 포함한 전달된 메시지는 말과 제스처를 결합하여 이루어집니다. 또 다른 일반적인 제스처 그룹은 덕어로 설명할 수 있습니다.

(A) 이 경우 제스처와 음성이 결합하여 현재의 물리적 공간이 아닌 공유 기억에만 존재하는 무언가를 성공적으로 참조할 수 있습니다.

(B) '직설적'이라는 용어는 '지적'을 의미하며, 우리는 대화할 때 종종 제스처를 사용하여 사물이나 사람을 가리킵니다.

(C) 나중에 "저 케이크 맛있었어요"라고 말할 때도 같은 제스처와 같은 테이블(케이크가 더 이상 올려져 있지 않음)을 사용할 수 있습니다.

(D) 현재 상황에서는 예를 들어 손으로 테이블(케이크가 그려진)을 가리키며 누군가에게 "케이크 드실래요?"라고 물을 때 딕틱을 사용할 수 있습니다.

이종현T의 독해 Point!

Pivot 문장 (B) : 개념 정의 및 전체 단락의 도입 역할 수행
(D) → (C) : 예시 나열, 시간 흐름상 현재 → 과거 순으로 배열
(A) : 맥락 요약, shared memory 언급은 (C)의 문맥에서 가장 자연스럽게 이어짐
전체는 정의 → 구체적 예시 → 일반화 순의 귀납적 구조

3.④ (A) 샬롯 퍼킨스 길먼의 작품을 읽는 모든 독자는 그녀가 같은 이야기를 반복한다는 것을 알고 있습니다. (B) 길먼의 소설에서 아날로그의 사용은 단순한 특정 줄거리나 주제의 반복 그 이상입니다. (C) 예를 들어, 그녀가 개인과 사회적 건강 사이의 관계를 다룰 때 특히 효과적입니다. (D) 그녀의 글의 이 특징을 아날로그의 글이라고 설명하고 싶습니다. [E] 그녀가 예술과 이념을 모두 조직하고 표현한 방식에 대한 이해는 매우 중요합니다.

이종현T의 독해 Point!

(A) 도입/문제 제기
→ "Gilman은 반복적인 이야기를 쓴다"
→ 현상 진술이자 글의 시작점
(D) 논리 중심
→ 이 반복적 특성에 'analogue'라는 이름을 붙임 (개념 명명)
(B) 개념 정의
→ analogue는 단순한 반복이 아닌 의미 있는 장치임을 설명
(E) 개념의 중요성 강조
→ 이 개념은 Gilman의 예술성과 이념을 이해하는 핵심
(C) 구체적 예시
→ 사회와 개인 관계를 다룰 때 analogue가 효과적으로 사용된다는 예

4.④ 고대 그리스인들은 자신들을 위해 수학과 천문학을 추구했습니다. 그들은 회계사나 계절 예측가가 되고 싶어서 수학을 공부한 것이 아닙니다. 그들의 유일한 욕망은 세상을 더 잘 이해하는 것이었습니다. 우리는 셰익스피어의 햄릿과 월트 휘트먼의 시를 읽었습니다. 그들의 대사는 하늘을 가로지르는 혜성처럼 아름다워서 모든 유명한 구절을 낭송할 수밖에 없었습니다.

(A) 하지만 저는 그리스인들에게 칭찬할 만한 점이 있다고 생각합니다. 그들은 호기심이 괴팍하다고 요구할 때 부끄러워하지 않았습니다. 그들은 항상 지식의 본질적인 이익을 물질적 이익보다 중요하게 여겼습니다. 수학적 지식이나 우리가 어떻게 살아야 하는지에 대한 지식을 면밀히 조사할 실질적인 이유가 없었습니다. 그들은 쓸모없는 지식이 문명을 가능하게 하는 데 필수적이며, 삶에서 바람직한 것을 함양하는 데 필수적이라고 제안합니다.

(B) 그렇다면 별과 기타 쓸모없는 지식에 대한 연구는 어떻게 문명을 가능하게 할까요? 별에 대한 연구는 도시의 빛 외에도 밤하늘에 본질적으로 우아하고 멋진 무언가가 있다는 것을 시사합니다. 수백만 년 전에 빛이 시작된 별의 화려함은 자연스러운 예술 작품으로 우리를 마주하게 합니다. 하지만 별에 대한 연구는 자연의 아름다움을 감상할 수 있게 해줄 뿐만 아니라 우리 안에 관조적인 마음의 습관을 만들어 냅니다.

(C) 현실로 돌아가서 그 구절들이 무슨 소용이 있을까요? 셰익스피어의 아름답게 쓰여진 대사를 기억하면 새로운 메르세데스가 탄생할까요? 자본주의의 병폐를 강조하는 데 도움이 될까요? 아니면 사회 계층의 최상위에 오르는 데 도움이 될까요? 안타깝게도 그렇지 않습니다. 제가 들은 바와 같이 지식은 우리에게 좋은 경력을 제공하기 위한 도구일 뿐입니다. 따라서 저는 실용적인 지식의 필요성에 굴복하고 예술과 인문학의 무용성을 소홀히 해야 합니다.

도시 생활은 빠르고 사람들을 불안하게 만듭니다. 사업가의 하루는 회의로 가득 차 있습니다. 그는 평온함 속에서 자신과 주변에서 일어나는 모든 일을 면밀히 살펴볼 시간이 거의 없습니다. 별을 바라보면서 그는 이전에 소홀히 했던 아름다움을 발견합니다. 별들이 가만히 서서 그를 바라볼 때, 그는 그들의 외딴 아름다움에 경외심을 품고 명상에 필수적인 마음의 평화를 얻을 수 있습니다. 별들에 대한 연구를 통해 세상을 감상함으로써 얻는 즐거움은 더욱 풍성해지고 풍성해집니다. 우리의 감수성을 높이고 영혼을 정화합니다. 우리를 문명화합니다.

이종현T의 독해 Point!

지문은 무용한 지식의 가치를 다루며, 그 예시로 별과 예술을 들고 있다. (C)는 현실적인 시각에서 출발하여 "아름다운 시구를 외워도 메르세데스를 사는 데 아무 소용이 없다"며 무용한 지식을 냉소적으로 부정하는 현실 인식으로 시작된다. 이 문장은 전체 글의 도입과 반어적 문제 제기 역할을 하며, 후속 문단을 위한 출발점이다. 이어지는 (A)는 이러한 냉소에 대해 반론을 제기하며, 그리스인들의 지적 자세를 예시로 들고, '무용해 보이는 지식이야말로 문명을 가능케 한다'는 핵심 논지를 제시한다. 마지막으로 (B)는 그 핵심 논지를 구체화하며, 별의 아름다움을 감상하는 사색적 사고의 확장을 통해 인간의 정신이 고양되고 문명이 이루어진다는 본문의 결론으로 이어진다. 전체 구조는 냉소적 현실 인식(C) → 고대의 지혜를 통한 반론 제시(A) → 철학적 · 심미적 구체화와 결론(B)의 논리적 흐름으로 전개된다.

5.③ 많은 사람들이 추운 겨울 아침에 자동차 시동을 거는 데 어려움을 겪습니다. 차가운 자동차에서는 엔진이 더 느리게 회전하고 때로는 전혀 회전하지 않는 경우가 있습니다. 자동차 소유자는 차가운 엔진을 탓할 수도 있지만, 진짜 문제는 시동 모터에 동력을 공급하는 차가운 배터리입니다. 이 모터는 일반적으로 배터리를 사용하여 회로에 연결됩니다.

(A) 이동하는 전자의 수를 늘리면 전류가 증가하여 모터에 사용

할 수 있는 전력의 양이 증가합니다.

(B) 모터가 배터리와 회로에 연결되면 전자가 회로를 통해 이동하여 전류를 생성합니다.

(C) 마찬가지로, 이동하는 전자의 수를 줄이면 사용 가능한 전력의 양이 줄어듭니다.

이종현T의 독해 Point!

이 지문은 겨울철 자동차 시동 문제의 원인이 배터리 전류와 관련 있다는 점을 설명한다. (B)는 배터리 회로에 연결된 모터에서 전자가 흐르며 전류를 생성한다는 전기 흐름의 기본 원리를 설명하며 전체의 출발점이 되는 pivot 문장이다. 이어지는 (A)는 전자의 흐름이 많아지면 전류가 세지고, 그만큼 모터에 공급되는 동력도 증가한다는 원리적 확장이다. 마지막으로 (C)는 (A)의 역방향 설명으로, 전류가 줄면 동력도 줄어든다는 대조적 정리다. 전체 구조는 원리 소개(B) → 강화될 때의 효과(A) → 약화될 때의 결과(C)로 이어지는 논리적 흐름이다.

6.② 여러 질병이 유전자 결함으로 인해 발생합니다. 유전자 치료의 목표는 장애를 치료하기 위해 환자의 세포에 올바른 유전자를 삽입하는 것입니다. 일부 초기 치료법은 성공적이었습니다. 하지만 유전자 치료에는 몇 가지 단점이 있습니다.

(A) 우선, 치료는 반복적으로 이루어져야 합니다.

(B) 이러한 장애물에도 불구하고 과학자들은 유전자 치료가 개별 환자에게 맞춤형 의료 치료를 제공할 수 있는 잠재력을 제공한다고 믿습니다.

(C) 또한 신체의 면역 체계가 부정적으로 반응하여 치료를 거부하고 환자를 사망에 이르게 할 가능성이 있습니다.

최근 망막 질환 환자의 시력 회복을 위한 노력이 성공적으로 이루어지고 있습니다.

이종현T의 독해 Point!

이 지문은 유전자 치료의 잠재력과 한계를 다루며, 단점의 열거와 희망적인 전망을 함께 제시한다. (A)는 반복적인 시술이 필요하다는 점을 들어 단점의 첫 번째 예를 제시하며, (C)는 치명적일 수 있는 면역 거부 반응이라는 두 번째 단점을 추가한다. 이 둘은 함께 'drawbacks'에 대한 구체적인 설명 역할을 한다. 마지막으로 (B)는 이러한 단점에도 불구하고 유전자 치료가 개별 환자 맞춤 치료로 이어질 수 있다는 전망을 제시하며 역전된 긍정적 결론으로 기능한다. 전체 흐름은 단점 제시(A → C) → 반전된 기대와 희망(B)의 구조를 따른다.

7.③ 12월이 다가왔습니다 : 상점 전면이 휴일 장식으로 장식되어 있고, 추위가 다가오고 있으며, 또 다른 해가 다가오고 있습니다. 12월은 고대 로마인들이 첫 달력을 세운 이래로 한 해의 끝과 겨울의 시작을 의미합니다. 어원에서 알 수 있듯이 12월은 라틴어 어근인 '십'에서 유래했지만, 12월은 우리의 열두 번째 달입니다.

(A) 고대 로마 달력은 3월에 시작된 1년 중 10개월만 사용했기 때문입니다. 결국 기원전 45년 율리우스력이 제정될 무렵에는 12월 다음 해 말에 1월과 2월이 추가되었습니다.

(B) 9월, 10월, 11월에도 이상한 숫자 차이가 나타나며, 이는 각각 9개월, 10개월, 11개월임에도 불구하고 "7개월", "8개월", "9개월"을 의미합니다.

(C) 1월과 2월은 연초에 등장하여 원래의 모든 달을 두 달 뒤로 밀어내고 원래 할당된 이름 그대로 두었습니다.

이종현T의 독해 Point!

이 글은 "December가 'decem(10)'이라는 어원을 가졌는데 왜 실제로는 12월이 되었는가?"라는 의문에서 출발한다. (B)는 이와 같은 달 이름과 실제 순서 사이의 불일치를 먼저 지적하며, 독자의 궁금증을 유발하는 문제 제기 역할을 한다. 이어서 (A)는 그 원인을 역사적으로 설명하며, 고대 로마의 달력은 원래 3월부터 시작했고 10개월만 있었기 때문에 December가 실제로는 10번째 달이었다는 배경을 제공한다. 마지막으로 (C)는 이후 달력 개편으로 1월과 2월이 맨 앞으로 이동하면서 달의 위치만 바뀌고 이름은 그대로 남게 되었다는 결과 정리로 마무리된다. 전체 흐름은 문제 제기(B) → 원인 설명(A) → 결과 정리(C)로 이어지는 자연스러운 한 줄 논리 구조다.

8.⑤ 어린 자녀에 관한 일련의 실험연구에서 부모들이 흔히 사용하는 급식 관행은, 뜻하지 않게 그들의 의도와 반대되는 행동을 조장하는 것으로 보였다.

(C) 예를 들어, 맛있는 음식에 대한 접근 제한은 이러한 '금지된 음식'에 대한 어린이의 선호와 섭취를 조장한다. 어린이에게 특정한 음식을 먹도록 강요하거나 압박하는 것은 그 음식들에 대한 선호를 감소시킨다. 어린이에게 싫어하는 음식을 먹은 것에 대해 보상해주는 것은 그 음식에 대한 선호도가 감소하도록 만든다.

(B) 다른 한편으로는, 어린이가 장려된 행동에 대한 보상으로서 달콤한 음식과 달지 않은 음식 둘 다를 받게 되면, 그 음식들에 대한 선호도가 높아진다.

(A) 미국 사회에서는 어린이가 긍정적인 행동을 한 상황에서 고지방 음식과 단 음식이 보상으로 거의 전적으로 사용되고 있고, 그러므로 이런 음식에 대한 선호를 더 강화시킨다.

이종현T의 독해 Point!

지문은 부모의 훈육 방식이 아이들의 음식 선호에 어떤 의도치 않은 영향을 주는지를 설명한다. (C)는 실험 결과를 바탕으로, 제한하거나 강요하거나 보상하는 방식이 오히려 원치 않는 선호 변화를 일으킨다는 핵심 내용을 제시하며, 글의 출발점이자 중심 논지(pivot) 역할을 한다. 이어지는 (B)는 (C)의 실험 결과 중 특히 "보상"의 사례를 확장하여, 보상으로 제시된 음식(달든 아니든)에 대한 선호가 강화된다는 심리 원리를 덧붙인다. 마지막 (A)는 이를 사회문화적 맥락으로 연결하여, 미국 사회에서는 단 음식이 긍정적 맥락에서 보상으로 사용되기 때문에 단 음식에 대한 선호가 더욱 강화된다고 설명한다. 전체 흐름은 실험 결과 제시(C) → 원리 정리(B) → 사회적 맥락 확장(A)의 논리적 구조로 구성된다.

9.③ 참이기를 바라는 것을 믿고 나서 그것을 정당화시켜줄 증거를 구하는 것은 일상 상황에서 최고의 접근법인 것으로 보이지는 않는다. 예를 들어 당신이 경마대회에 있을 때, 당신이 가장 빠르다고 생각하는 말에 돈을 거는 것이 이성적이겠지만, 당신이 어떤 말에 돈을 걸었기 때문에 그 말이 가장 빠르다고 믿는 것은 말이 안 된다.

(B) 마찬가지로, 매력적이라고 생각하는 직장을 선택하는 것은 이치에 맞지만, 당신이 제안을 수락했기 때문에 직장이 매력적이라고 믿는 것은 비이성적이다.

(C) 그래도 비록 각 경우에 후자의 접근법이 이성적으로 말이 되지 않지만, 아마 당신을 더 행복하게 해 줄 것은 바로 그 비이성적인 추론일 것이다. 그리고 정신은 일반적으로 행복을 향하여 작동하는 것 같다.

(A) 이러한 예 둘 다에서, 연구에 의하면, 사람들이 선택할 가능성이 있는 것은 바로 후자의 선택이다. 인간 사고 과정의 '인과관계의 화살'은 일관적으로 앞이 아니라 뒤를 가리키는 경향이 있다.

이종현T의 독해 Point!

지문은 바람이 판단을 이끄는 비합리적 사고 — 즉 '내가 선택했기 때문에 그게 옳다'는 식의 거꾸로 된 인과 — 에 대해 논하고 있다. (B)는 도입에 제시된 '경마' 예시와 논리적으로 평행한 직업 선택에 관한 새로운 예시를 제시하면서 글의 서론과 자연스럽게 연결된다. 이어지는 (C)는 이 비합리적 사고 방식이 비논리적이지만 오히려 행복을 증진시킨다는 심리학적 통찰을 덧붙이며 글의 핵심 주장을 확장한다. 마지막 (A)는 실험 연구 결과를 통해 이 모든 사고 경향이 "일관되게 '원인 → 결과'가 아닌 '결과 → 원인'으로 작용한다는 점(역인과성)"을 정리하며, 전체 논지에 대한 귀결 및 일반화 역할을 한다. 전체 흐름은 새 예시 제시(B) → 통찰과 의미 확장(C) → 실증적 정리(A)의 순서로 전개된다.

10.② 우리가 느낀 첫인상에 따라 사람들에게 꼬리표를 붙이는 것은 인지 과정의 불가피한 부분이다. 이러한 꼬리표는 해석을 하는 한 방법이다. '그녀는 명랑한 것 같아.' '그는 진실해 보여.' '그들은 끔찍할 정도로 자만심이 강해.'

(B) 그것들이 정확하다면, 이러한 인상은 미래의 사람들에게 가장 잘 대응하는 방법을 결정하는 유용한 방법일 수 있다. 그러나 우리가 붙이는 꼬리표가 부정확할 때 문제가 발생하는데, 왜냐하면 우리가 누군가에 대한 의견을 형성한 후, 우리는 그것을 고집하고 어떠한 상충하는 정보도 우리의 이미지에 들어맞게 만드는 경향이 있기 때문이다.

(A) 예를 들어 당신이 친구에게 당신의 새로운 이웃의 이름을 언급한다고 가정 해 보자. "아, 나 그 사람 알아." 당신의 친구가 대답한다. "그는 처음엔 친절한 것 같지만 그건 전부 연기였어." 아마 이러한 평가는 완전히 틀릴지도 모른다.

(C) 판단이 정확하든 그렇지 않든, 당신 친구의 평가를 받아들이고 나면, 그것은 십중팔구 당신이 그 이웃에게 대응하는 방식에 영향을 줄 것이다. 당신은 당신이 들었던 위선의 예를 찾아볼 것이며 십중팔구 그것을 찾아낼 것이다.

이종현T의 독해 Point!

지문은 우리가 첫인상으로 사람들에게 '레이블'을 붙이는 과정이 지각의 일부이자, 때론 부정확한 평가를 고착시킨다는 심리적 메커니즘을 설명한다. (B)는 이 현상에 대한 정의와 장단점, 특히 " '문제는 부정확한 평가가 굳어질 때 생긴다'는 핵심 논지(pivot)"를 명확히 제시한다. (A)는 이러한 현상이 실제 상황에서 어떻게 나타나는지를 보여주는 사례 제시이며, 친구의 평가가 정확하든 아니든 그 평가가 행동에 영향을 준다는 점을 설명한다. 마지막 (C)는 그 영향이 어떻게 작용하는지를 분석하며, 고정된 평가가 이후의 관찰마저 왜곡하게 만든다는 인지 편향의 심리적 결론으로 마무리한다. 전체 구조는 핵심 주장(B) → 예시(A) → 결과(C)의 논리적 흐름이다.

11.③ 물론, 사람들은 많은 다양한 종류의 식사를 하고, 알맞은 청중에게 알맞은 메시지를 전달하려는 의도로 그것들을 선택한다.

(B) 혼자 서두르며 먹는 일상의 음식을 위해서 사치스러운 재료에 거금을 쓰지 않는 것처럼, 연인이 될 가능성이 있는 사람에게 깊은 인상을 주려고 애쓸 때, 반 정도 먹다 남은 음식을 다시 데우지는 않을 것이다. 어떤 의미에서 모든 음식은 그 자체의 부호화된 메시지를 지닌다.

(C) 그러나 이것이 언제나 다른 사람에 의해 쉽사리 인식되거나 정확하게 이해된다고 말하는 것은 아니다. 식사를 준비하는 사람에게는 편안한 약식 행위로 의도될지도 모르는 것이 초대받은 손님에게는 게으름으로 해석될지도 모른다.

(A) 마찬가지로, 채식주의자에게 제공된 구운 소고기로 구성된 식사는 고의적인 모욕으로 해석될 수도 있다. 모든 언어에서처럼, 잘못된 전달이 있을 수 있다. 이것(잘못된 전달이 있음)에도 불구하고, 먹는 일을 관찰하거나 의견을 말하는 외부인은 아주 큰 어려움 없이 보통 의도된 메시지를 해독할 수 있다.

이종현T의 독해 Point!

이 글은 식사가 일종의 커뮤니케이션 수단으로 작용한다는 전제를 바탕으로, 그 메시지가 의도와 다르게 해석될 수 있다는 점을 설명한다. (B)는 구체적인 예시를 통해 식사의 구성과 맥락이 특정한 '의미'를 전달한다는 주장을 시작하며, 글의 도입이자 핵심 논지(pivot) 역할을 한다. 이어지는 (C)는 그 메시지가 항상 제대로 해석되지 않을 수도 있다는 점을 보완적으로 설명하며, 의도와 해석 사이의 간극을 강조한다. 마지막 (A)는 이러한 오해 가능성을 확장하여, "극단적인 예시(채식주의자에게 고기 제공)"를 통해 잘못된 해석이 모욕이 될 수도 있다는 사례를 들고, 그럼에도 불구하고 보통은 해석이 어렵지 않다며 정리한다. 전체 흐름은 (의미 있는 식사 선택) → (해석 오류 가능성) → (실제 사례와 일반적 결론)으로 이어지는 논리적 전개다.

12.② 지중해에 있는 국가에서 고대의 난파선은 오랫동안 다른 어떠한 고고학적 유적지처럼 다루어져 왔다. 그것의 기원과는 관계없이, 고대의 난파선은 그것이 자리잡고 있는 영해의 국가에 속한다.

(B) 그것을 어느 방식으로든 건드리기 위해서는, 외국이나 국내의 고고학자들은 그 나라 정부의 고고학 부처로부터 공식 허가를 받기 위해 적절한 증명서를 가져야 한다.

(A) 지난 세기에 너무나 많은 고대 유물이 이런 국가들에서 외국의 박물관과 수집품으로 빼앗겼기 때문에, 이 접근법이 안전장치로 개발되었다.

(C) 따라서 비록 불법적인 고대 유물의 약탈이 주변의 육상에서처럼 지중해 아래에서도 실제로 일어나기는 하지만, 많은 지역에서보다 지중해에서 더 적은 보물 약탈이 있었다.

이종현T의 독해 Point!

지문은 고대 지중해 선박 침몰 유적이 국가의 고고학적 자산으로 다뤄지는 방식과 그 배경, 결과를 설명한다. (B)는 "이 유적을 조사하려면 반드시 정부의 허가를 받아야 한다"는 현행 규정을 설명하며, 글의 구체적 정책 설명이자 pivot 역할을 한다. 이어지는 (A)는 이러한 엄격한 규정이 왜 생겨났는가에 대한 역사적 배경을 제공하며, 외국으로의 유물 유출을 막기 위한 보호 장치였음을 밝힌다. 마지막 (C)는 이러한 제도적 배경과 규제가 실제로 어떤 결과를 낳았는지를 설명하며, "보물 사냥이 줄어들었다"는 긍정적 효과와 "불법 도굴은 여전히 존재한다"는 현실을 균형 있게 덧붙인다. 전체 논리는 (규정 설명) → (정책의 기원) → (정책의 결과)로 이어지는 구조적 흐름을 따른다

13.② 어떤 사람이 성인기의 어떤 지점에서 어떻게 행동하는지는 그의 과거 경험과 그가 당면한 문제에 의해 강하게 영향을 받는다. 이러한 생의 주기적 요소들은 성인들의 행동을 평가할 때 고려되어야 한다. 예를 들어, 학교로 돌아가기로 선택하는 중년 여성은 적응 장애를 겪고 있는 것이 아닐지도 모른다. 그녀는 단지 자신의 새로운 면을 계발하고 싶은 건지도 모른다.

(B) 어떤 사람들은 그것이 전혀 사실이 아닌데도 그녀의 결정을 자신의 현재 생활 상황을 처리하지 못하는 것으로 해석할지도 모른다. 그게 아니라 그녀는 자신의 생활을 이성적으로 평가하고, 예컨대 자신의 직업에서 앞으로 나아가기 위하여 학위가 필요하다고 깨달은 것이다.

(A) 마찬가지로, 사적인 질문에 모호한 답변을 내놓는, 더 나이 든 남자는 저항하는 게 아닐지도 모른다. 그는 단지 자신의 내적 자아를 낯선 사람에게 드러내지 않으려는 그의 세대의 경향을 반영하고 있는 것일지도 모른다.

(C) 가장 중요한 것은, 특정 징후의 의미가 나이에 따라 바뀔 수도 있다는 것이다. 예를 들어 아침에 일찍 일어나는 문제는 젊은 성인에게는 우울증을 나타내는 것일지도 모르지만 더 나이든 성인에게는 단지 정상적인 노화의 결과일지도 모른다.

이종현T의 독해 Point!

지문은 성인의 행동을 평가할 때 반드시 과거 경험과 생애주기적 요인을 고려해야 하며, 그렇지 않으면 오해가 발생할 수 있다는 점을 강조한다. (B)는 지문에 제시된 중년 여성 사례에 대한 오해 가능성과 그 현실적 동기를 구체화하며, 글의 '핵심 주장(pivot)'을 구체적으로 전개한다. 이어지는 (A)는 또 다른 사례로, 노년 남성의 비개방적 태도가 세대 문화의 반영일 수 있음을 보여주며 동일 논리를 확장한다. 마지막 (C)는 구체적 사례에서 벗어나, 증상 해석이 연령에 따라 달라질 수 있다는 일반 원칙을 제시하며 글의 논지를 추상화 및 귀결 형태로 정리한다. 전체 흐름은 (중년 여성 사례 구체화) → (노년 남성 사례 확장) → (연령별 증상 해석의 원리)로 이어지는 구조다.

14.④ 1980년대 초반, 개인용 컴퓨터가 처음 이용 가능해졌을 때 소프트웨어 발행자들은 자신들의 지적 재산이라 여기는 것(즉, 프로그램의 핵심 코드)을 해커들이 복제할지도 모른다고 우려했다.

(C) 프로그램의 핵심 코드에 접근하는 것은 꽤 간단했으며, 그것을 규제하는 법이 그 당시에는 그다지 명확하지 않았다. 그래서 응용 프로그램이 출시되기 전에 기록되지 않은 작은 특징이 추가되었다.

(A) 이렇게 하여, 그 핵심 코드가 도난당해 다른 응용 프로그램으로 개조되면, 그 기록되지 않은 특징도 새 프로그램에 포함될 것이었다. 그리고 그것은 절도의 증거를 구성할 것이었다.

(B) 그 관행은 프로그래머들이 자신들이 한 작업에 대해 항상 공식적인 인정을 얻지는 못했던 1980년대 후반에 정말 큰 인기를 얻었다. 자신들이 관련돼 있음을 증명하기 위해서, 단지 자신들이 처음에 거기에 있었음을 보이고자 그들은 코드 안에 작은 무언가를 심곤 했다.

이종현T의 독해 Point!

지문은 1980년대 초 컴퓨터 프로그램의 저작권 보호가 느슨했던 시절, 프로그램 도난을 막기 위해 숨겨진 코드(undocumented feature)를 삽입하는 관행이 생겨났음을 설명한다. (C)는 당시 코어 코드를 훔치기 쉬웠고 법적 제재도 불분명했기 때문에, 미리 숨겨진 기능을 삽입했다는 배경 설명이자 전환의 중심(pivot) 역할을 한다. 이어지는 (A)는 이런 숨겨진 기능이 도난이 발생했을 때 증거로 기능한다는 원리를 설명하며, (C)의 내용에 기능적 목적을 더한다. 마지막 (B)는 이 관행이 이후에는 도난 방지 목적뿐 아니라, 자신이 만든 코드임을 증명하려는 수단으로 확장되었다고 설명하며 역사적 발전을 덧붙인다. 전체 흐름은 (당시 상황 설명) → (방지 목적) → (개발자 신원 증명 수단으로의 확장)이라는 논리적 전개다.

15.② 훌륭한 언어적 의사소통은 그것이 개인적인 관계이건 직업적인 관계이건 모든 성공적인 관계의 기초라고 알려져 있다. 그러나 우리가 의사소통할 때 가장 크게 말하는 것은 우리의 비언어적인 단서들이다.

(B) 우리가 다른 사람과 소통할 때, 우리는 계속해서 그러한 말 없는 신호를 주고받는다. 우리의 비언어적인 행동의 모든 것, 다시 말해, 우리의 몸짓, 우리가 앉는 방식, 우리가 얼마나 빨리 또는 얼마나 크게 말하는가, 우리가 얼마나 가까이 서 있는가, 우리가 얼마나 많이 눈을 마주치는가는 강한 메시지를 보낸다.

(A) 이러한 메시지는 여러분이 말하는 것을 멈출 때 멈추지 않는다. 여러분이 아무 말도 하지 않을 때도 여전히 비언어적으로 소통하는 것이다. 자주 우리의 입으로 나오는 것과 우리의 몸짓을 통해 의사소통하는 것은 둘이 전적으로 다르다.

(C) 이러한 혼합된 신호에 직면했을 때, 듣는 사람은 언어적인 메시지를 선택해야 할까 비언어적인 메시지를 선택해야 할까를 선택해야 하는 데, 어떤 주어진 순간에 우리의 진정한 감정과 의도를 무심코 누설하는 것은 자연스럽고 무의식적인 언어이기 때문에 그 사람은 많은 경우에 비언어적인 메시지를 선택한다.

이종현T의 독해 Point!

지문은 비언어적 신호가 언어보다 강한 메시지를 전달한다는 사실을 강조한다. (B)는 우리가 일상적으로 비언어적 신호를 주고받고 있으며, 그 예시(자세, 말투, 눈맞춤 등)를 제시함으로써 비언어적 소통의 범위와 중요성을 설명하는 도입이자 논리 중심 pivot 문장이다. 이어지는 (A)는 이러한 비언어적 메시지가 말을 멈춘 후에도 계속되며, 심지어 말과 충돌할 수 있다는 점을 부연 설명하면서 (B)의 내용을 자연스럽게 확장한다. 마지막 (C)는 이러한 언어-비언어 불일치 상황에서 사람들은 대부분 비언어적 메시지를 더 신뢰한다는 심리적 결론을 제시하며, 전체 논지를 강조와 귀결로 마무리한다. 전체 흐름은 (비언어 신호의 범위와 예시) → (침묵과 불일치까지 포함한 확장) → (비언어가 더 신뢰받는 이유)로 구성된다.

16.② 곤충에게서 휴식이라기보다는 수면, 그래서 '무의식(의 상태)'(이 용어가 사용될 수 있는 때)이 확실히 발견될 수 있다.

(A) 예를 들어, 야간에 벌은 약 6시간에서 8시간가량 잠을 자는데 그때 흔히 그것은 더듬이를 '축 늘어뜨리고', 자신에게 충돌하는 다른 벌들에 대해 거의 반응을 보이지 않는다. 대부분 곤충이 시력이 아주 좋지만, 눈꺼풀이 없어서 눈을 보고서는 그것들이 자고 있는지를 분간할 수 없다.

(C) 하지만, 더듬이가 눈만큼이나, 그리고 아마도 눈보다 더 중요하기 때문에, 축 늘어진 더듬이는 그 동물이 현실과 접촉한 상태가 아니고 단지 쉬고 있는 것이 아니라는 것을 확실히 보여준다. 예를 들어 벌은 끊임없이 움직이는 병에 그것들을 가둬두어 그 곤충들이 내내 날아다녀야 하게 만듦으로써 쉽게 잠을 빼앗 기게 할 수 있다.

(B) 병이 움직임을 멈출 때, 그것들은 편안히 자리를 잡고 병의 추가적인 부드러운 흔들림에 대해 보통 때보다 훨씬 덜 반응을 한다. 그것은 마치 그것들의 수면 상태가 손실에 대한 보상으로 더 깊어진 것 같다.

이종현T의 독해 Point!

이 글은 곤충, 특히 벌의 수면 상태가 단순한 휴식이 아닌 의미 있는 무의식 상태라는 점을 논리적으로 보여주는 글이다. (A)는 글의 pivot 문장으로, 벌이 6~8시간 동안 수면 상태에 있으며 '안테나가 축 처지고, 자극에도 무반응하다'는 관찰 사례를 구체적으로 제시하며 글의 주제를 본격적으로 전개한다. 이어지는 (C)는 (A)에서 언급된 안테나의 변화가 '단순한 휴식이 아님'을 더 강하게 주장하면서, 눈 대신 안테나가 수면 판단의 기준이 될 수 있음을 논리적으로 설명하고, 수면 박탈 실험의 시작을 제시한다. 마지막 (B)는 그 실험의 결과로, 벌들이 수면을 방해받은 뒤 더 깊은 반응 둔화 상태에 빠진다는 관찰을 통해 곤충 수면의 실재성과 보상 메커니즘까지 입증한다.

전체 흐름은 수면 관찰 사례(A) → 논리적 해석과 수면 박탈 실험(C) → 수면 보상 결과(B)로 이어지는 구조다.

17.② 조직 안에서의 (일) 처리의 능숙함과 관련된 흥미로운 하나의 질문은 조직이 그들의 직원과 고객의 의견을 어떻게 평가하는지에 관련된 것이다. 다음의 예를 살펴보자.

(B) 한 관리자가 한 직원으로부터 회사 정책이 바뀌어야 한다는 요청을 끊임없이 받는다. 그러한 요청으로, 그 관리자는 조직 안에서의 다른 사람들이 문제가 되고 있는 이 사안에 대해 어떻게 느끼는지를 판단해야 한다.

(A) 강경하게 의견을 밝히는 직원의 잦은 요구는 조직 안에서의 나머지 사람들 이 그 정책에 대해 어떻게 느끼는지에 대한 관리자의 인식에 편견을 갖게 할 것인가? Weaver, Garcia, Schwartz, 그리고 Miller의 연구가 그 답은 그렇다는 것을 시사한다.

(C) 여섯 차례의 연속된 실험에서, 그들은 인지된 친숙함이 특히 강경하게 의견을 밝히는 한 구성원에게서 나오는 결과라고 할지라도, 사람들은 친숙한 의견이 일반적인 의견이라고 추론하는 경향이 있다는 것을 입증했다.

이종현T의 독해 Point!

지문은 조직 내에서 한 사람의 반복된 의견이 전체 구성원의 의견처럼 잘못 해석될 수 있다는 점을 설명한다.

(B)는 글의 논리적 pivot으로, "한 직원의 반복된 요청을 보고, 관리자는 전체 구성원이 어떻게 느끼는지를 유추해야 한다"는 문제 상황을 구체적으로 설정한다.

(A)는 이 상황에 대한 의문을 던지고 바로 연구 결과로 연결하며, "그렇다"는 답과 함께 이 문제의 현실성을 부각시킨다.

(C)는 Weaver 등의 실험을 통해 한 사람의 반복된 메시지가 의견의 '친숙성'을 만들어내고, 그것이 '대다수의 의견'처럼 느껴지게 만든다는 심리학적 원리를 설명하며 논리를 귀결한다.

전체 구조는 사례 도입(B) → 질문 및 정답 제시(A) → 이론적 근거(C)로 구성되어 있다.

18.④ 어느 따뜻한 봄날, 한 테니스 코치가 학생과 공을 서브하는 기술을 연습하고 있었다. 학생이 반복해서 공을 던지고 치는 동안, 코치는 학생의 움직임과 스윙을 이루는 각 부분에 주의를 쏟았다.

(C) 코치는 학생의 실수에 대해서 절대 비판하지 않았으나, 그 대신 매번 공을 칠 때마다 라켓의 위치, 공을 던져 올리는 높이, 라켓이 공을 칠 때의 각도, 그리고 라켓의 마무리 동작 때 학생의 움직임에 대해 피드백을 주었다. 테니스에서는 성공적인 타구로 평가받기 위해 공이 서비스 코트 안으로 떨어져야 한다.

(A) 하지만 놀랍게도, 코치는 학생의 서브 이후에 공이 어디에 착지하는지 보기 위해 한 번도 확인하지 않았다. 그 대신에, 코치는 학생의 서비스 타격법의 각 부분을 향상시키기 위한 방법에 관한 피드백에만 오로지 집중했다.

(B) 그 코치는 학생이 일단 관련된 각각의 기술을 배우면, 학생

은 그것들을 결합하여 공이 목표 지역에 일관되게 도달하게 할 수 있을 거라 확신하였다.

이종현T의 독해 Point!

지문은 테니스 코치가 학생의 서브 훈련을 지도하면서 결과보다 과정에 집중하는 방식을 보여준다.
(C)는 글의 pivot 문장으로, 코치가 실수를 지적하기보다 각 동작 요소(라켓 위치, 토스 높이 등)에 대한 피드백을 주었다는 핵심 행동을 상세히 설명한다. 또한 "In tennis, the ball needs to land..."라는 문장으로 결과의 중요성도 잠시 상기시키며 주제를 전환할 준비를 한다.
(A)는 이러한 지도 방식의 특징을 요약하며, 코치가 공이 어디로 가는지를 전혀 보지 않았다는 점을 강조하고, 과정 중심 피드백에 초점을 맞췄다는 사실을 부각시킨다.
마지막으로 (B)는 그 이유를 해설하며, 코치는 각각의 기술이 숙달되면 자연히 정확한 결과로 이어질 것이라는 신념을 보여준다.
전체 흐름은 (행동 구체화 → 핵심 특징 강조 → 그 이유 설명)의 논리 구조이며, 중심은 (C)가 잡고 있다.

19.④ 지난 이십 년 동안, 우리는 세금 정책의 변화, 해외 경쟁 증대, 억제하지 않은 정부의 낭비, 그리고 월스트리트의 도둑질을 보아 왔다. 그러나 자료와 연구를 들 여다보면 이것들 중 어느 것도 불평등 증대의 주요 동인이 아니라는 것을 깨닫게 된다.

(C) 대신에 주요 동인은 우리의 경제 체제의 기저를 이루는 과학기술에서의 기하급수적이고 디지털적이며 조합적인 변화이다. 이러한 결론은 비슷한 경향이 대부분의 선진국에서도 보인다는 사실에 의해 강해진다.

(A) 예를 들어 스웨덴, 핀란드, 독일에서는 미국에서보다 수입 불평등이 지난 20년에서 30년 동안 실제로 더 빠르게 상승했다.

(B) 이러한 국가들은 수입 분배에서 불평등이 덜한 상태로 출발했기 때문에 계속해서 미국보다 덜 불평등한 상태로 있지만, 놀라울 정도로 다른 기관, 정부 정책, 문화 전반에 걸쳐 근본적인 경향은 전 세계적으로 비슷하다.

이종현T의 독해 Point!

지문은 소득 불평등의 주요 원인이 흔히 지목되는 요인들(세금 정책, 정부 낭비, 월가 등)이 아니라, 기술 변화에 있다는 점을 강조한다.
(C)는 글의 중심 pivot 문장으로, "진짜 원인은 기술 발전이다"라는 핵심 주장을 명확히 밝히며 전체 논리 전환을 이끈다. 또한 이 주장을 강화하기 위해 "이러한 경향은 다른 선진국에서도 동일하게 나타난다"고 말하며 다음 문장들의 비교 사례를 준비한다.
(A)는 구체적 예시로 스웨덴, 독일, 핀란드에서 미국보다 더 빠르게 불평등이 증가했다는 사실을 제시하며, (C)의 논지를 실증적으로 뒷받침한다.
(B)는 이 국가들의 절대적 불평등 수준은 아직 미국보다 낮지만, 그 증가 추세는 동일하다는 점을 정리하며, 제도나 문화가 달라도 기술 변화라는 공통 요인이 핵심임을 다시 강조한다.
전체 흐름은 핵심 주장(C) → 구체적 예시(A) → 예외적 반론 대비 및 정리(B)로 전개된다.

20.④

(A) 지나치게 오랫동안 빗속에 있어 봤거나 몇 시간 동안 욕조에서 몸을 흠뻑 적셔 본 사람은 누구라도 그들의 손과 발이 주름지게 될 수 있다는 사실을 알고 있다. 일반적 통념은 그것이 단지 피부가 물을 흡수한 것에 지나지 않는다고 말한다.

(D) 그러나 많은 의문이 과학자들을 혼란스럽게 했다. 왜 '젖은 주름'은 손과 발에만 나타나는가? 그리고 왜 가장 두드러진 주름은 손가락과 발가락 끝에 나타날까?

(B) 이제 '두뇌, 행동 그리고 진화'라는 학술지에 실린 한 논문이 젖은 주름이 도움이 된다는 증거를 제공한다. 타이어의 접지면과 유사하게, 그것들은 정지 마찰력을 향상시킨다. 그 연구에서, 한 진화 신경생리학자와 그의 공동 저자들이 물로 인해 주름진 28개의 손가락을 조사했다.

(C) 그들은 손가락들이 모두 나무의 가지처럼 갈라지는 주름 패턴을 지녔음을 발견했다. 이 가지 형태의 패턴은 물이 손끝에서 빠지게 하고, 더 많은 피부 접촉을 돕고 (물건을) 더 잘 쥐게 해준다.

이종현T의 독해 Point!

지문은 "물이 닿으면 손과 발이 쪼글쪼글해지는 현상"이 단순한 수분 흡수 때문이 아니라 기능적인 목적이 있다는 과학적 설명으로 전환되는 구조다.
(A)는 글의 도입이자 pivot 전 단계로, "기존에는 단순히 물을 흡수해서 생기는 현상이라 여겼다"는 일반적 통념을 제시한다.
(D)는 그런 통념에 의문을 제기하는 전환점으로, "왜

손과 발에만 나타나는가?"라는 과학적 질문을 제기하며 논지를 전환하고,
(B)는 본격적으로 과학적 연구 결과를 소개하며 물주름의 기능성(접지력 향상)을 주장하는 핵심 pivot 역할을 한다.
(C)는 실험 결과를 구체적으로 설명하며, 주름이 가지처럼 갈라져 물을 배출하고 그립감을 높인다는 결론을 제공한다.
전체 흐름은 기존 인식(A) → 의문 제기(D) → 과학적 주장 제시(B) → 실험 기반 설명(C)으로 이어지는 구조다.

21.② 꽤 빈번한 경우에 우리는 관찰에서 실수를 한다. 예를 들어, 수업 첫 날 당신의 강사가 무슨 옷을 입고 있었는가? 당신이 추측해야 한다면, 그것은 우리의 일 상적인 관찰의 대부분이 건성이고 반만 의식하는 것이기 때문이다.

(B) 당신이 당신 강사가 무엇을 입고 있는지 관찰하고 기록하겠다는 의식적 계획을 가지고 첫 수업에 갔다면, 당신은 훨씬 더 정확해질 것이다. 많은 경우에 단순한 측정 장치와 복잡한 측정 장치 둘 다 부정확한 관찰에 맞서는 데 도움이 된다.

(A) 그뿐만 아니라, 그것들은 보조를 받지 않은 인간 감각의 능력을 훌쩍 넘어선 정도의 정확성을 더해준다. 예를 들어 당신이 그날 당신 강사의 컬러 사진을 찍었다고 가정해 보라.

(C) 무심한 인간의 탐구와는 반대로, 이와 같은 과학적 관찰 기법은 의식적 활동이 된다. 그것은 당신으로 하여금 당신의 모든 주의를 특정 주제에 맞추도록 요구한다.

이종현T의 독해 Point!

지문은 일상적인 인간 관찰이 부정확할 수 있음을 전제로, 정확한 관찰을 위한 의식적·과학적 방법의 필요성을 설명한다.
(B)는 글의 pivot 문장으로 "처음부터 관찰할 계획을 세우면 더 정확하게 기억할 수 있으며, 측정 기기가 이를 보완해준다"는 내용을 통해 글의 핵심 논지 - 정확한 관찰은 의도와 도구를 통해 달성된다 - 를 명확히 제시한다.
(A)는 이러한 논지를 강화하는 예시 문장으로, 색상 사진처럼 감각을 넘어선 도구가 정확성을 높인다는 사실을 구체화한다.
(C)는 글을 마무리하며, 과학적 관찰은 일상적 관찰과 달리 집중과 의도를 필요로 하는 의식적인 행위임을 이론적으로 정의한다.
전체 흐름은 (논지 제시 B) → (구체적 사례 A) → (개념적 정리 C)의 순서로, 한 줄 논리로 완결되는 구조다.

22.②

(D) 당신은 단 하나의 경험, 특히 다른 이의 것(=경험)으로부터 일반적인 규칙을 추론할 수는 없다.

(B) 일화적인 증거는 대단히 설득력 있고 흥미진진하게 들릴 수 있는 다른 어떤 사람의 개인적 경험에 근거하기 때문에 보통 무시하기가 가장 어려운 충고이다. 만약 여러분의 옆집 사람이 수박 식이요법 이후에 암에서 회복되었다면, 그것은 매우 설득력 있게 들릴 수 있다.

(A) 그러나 우리는 이미 원인과 결과를 당연하다고 생각하는 것의 위험성, 즉 그녀가 회복되기 전에 수박을 먹었다는 단지 그 이유가 그녀의 회복을 일으켰다는 것을 의미하지 않는다는 것을 알고 있다. 또한, 단지 생존자만이 말한다는 것을 기억하라. 아마도 50명의 다른 사람들은 '기적의 수박 치료'를 시도한 후에 암으로 사망했을 것이다.

(C) 일화적인 이야기는 균형이 맞지 않는 시각을 줄 수 있다. 그런데 만약 수박을 먹은 환자가 두 배 더 오래 생존했다는 것을 보여주는 무작위 통제 실험이 있었다면, 그것은 다른 이야기였을 것이다.

이종현T의 독해 Point!

이 글은 일화적 증거(anecdotal evidence)의 위험성과 그에 현혹되지 말아야 할 이유를 설명하는 구조다.
(D)는 글의 pivot 문장으로, "타인의 단일 경험에서 일반 법칙을 추론할 수 없다"는 핵심 원칙을 가장 먼저 제시하며, 글의 중심 논리를 확립한다.
(B)는 (D)의 원칙을 실제 예시로 연결하여, "이웃이 수박 다이어트로 암을 극복한 경험처럼, 일화적 증거는 감정적으로 매우 설득력 있게 다가온다"고 설명하며 현실에서 쉽게 빠지는 오류를 보여준다.
(A)는 그 오류에 대해 논리적으로 반박하며 "그 사람이 살아남았다고 해서 수박이 원인이라는 보장은 없고, 실패한 사람은 말할 기회조차 없다"는 생존자 편향의 함정을 지적한다.
(C)는 마지막으로 해결책을 제시하며, "진짜 믿을 만한 결론은 통제된 과학적 실험이 필요하다"는 점을 강조하며 글을 마무리한다.
전체 흐름은 (원칙 제시 D) → (사례 B) → (반박 A) → (대안 C)의 구조다.

23.⑤ 사이에 낮은 계곡을 가지고 있는 산악 지역들은 에워싸고 있는 평평한 지역보다 더 많은 종의 풍부함을 가지는 경향이 있다는 것은 의심할 여지가 없다.

(C) 이것은 부분적으로 더 다양한 환경이 있고, 각각의 환경은 그 자체의 특 징적인 종의 집단을 가지고 있기 때문이다. 우선, 산에는 다양한 기후대가 있는데, 평평한 저지대에는 오직 한 가지 기후만 있다.

(B) 예를 들어, Arizona 주의 Santa Catalina 산맥에는, 많은 다양한 식물 종이 똑같은 산이지만 별개의 고도에 존재하는데, 각각의 종은 그 자체의 기후 최적 조건에 있다.

(A) 고도에 따른 종 구성의 비슷한 다양성은 Oregon 주의 Siskiyou 산맥과 사실상 거의 모든 높은 산에서 발견되는데, 그것은 단지 그곳에 광범위한 기후가 있기 때문이다.

이종현T의 독해 Point!

이 글은 왜 산악 지역이 평지보다 종 다양성이 높은가에 대한 과학적 설명을 전개한다.
(C)는 글의 pivot 문장으로 "산악 지역은 다양한 환경이 존재하기 때문에 종 다양성이 높다"는 핵심 원인을 제시하며 글의 중심 논지를 형성한다.
이후 (B)는 Santa Catalina Mountains라는 실제 사례를 통해 고도가 다른 지점마다 각기 다른 식물들이 분포한다는 관찰 결과를 제시하며 (C)의 이론을 실증적으로 뒷받침한다.
(A)는 이 현상이 특정 지역에만 국한된 것이 아니라 Oregon의 Siskiyou Mountains 등 다양한 산지에서 반복적으로 나타나는 일반적 패턴임을 말하며, (B)에서 제시된 사례를 확장하고 글을 마무리한다.
전체 구조는 (이론 제시 C) → (구체 사례 B) → (범세계적 일반화 A)로, 한 줄 논리 흐름이 매끄럽게 전개된다.

24.② 1980년대 말 공산주의의 붕괴와 함께, 정부에 대한 민주주의적 접근법과 경제 상태에 대한 시장 접근법과 같은 특정 관점이 전 세계적으로 점점 더 우세해졌다. 민주주의의 옹호자로서, 우리는 전체주의 정권의 쇠퇴와 민주주의의 성공에 고무된다.

(B) Winston Churchill이 마땅히 진술한 대로, 민주주의는 불완전한 정부 형태일지 모르지만, 다른 모든 것들은 더 나쁘다. 우리는 경제 분야에서는 시장 운용에 대한 근본적인 불만이 없다.

(A) 예를 들면, 우리는 출판사들 또는 제약회사들 사이의 경쟁에서 시장이 할 수 있는 긍정적인 역할을 이해한다. 그리고 많은 다른 것들처럼, 우리는 융통성 있고, 비교적 자유방임주의적인 경제 체제로부터 개인적으로 혜택을 받아 왔다.

(C) 하지만 삶의 모든 영역이 시장 모델로 가장 잘 운영되는 것은 아니다. 의학, 과학, 교육, 예술과 같은 주요한 전문 영역은 영리 기업들이 하는 것과 같은 방식으로 작용해서는 안 된다.

이종현T의 독해 Point!

이 글은 민주주의와 시장경제의 확산을 긍정적으로 바라보면서도, 시장 모델이 삶의 모든 영역에 적용되기에는 한계가 있다는 점을 주장하는 구조다.
(B)는 글의 pivot 문장으로, "Churchill의 말처럼 민주주의는 완벽하지 않지만 대안이 없다"는 정치적 입장과 함께, 시장경제에 대해서도 본질적인 거부감은 없음을 명확히 하며 글의 전제와 입장을 확립한다.
(A)는 (B)의 입장을 부연하며, 시장이 경쟁을 촉진하고 유연성을 제공한다는 점에서 시장경제의 이점을 구체적 사례로 뒷받침한다.
(C)는 그러나 전환점 역할을 하며, "삶의 모든 영역이 시장 모델에 적합한 것은 아니다"라는 주장으로 글의 핵심 비판을 제시하며 마무리한다.
전체 흐름은 (기본 입장 제시 B) → (구체적 동의 근거 A) → (비판적 예외 제시 C)의 구조로, 전형적인 양면적 논증 전개다.

25.② Adam Smith는 사회의 가난한 사람들조차 읽기, 쓰기, 그리고 연산의 필수 기술을 습득할 수 있도록 주로 정부가 비용을 대는 보편적인 공교육의 설립을 권장했다.

(B) 이러한 제안은 영국지배층 사이에 널리 퍼진 지식에 반하는 것이었는데, 그들은 그것이 복종하려는 의욕을 꺾을 것이라고 두려워했다. 하지만 Smith가 교육을 의무적인 것으로 만들자고 주창한 것은 아니다.

(A) 대신에 그는 교육을 더 접근하기 쉽고 더 실용적으로 만들려는 계획을 내놓았다. 그는 부모들이 자녀를 교육시키도록 권장하는 지원을 제공할 것을 제안했다.

(C) 그러한 보상은 필요했는데, 왜냐하면 Smith가 알고 있었듯 분업으로 뒷받침되는 제조업의 확산은 아이들이 소득을 창출하는 일에 고용되는 것을 가능케 함으로써, 부모가 심지어 매우 어린 자녀들까지도 일자리로 내몰게 했기 때문이다.

이종현T의 독해 Point!

이 글은 아담 스미스가 공교육을 왜 강조했는지, 그리고 그에 따르는 사회적 맥락과 현실적 고려를 설명하는 구조다.
(B)는 글의 pivot 문장으로 "스미스의 제안은 당대 지배계급의 관점과 충돌했지만, 그는 의무 교육까지는 주장

하지 않았다"는 핵심 입장을 설명하며 논점이 전개되는 전환 지점이다.
(A)는 (B)의 뒤를 이어 스미스가 강제 대신 장려를 택했고, 실용적이고 접근 가능한 교육을 위한 구체적 방법(부모 지원책 등)을 제시했음을 보여주는 실천적 대안 설명이다.
(C)는 마지막으로 이 장려가 왜 필요한지를 설명하는 사회경제적 배경 설명으로, 분업 기반 산업 구조가 아이들을 노동시장으로 내몰았기 때문에 부모가 교육 대신 노동을 선택하게 되는 현실을 지적한다.
전체 구조는 (비판적 배경 및 입장 정리 B) → (실천적 대안 A) → (그 대안이 필요한 사회적 이유 C)로 이어지는 논리적 흐름이다.

26.⑤ 연극 작품을 관람할 때 여러분은 '불신의 자발적 중지'라고 불리는 것에 관여한다. 즉 여러분의 의식적인 마음은, 묘사되고 있는 사건들은 극작가가 쓴 것이고 실제로는 결코 일어나지 않았을 수도 있다는 것을 충분히 이해하고 있다.

(C) 하지만 여러분은 작품에 끌어들여져서 여러분이 가진 모든 감정으로 이야기를 경험하도록 무대에서의 연기에 대한 여러분의 불신을 기꺼이 중지시킨다.

(B) 배우들이 그들의 일을 성공적으로 하고 있으면 여러분은 여러분 앞에서 일어나는 것이 실제이고 여러분이 보고 있는 사건과 상호 작용이 오로지 바로 지금 처음으로 일어나고 있는 중이라고 잠시 실제로 믿을 수 있다.

(A) 하지만 반면에 배우들이 자기만족에 빠져 연기가 지루해지면 여러분은 불신을 완전히 중지시키지 못할 것이고 단지 암기한 대사를 암송하고 있는 배우를 보고 있다는 불편한 인식을 하게 될 것이다.

이종현T의 독해 Point!

이 글은 연극을 볼 때 관객이 스스로 믿음을 유보하며 몰입하는 심리 현상, 즉 "willing suspension of disbelief"를 설명하는 구조다.
(C)는 글의 pivot 문장으로 "관객은 무대 위 상황이 실제가 아님을 알면서도 감정적으로 몰입하기 위해 기꺼이 믿음을 유보한다"는 핵심 개념을 정리하며 논지를 본격적으로 전개하는 중심 문장이다.
(B)는 그 몰입이 성공적으로 이루어졌을 때의 효과를 설명하며, 관객이 실제 사건처럼 느끼게 되는 몰입의 심리적 경험을 구체화한다.
(A)는 반대로 연기가 무기력하고 몰입이 되지 않을 때, 관객은 배우들이 대사를 외우고 있다는 사실을 인식하게 되고 몰입이 깨진다는 부정적 상황을 제시하며 글을 마무리한다.
전체 흐름은 (핵심 개념 정의 C) → (몰입이 성공한 경우 B) → (몰입이 실패한 경우 A)의 구조로, 한 줄 논리 흐름이 자연스럽게 이어진다.

27.④ 어떤 동물이 다쳤을 때, 그것이 할 수 있다면 가장 먼저 할 일은 재빨리 일어나는 것이다.

(B) 이러한 행동이 아마 더한 통증을 야기할 것이라는 사실에도 불구하고 일어나고자 하는 본능이 그 동물을 몰아붙이는데, 왜냐하면 일어나려는 동작을 전혀 취하지 않는 또 다른 선택사항은 무방비 상태의 그 동물을 죽여서 먹어치울 포식자를 불러들이는 것이기 때문이다.

(C) 감정적인 면에서 우리들도 (동물들과) 똑같이 한다. 흔히 이제 막 부상 또는 엄청난 충격이나 상실을 겪은 사람은 "어떻게 지내니?"라는 질문을 받을 때 "좋아"라고 대답할 것이다.

(A) 이것을 단지 부인이라고 규정하는 것은 보다 심오한 사실을 놓치는 것이다. 동물이든 사람이든 유기체들은 공격을 피하기 위해 괜찮아 '보이려고' 노력할 뿐만 아니라 괜찮은 상태에 '있으려고' 노력한다.

이종현T의 독해 Point!

이 글은 동물의 생존 본능과 인간의 감정 반응이 "상처를 입고도 괜찮은 척하는 행동"이라는 공통된 본능에서 비롯된다는 것을 설명한다.
(B)는 글의 pivot 문장으로, 동물이 다친 직후 일어나려는 행동이 고통을 무릅쓰고라도 포식자로부터 자신을 지키기 위한 본능적 반응임을 설명하며, 글의 중심 논지를 설정한다.
(C)는 그 논리를 인간에게 확장하며, 큰 상실이나 충격을 입은 사람도 "I'm fine"이라고 반응하는 정서적 대응이 동물과 같은 본능에서 비롯된다는 유비적 연결을 제공한다.
(A)는 이런 반응을 '부정(denial)'으로 단순화하는 것이 아니라, 자신을 실제로 괜찮게 만들려는 깊은 생존 욕구의 표현이라고 해석해야 한다는 주장을 덧붙이며 글을 마무리한다.
전체 구조는 (본능적 생존 반응 B) → (인간의 감정 반응과의 연결 C) → (그 반응의 본질적 의미 A)로 이어지는 한 줄 논리 흐름이다.

28.② 우리의 전통은 우리가 정의를 모든 개인이 자신이 원

하는 것이면 무엇이나 추구할 동등한 기회의 문제로 생각하도록 부추긴다. 동등한 기회는 공정한 법과 정치적 절차, 즉 모든 사람에게 같은 방식으로 적용되는 법과 절차에 의하여 보장된다.

(B) 그러나 정의에 대한 이러한 사고방식은 본질적으로, 개인이 꿈을 추구할 동등한 기회를 가진다면 사회에서의 재화의 분배가 결국 어떤 모습이 될지에 대한 비전을 제시해주지 못한다.

(A) 따라서 모든 사람이 보수가 좋은 일자리를 얻을 동등한 기회가 있는 어떤 공정한 사회에서 다른 직업의 사람들에게 주어지는 임금에서 큰 차이가 있을 수 있다.

(C) 그러나 현재 고통스럽게 명백해지고 있는 것처럼 흥미로운 직업에서의 빈자리보다 더 많은 자격 있는 지원자들이 존재한다면, 정의를 확실히 하는 데 평등한 기회가 충분한 것일까? 출발선에 한참 못 미치는 곳에 남겨졌기 때문에 공정한 경주의 기회를 얻을 수 없는 곳에 있는 사회적 약자들은 어떻게 되는가?

이종현T의 독해 Point!

이 글은 기회 평등이라는 정의 개념이 과연 충분한가를 비판적으로 탐색한다.
(B)는 글의 pivot 문장으로 "기회 평등이라는 정의관은 그 결과가 실제 사회에서 어떻게 나타날지를 설명해주지 않는다"며 전통적 정의관의 구조적 한계를 지적하고 논지를 전환한다.
(A)는 그 한계를 전통 정의관의 내적 논리로 설명하며, "기회가 공정하기만 하다면 결과적 불평등(직업 간 임금 격차 등)은 정의롭다고 간주될 수 있다"는 입장을 제시한다. 이는 (B)에서 제기한 비판을 뒷받침하는 기존 시각의 입장을 구체화한 것이다.
(C)는 그 전통적 정의관이 현실에 충분하지 않다는 문제를 날카롭게 제기하며, "모두에게 평등한 기회가 주어진다 해도, 출발선조차 설 수 없는 사람들이 실제로 존재한다"는 점에서 정의에 대한 새로운 질문을 제기한다.
전체 구조는 (기존 정의관의 한계 제기 B) → (그 논리적 구조 설명 A) → (현실에서 그 정의관이 실패하는 지점 C)로 이어진다.

29.④ 대부분의 중세 이야기꾼들과 삽화가들은 동물학자가 아니었으며, 그런 척하지도 않았다.

(C) 그들의 목표는 독자들을 즐겁게 해주거나 그들에게 종교적, 도덕적 교훈을 제공해 주는 것이었다. 그들은 사람들이 놀라고 겁에 질리는 것을 좋아한다는 것을 알고 있었다.

(A) 그래서 불을 내뿜는 용은 완벽히 그들의 요구에 걸맞았다. 어떠한 독자도 용을 만난 적이 없었지만, 그러한 만남이 가능할지도 모른다는 바로 그 생각만으로도 겁을 주기에 충분했으며, 그것이 일어날 수 없다고 증명할 방도가 없었다.

(B) 반면에, 작가들은 친근한 동물들이 단지 사람들이 그들과 친숙하고 같이 지내는 것에 익숙해졌다는 이유만으로 친숙한 동물들에 의한, 심지어는 특히 곰과 늑대와 같은 사나운 동물들에 의해 제기되는 위험도 과장할 수가 없었다.

이종현T의 독해 Point!

지문은 중세의 이야기꾼들이 왜 사실적인 동물보다 환상적인 괴물들(예 용)을 더 자주 등장시켰는지 설명하는 글이다.
(C)는 글의 pivot 문장으로, 중세 이야기꾼들의 목적은 정확한 동물 묘사가 아니라 독자를 놀라게 하고 종교적·도덕적 메시지를 전달하는 것이었다고 밝히며 글의 핵심 관점을 제시한다.
(A)는 (C)의 논리를 뒷받침하는 대표 사례로, 독자는 실제로 본 적 없는 존재인 용에 더욱 강한 공포를 느꼈고, 이 상상력이 전달력에 효과적이었다는 점을 설명한다.
(B)는 (A)와 대조되는 반례로, 곰이나 늑대처럼 실제로 존재하는 동물은 사람들이 익숙하게 여겨서 이야기 속 공포 효과를 내기에 한계가 있었다는 점을 부연하며 글을 마무리한다.
전체 흐름은 (이야기꾼의 목적 C) → (환상 동물의 효과 A) → (현실 동물의 한계 B)라는 전형적인 주장-사례-대조 구조를 따른다.

30.③ 한 전통적 정의에 의하면, '미학'은 아름다움, 특히 예술의 아름다움을 다루는 철학의 분야이다. 예를 들어, '모나리자'나 꼭대기가 눈에 덮인 산의 유쾌한 특징들을 살펴보는 것이 미학의 범위에 해당될 것이다.

(B) 하지만, 예술 작품들과 자연의 물체가 아름답다는 것 외에 다른 특징을 가지고 우리의 관심을 끌 수 있기 때문에 그러한 정의는 너무 좁아 보인다. 아름다움에 대한 경탄을 불러일으키는 대신에, 예술가들은 당혹, 충격, 심지어 혐오감을 불러일으킬 수도 있다.

(C) 스페인 내란 동안에 독일과 이탈리아의 전투기들에 의한 스페인 민간인 대량 학살에 대응하여 피카소가 그린 검은색, 흰색, 회색으로 이루어진 거대한(11피트×25.6피트) 그림인 피카소의 '게르니카'에 대해 생각해보라. 죽어가는 군인들과 비명을 지르는 사람들의 이미지가 캔버스를 지배한다.

(A) 이 작품은 널리 칭송되고 있으나 아름답기 때문이 아니다. 그러므로 미학에 대한 더 나은 정의는, 미학이란 사물이 경험되면서 사람들을 즐겁게 하는 방식을 연구하는 철학의 분야라는 것이/될 것이다.

이종현T의 독해 Point!

지문은 전통적 미학의 정의 – 즉, "아름다움을 다루는 철학의 한 분야"라는 관점 – 이 예술작품의 다양한 감정적 효과를 포괄하기에 지나치게 협소하다는 점을 비판한다.
(B)는 글의 pivot 문장으로 "예술이 반드시 아름다움을 추구하는 것은 아니며, 혼란 · 충격 · 혐오감 등을 유발할 수도 있다"는 점을 통해 기존 정의의 한계를 지적하고 논지를 전환한다.
(C)는 그 주장에 대한 대표 사례로, 피카소의 〈게르니카〉가 아름다움을 표현하기보다는 전쟁의 참혹함을 드러내는 작품임을 설명하며 (B)의 주장을 실증적으로 뒷받침한다.
(A)는 이러한 전환을 종합하며, 미학을 단순히 '아름다움'이 아닌, '경험 속에서 인간에게 쾌감을 유발하는 방식 전반을 탐구하는 철학 분야'로 재정의해야 한다는 결론을 제시한다.
전체 흐름은 (전통 정의 비판 B) → (예시 제시 C) → (정의 재구성 A)의 한 줄 논리 구조로 이어진다.

31.④ 당신은 당신의 아이가 태어날 때 가졌던 모든 지능을 가지고 성장하기를 바란다. 그렇지 않은가? 그러한 지능을 활성화하기 위해서는 아이가 적극적이어야 한다.

(C) 실험해 볼 기회를 더 많이 가질수록, 그는 점점 더 똑똑해질 것이다. 나의 '똑똑한 아이를 위한 공식'은 내가 '우수성을 위한 여섯 가지 E'라고 부르는 것으로 구성되어 있다. 곧, 탐구(Exploration)와 실험(Experimentation)을 권장하는(Encourage) 환경(Environments)과 경험(Experiences)에 아이를 노출시키라(Expose)는 것이다.

(A) 이러한 관점에서 봤을 때, 유감스럽게도 텔레비전은 기대에 부응하지 못한다. 텔레비전은 탐구와 실험을 억누르는 전자적 환경을 만든다. 내가 말하고 있 는 것을 증명하려면, 그저 자리 잡고 앉아 아이가 텔레비전 보는 모습을 보라.

(B) 생기 없는 표정이 보이는가? 힘이 없는 손이 보이는가? 어떠한 창의적이고 건설적인 행동이 결여된 것이 보이는가? 당신은 아이가 시간을 낭비하는 것을 보게 되는데, 시간이란 그것을 가지고 재능을 계발할 인간 정신이 가진 전부이다.

이종현T의 독해 Point!

이 글은 유아의 지능 발달을 위해서는 능동적 탐색과 실험의 기회가 중요하며, TV는 그 반대의 환경이라는 점을 강조한다.
(C)는 글의 pivot 문장으로 "스마트한 아이를 만드는 공식은 '탐색과 실험을 장려하는 환경과 경험'에 노출시키는 것"이라는 핵심 주장을 제시하며 글의 중심 논지를 이끈다.
(A)는 이 주장에 반하는 매체로 TV를 지목하며, TV는 탐색과 실험을 억제하는 환경을 만든다는 점을 설명하고, 독자에게 "아이들이 TV를 보는 모습을 직접 보라"는 요청으로 이어진다.
(B)는 그 관찰 결과를 묘사하며, 창의성과 활동성이 사라진 표정, 자세, 행동을 나열하면서 TV 시청이 정신적 시간 낭비임을 강조하며 글을 마무리한다.
전체 흐름은 (핵심 주장 C) → (TV의 반례 A) → (관찰에 의한 경고 B)의 순으로 전개된다.

32.② 일부 사람들은 살면서 의도적인 변화를 거의 하지 않는다. 물론, 시간이 흐르면서 그들은 더 살이 찌고, 주름살이 늘어나고, 그리고 머리가 희끗희끗해질 것이다.

(B) 그러나 그들은 편안하고 예측 가능한 삶이 쉽다는 이유만으로 똑같은 방식으로 머리를 하고, 똑같은 상표의 신발을 사고, 똑같은 아침을 먹으며 판에 박힌 일상을 고수한다. 하지만 연구와 실제 삶이 모두 보여주듯이, 많은 다른 사람들은 실제로 중요한 변화를 한다.

(A) 그들은 마라톤을 위해 훈련을 하고, 담배를 끊고, 분야를 바꾸고, 희곡을 쓰고, 기타를 배우고, 또는 살면서 전에 한 번도 춤을 춰 본 적이 없다고 해도 탱고를 배운다. 이 두 집단의 사람들 사이에 있는 차이는 무엇인가?

(C) 그것은 그들의 관점이다. 변화하는 사람들은 변화가 가능한지를 묻지 않으며 변화할 수 없는 이유를 찾지 않는다. 그들은 그저 자신이 원하는 변화를 결정하고 그것을 성취하는 데 필요한 것을 한다. 항상 확고한 결심에서 비롯되는 변화는 최우선의 것이 된다.

이종현T의 독해 Point!

이 글은 변화를 거의 하지 않는 사람들과 활발히 변화하는 사람들의 차이를 제시하고, 그 차이가 행동이 아닌 사고방식(perspective)에서 비롯된다는 점을 강조한다.
(B)는 글의 pivot 문장으로, 처음 제시된 "변화를 거의 하지 않는 사람들"의 일상을 묘사한 뒤, "하지만 실제로 많은 사람들은 변화한다"는 전환의 흐름을 자연스럽게

만들어내며 글의 중심 전환점을 이룬다.
(A)는 (B)의 "변화하는 사람들"에 대한 구체적 예시를 나열하며, 운동, 금연, 악기, 예술 등 다양한 자기 변화의 모습을 보여준다. 그리고 마지막에 두 집단의 차이가 무엇인지 질문을 던지며 (C)로 연결된다.
(C)는 그 질문에 대한 결론이자 글의 핵심 논지로, 변화하는 사람들은 '가능한가?'를 묻지 않고 그냥 해낸다는 점, 즉 관점(perspective)의 차이가 행동의 차이를 만든다는 주장을 정리하며 마무리된다.
전체 구조는 (두 집단 소개 및 전환 B) → (변화하는 사람들 예시 A) → (변화의 핵심 요인 정리 C)로 한 줄 흐름이 매끄럽게 완성된다.

33.③

(D) 여러분이 새 컴퓨터를 찾아 가게로 들어갔는데 만난 첫 번째 판매원이 즉시 한 무더기의 컴퓨터를 가리키면서 "저것들은 다 좋아요."라고 말한 뒤가 버린다면, 여러분도 나가 버릴 가능성이 크며, 그럴 만한 충분한 이유가 있다.
(B) 왜 그런가? 여러분은 무엇을 찾고 있는지, 얼마나 돈을 쓸 수 있는지, 또는 컴퓨터가 사업용인지 오락용인지 아니면 아이의 숙제용으로 사용될 것인지 한 번도 질문을 받지 않았다.
(C) 간단히 말해, 그 판매원은 여러분의 필요와 선호도에 대해 전혀 고려하거나 묻지 않았다. 잠재적 고객의 필요에 무관심한 판매원이 곧 일자리를 잃게 되는 것이 놀라운 일로 다가오지 않는 것처럼, 독자를 무시하는 필자에게도 똑같은 것이 적용된다.
(A) 즉 독자는 필자의 '고객'이며 그 고객의 관심사나 인정은 우리가 추구할 필요가 있는 것이다. 여러분이 독자에 대해 더 많이 알면 알수록, 여러분이 독자의 필요와 기대를 충족시킬 가능성이 더 커진다.

이종현T의 독해 Point!

이 글은 글쓰기에서 독자의 입장을 고려하지 않는 글이 실패할 수 있다는 점을, 매장 판매의 예시를 통해 설명한다.
(D)는 글의 도입 및 pivot 문장으로, 독자가 경험할 법한 상황 — 무관심한 판매원의 부실한 응대 사례를 생생하게 보여주며 독자의 주의를 끌고 중심 주제를 암시한다.
(B)는 그 행동이 왜 문제인지 구체적으로 분석하며, 판매원이 고객의 필요를 묻지 않았다는 점을 지적한다.
(C)는 그 문제 행동에 대한 일반적인 판단을 제시하며, "고객을 고려하지 않은 판매원은 실직할 것이다"라는 결론을 이끌고, 이 판단을 글쓰기 상황에 비유로 연결한다.
(A)는 이 비유의 본론이자 결론으로, 작가에게 독자는 '고객'이며, 독자의 기대를 고려하지 않는 글쓰기는 실패할 수밖에 없다는 글의 주장을 분명히 정리한다.
전체 구조는 (사례 제시 D) → (문제 지적 B) → (판단과 유비 C) → (글쓰기 적용 A)로, 깔끔한 한 줄 논리 흐름이다.

34.② 문화적인 특징은 부모로부터 자식에게 전달될 뿐만 아니라 전하는 말이나 글을 통해 어느 한 개인으로부터 다른 개인에게 전달될 수 있다.
(B) 그래서 일부 문화적인 변화는 전체 인구에 의해 상당히 빠르게 채택될 수 있다. 문화의 전달은 전염병의 전염과 다소 비슷하다. 유행성 독감과 감기는, 특히 사람들이 서로 갖는 접촉의 양이 많은 현재 상황에서, 매우 빠르게 퍼진다.
(A) 그러한 전염성 질병들처럼 대중음악의 선호와 의상의 유행 같은 문화적인 관습은 오늘날 특히 라디오와 텔레비전이라는 매체를 통해 매우 빠르게 전파될 수도 있다.
(C) 그러나 민족과 민족적 하위 집단의 다른 뿌리 깊은 문화적인 특징은 변화시키기가 훨씬 더 어렵다. 이것들은 변화에 너무나 저항적이어서 선천적인 것처럼 보이는 문화 양상이다.

이종현T의 독해 Point!

이 글은 문화가 감염처럼 전파되며, 어떤 문화는 빠르게 확산되지만 어떤 것은 매우 변하기 어렵다는 점을 설명한다.
(B)는 글의 pivot 문장으로 "문화는 감염처럼 퍼질 수 있다"는 핵심 비유를 제시하며 글의 중심 논리를 정립한다.
이어서 (A)는 그 비유를 구체화하며, 감염처럼 빠르게 퍼지는 문화의 대표적 예시(대중음악, 패션 등)를 제시하고, 매체를 통한 확산 속도를 강조한다.
(C)는 이와 대조적으로, 깊이 뿌리박힌 문화적 특성(예 인종적 하위문화)은 쉽게 변하지 않는다는 점을 설명하며 문화 전파의 양면성을 정리한다.
전체 흐름은 (핵심 비유 제시 B) → (빠른 문화 확산의 예시 A) → (변화 어려운 문화에 대한 예외적 설명 C)의 구조로, 논리 전개가 매끄럽다.

35.④

(D) 색깔의 영향은 수십 년 동안 연구되어 왔다. 예를 들어, 어떤 공장에서 온도가 화씨 72℉로 유지되었으며 벽은 시원한 청록색으로 칠해졌다. 직원들은 춥다고 불평했다.
(C) 온도는 동일한 수준으로 유지되었지만, 벽을 따뜻한 산호색으로 칠했다. 직원들은 온도에 관한 불평을 하지 않았고

그들은 아주 편안하다고 보고했다.

(A) 따뜻하고 시원한 색조의 심리적 효과는 Notre Dame 미식축구팀 코치들에 의해서 효율적으로 사용되는 것 같다. 하프타임 휴식시간에 사용되는 라커룸들이 특정한 색조의 감정적 영향을 이용하기 위해서 칠해졌다고 한다.

(B) 홈팀의 라커룸은 밝은 빨간색으로 칠해졌는데, 이것이 팀원들을 흥분하거나 심지어 분노에 찬 상태로 있게 했다. 원정팀의 라커룸은 청록색으로 칠해졌는데, 이것이 팀원들을 차분하게 하는 효과를 나타냈다. 이런 색깔 적용의 성공은 Notre Dame 미식축구팀의 전적에서 찾아볼 수 있다.

이종현T의 독해 Point!

이 글은 색채가 인간의 심리와 행동에 미치는 영향을 설명하면서, 공장과 스포츠 현장의 사례를 통해 구체적으로 전개하는 구조다.
(D)는 글의 pivot 문장으로, 색채 심리학의 연구를 소개하며 "72도에서 벽 색이 차가운 색일 때 사람들이 춥다고 느낀다"는 현상을 설명하고 글의 중심 주제를 제시한다.
(C)는 같은 조건에서 벽 색을 따뜻한 색으로 바꿨을 때, 사람들의 반응이 달라졌다는 후속 실험 결과를 보여주며, 색채가 실제로 심리에 영향을 준다는 논거를 강화한다.
(A)는 이 원리가 스포츠에서도 활용됨을 보여주며, 노트르담 미식축구팀이 감정 자극을 위한 색채 전략을 적용했다는 사례를 소개한다.
(B)는 그 전략의 구체적인 적용 방식과 효과, 즉 홈팀과 원정팀에 각각 다른 색을 적용한 결과, 실제 성적이 좋아졌다는 정황을 설명하며 글을 마무리한다.
전체 흐름은 (색채 효과 연구 소개 D) → (그 실험적 증거 C) → (스포츠 응용 사례 A) → (전략적 효과 B)의 순으로, 중심 논지가 논리적이고 점층적으로 확장되는 구조다.

36.② 우리는 모두 '함께 놀이하는 가족은 함께 있게 된다.'라는 말을 들어보았다. 이 말 속에 담긴 지혜는 사회적인 놀이는 사람들 사이에 지속적이고 중대한 유대를 형성한다는 것이다.

(B) 이러한 지혜는 인간의 가족 밖에 서도 적용된다. 예를 들면, 얼룩다람쥐 한 마리가 멀리 있는 포식자를 발견하면, 그것은 다른 다람쥐들이 숨을 곳을 찾아 뛰도록 알리는 경보를 발 할 것이다. 그것은 위험한 행동이다.

(A) 큰 소리를 낼 때, 위험을 감지한 그 다람쥐는 자신을 주목하도록 하는데, 그것은 포식자의 주의를 끌 가능성이 클 것이다. 과학자들은 동물들이 오직 공통 유전자를 나눠 가진 종족을 위해서만 이처럼 생명을 건 위험을 무릅쓸 것으로 생각했었다.

(C) 그러나 새로운 증거는 다람쥐들이 유전적으로 관련 없는 이전의 놀이 동무를 위해서도 또한 경보를 발함을 보여준다. 이 다람쥐들은 놀이를 하면서 사회적인 자산을 형성했기에, 이 친구들은 놀이 동무를 구하기 위하여 죽음을 무릅쓸 것이다.

이종현T의 독해 Point!

이 글은 사회적 유대감이 인간뿐 아니라 동물 사이에서도 생존 행동에까지 영향을 미친다는 점을 설명한다.
(B)는 글의 pivot 문장으로, 인간 가족의 놀이 유대에 대한 속담을 동물 세계로 확장하며, "다람쥐가 포식자를 보면 위험을 무릅쓰고 경고음을 낸다"는 사례를 도입하면서 본격적으로 주제를 전개한다.
(A)는 이 행동이 왜 위험한지를 설명하며, 이전까지 과학자들이 이타적 행동은 오직 유전적으로 연결된 개체 사이에서만 나타난다고 믿었다는 전통적 관점을 설명한다.
(C)는 최신 연구 결과를 통해 기존 가설을 반박하며, 다람쥐가 유전적 관련이 없는 '놀이 친구'에게도 경고음을 보내는 이유는, 놀이를 통해 사회적 유대를 형성했기 때문이라는 새로운 결론을 제시하며 글을 마무리한다.
전체 구조는 (행동 사례 도입 B) → (기존 이론 A) → (새로운 해석 C)의 전형적인 비교-반박 구조다.

37.④

(D) 때때로 처벌이 몇 번 가해진 후에는 그것(처벌)이 계속될 필요가 없는데, 왜냐하면 처벌하겠다는 단순한 위협만으로도 바라는 행동을 끌어내기에 충분하기 때문이다.

(C) 심리학자들은 당사자가 처벌 결과의 가능성을 피하는 법을 배우고 있으므로 이것을 회피 훈련이라고 부른다. 일상의 많은 행동들이 회피 훈련에 기인한다. 그것(회피 훈련) 때문에 여러분은 비가 올 것 같으면 젖게 되는 처벌을 피하려고 우산을 가져가고, 화상의 처벌을 피하기 위해 뜨거운 다리미에서 손을 멀리하는 법을 배웠다.

(A) 그러나 회피 훈련이 항상 우리에게 유리하게 작용하는 것은 아니다. 예를 들어 수학에서 부진한 (학업) 성취로 반복해서 야단을 맞은 아이는 더 심한 처벌을 피하기 위해 어려운 수학 문제를 요리조리 피하는 방법을 배우게 될 것이다.

(B) 불행하게도 이러한 회피 때문에 그 아이는 자신의 수학 기술을 발전시키지 못하고, 따라서 자신이 가진 능력을 개선하지 못하게 되며, 그래서 악순환이 시작되는 것이다. 이 (악

순환의) 고리를 끊기 위해서는 수학에서의 몇 가지 긍정적인 경험을 통해 회피를 배우지 않았던 상태로 되돌려져야 한다.

이종현T의 독해 Point!

이 글은 처벌이 사람의 행동에 미치는 영향, 특히 '회피 학습(avoidance training)'이 형성되고 그것이 어떻게 긍정적/부정적으로 작용할 수 있는지를 설명하는 구조다.
(D)는 글의 pivot 문장으로 "처벌은 몇 번만 가해져도 그 '위협'만으로 행동을 유도할 수 있다"는 핵심 아이디어를 제시하며, 회피 학습의 작동 방식을 본격적으로 열어주는 전환점이 된다.
(C)는 회피 학습의 정의와 일상적 예시를 제시하며, 처벌을 피하기 위해 행동이 형성되는 구체적 상황들(우산, 뜨거운 다리미 등)을 설명해 주제를 본격화한다.
(A)는 회피 학습이 부정적으로 작용하는 사례로 전환하며, 수학에 대해 반복적으로 부정적 피드백을 받은 아이가 문제 자체를 회피하게 되는 사례를 소개한다.
(B)는 그 회피 행동이 어떻게 학습 기회를 차단하고 악순환으로 이어지는지를 설명하고, 이를 극복하려면 긍정적 경험이 필요하다는 해결책을 제시하며 글을 마무리한다.
전체 흐름은 (처벌의 작동 방식 D) → (회피 학습의 정의 및 예 C) → (부정적 사례 A) → (결과 및 해결책 B)의 구조로, 논리적으로 매우 명확하게 전개된다.

38.④

(D) 긍정적 행동 대(對) 부정적 행동의 타이밍은 매력도에 영향을 주는 것처럼 보인다. 득실 효과라 불리던 것이 몇몇 연구에 의해 확인되었다.

(C) 이 효과는 어떤 사람의 행동이 긍정적에서 부정적으로 또는 부정적에서 긍정적으로 이동할 때 매력도에 어떤 일이 발생하는지를 반영한다. 예를 들면 어떤 사람이 상호작용 초기에는 당신에게 매우 친절해 보였지만, 그 후에 얼간이처럼 행동하기 시작한다면 당신은 그 사람이 처음부터 얼간이일 때보다 그 사람에게 더 끌리게 될까?

(A) 연구는 당신이 그렇지 않을 거라고 보여준다. 사실 사람들은 초기에는 긍정적으로 행동한 후 부정적 행동으로 바뀌는 사람보다 일관되게 부정적인 사람에게 더 끌린다.

(B) 그 이유는 다음과 같다. 초기에 친절한 사람들은 우리의 기대를 부풀리고, 따라서 그들이 친절하지 않다는 사실을 발견할 때 우리가 경험하는 실망감은 그들이 처음부터 나쁘게 행동했을 때보다 상황을 더 악화시킨다.

이종현T의 독해 Point!

이 글은 사람에 대한 호감 형성이 행동의 '순서'(처음 긍정적 → 나중 부정적 vs. 그 반대)에 따라 달라진다는 심리학적 현상, 즉 "loss-gain effect"를 설명한다.
(D)는 글의 pivot 문장으로 "긍정적 vs. 부정적 행동의 '타이밍'이 호감도에 영향을 준다"는 핵심 개념과 'loss-gain effect'라는 용어를 처음 도입하면서 글의 주제를 명확히 제시한다.
(C)는 이 이론에 대한 구체적 예시 질문으로, 처음에 좋았다가 나빠진 사람과 처음부터 안 좋았던 사람 중 누가 더 호감가는지 묻고, 심리적 맥락을 상상하게 한다.
(A)는 실제 연구 결과를 통해, 사람들은 일관되게 부정적인 사람보다, 처음만 좋고 나중에 실망을 주는 사람에게 더 부정적인 반응을 보인다는 연구 결과를 소개한다.
(B)는 그 이유를 설명하며, "기대가 무너질 때의 실망감이 더 크기 때문에 차라리 처음부터 안 좋았던 사람이 더 나아 보인다"는 심리 메커니즘을 해설하고 글을 마무리한다.
전체 구조는 (핵심 이론 제시 D) → (예시 질문 C) → (연구 결과 A) → (심리적 이유 B)의 한 줄 논리 흐름이다.]

39.② 음식은 여러분이 야외 활동을 얼마만큼 즐기는가에 많은 역할을 한다. 가능성은 무한하므로 끊임없이 식단을 다양화할 수 있다.

(B) 야외에서의 식사는 양극단이 있을 수 있는데, 그것은 미식가와 생존을 위해 먹는 사람이다. 첫 번째(미식가)는 야외 화덕을 설치하기 위한 몇 시간을 확보하려고 점심 무렵에 텐트 치는 것을 좋아한다. 그리고 케이크와 빵을 굽고 여러 단계의 코스로 저녁식사를 요리한다.

(A) 그들은 매일 단지 몇 마일 만을 걸으며 같은 야영장에서 며칠 밤을 보낼 수도 있다. 생존을 위해 먹는 사람들은 아침 식사로 건조된 약간의 시리얼을 먹고 잠에서 깬 지 수분만에 일어나서 걷는다.

(C) 그들은 매일 수십 마일을 걷고 점심은 이동하면서 먹는 일련의 데우지 않는 차가운 간식으로 이루어진다. 저녁식사는 용기 안에 뜨거운 물을 부어 '조리되는' 동결건조 식사로 이루어진다.

이종현T의 독해 Point!

이 글은 야외 활동 중 음식 방식이 어떻게 다를 수 있는지를 설명하면서, '고급 식사파'와 '생존 식사파'라는 두 극단적 유형의 캠핑 식사 스타일을 대조하는 구조로 이루어져 있다.

(B)는 글의 pivot 문장으로, 야외 식사의 두 스타일인 "gourmet eaters"와 "survival eaters"라는 구분을 처음 도입하며 전체 글의 비교 구도를 설정하는 중심 문장이다.
(A)는 survival eaters의 특징을 먼저 설명하면서 그들의 빠른 아침, 간단한 식사, 짧은 이동 거리 등을 구체적으로 묘사한다.
(C)는 같은 그룹인 survival eaters 중 더 극단적인 유형을 이어 설명하며, 점심은 이동 중 간식, 저녁은 뜨거운 물 부어 먹는 동결식 식사 등을 추가해 비교를 완성한다.
전체 흐름은 (두 집단 도입 B) → (생존파 기본 특징 A) → (생존파의 극단적 버전 C)로 이어지는 한 줄 논리다.

40.⑤ 문제 해결력에 있어서 집단 작업이 가장 숙련된 집단 구성원들의 개별 작업보다 더 우수하기 때문에 학생들이 협력할 때 더 잘 배운다는 것은 놀라운 일이 아닐 것이다. 그렇지만, 더 깊은 고려가 필요한 한 가지 문제가 있다.
(C) 구체적으로 말하면, 학생들이 서로 돕게 하는 방법은 실력이 더 높은 학생들을 희생시켜서 실력이 낮은 학생들이 도움을 받게 하는 것은 아닌가 하는 의문이 생기게 한다. 이것이 사실일까?
(B) 절대 그렇지는 않다. 다행히 지식은 제로섬 게임의 산물이 아니다. 실력이 더 높 은 학생들은 실력이 더 낮은 학생들을 가르침으로써 자신의 지식을 강화시킬 수 있다.
(A) 그러한 이득 외에도, 실력이 더 낮은 학생들을 도와주는 것은 흔히 실력이 더 높은 학생들을 그 자료에 대해 보다 더 정교하게 이해하도록 이끈다. 교사가 그들의 학생들만큼 많이 배운다는 상투적인 말은 분명히 사실이다.

이종현T의 독해 Point!

이 글은 협동 학습이 전반적으로 효과적이지만, 상위권 학생이 하위권 학생을 돕는 구조가 오히려 상위권에게 불이익일 수 있다는 우려에 대해 논박하는 글이다.
(C)는 글의 pivot 문장으로 "능력 낮은 학생을 돕는 것이 높은 학생에게 손해인가?"라는 핵심 문제를 제기하며 글의 논의 방향을 본격적으로 설정한다.
(B)는 그 질문에 대한 직접적인 반박으로, 지식은 제로섬 게임이 아니며, 오히려 상위권 학생이 설명하는 과정에서 자신의 지식이 강화된다는 논지를 전개한다.
(A)는 그 논지를 더 확장하며, 하위권 학생을 가르치면서 상위권 학생이 더 정교한 이해에 도달하게 되고, 이는 '가르치는 사람이 더 많이 배운다'는 교육의 진리와 일치함을 강조하면서 글을 마무리한다.
전체 흐름은 (문제 제기 C) → (반박 및 원리 설명 B) → (확장 및 귀결 A)로 이어지는 정형적인 문제-해결 구조다.

41.③ 엄마와 아빠가 멋진 식당으로 저녁식사를 하러 가셨다. 처음으로 혼자 있게 된 그날 밤에, 아빠는 자신의 영사기와 모든 필름 통들을 내게 맡기셨다.
(B) 그는 그날 밤에 내가 모든 것을 스스로 할 수 있다고 말씀하셨다. 그래서 나는 거실의 한쪽 끝에 영사막을 설치했다. 나는 영사기를 켜고, 전 등을 끄고, 무릎에 팝콘 그릇을 놓고는, HAT TIE-1951이라는 이름표가 붙은 필름을 보기 위해 자리를 잡았다.
(C) 그것은 내가 특히 좋아하는 것 중의 하나인데, 내 세 번째 생일 파티가 들어 있고 우리의 늙은 고양이 Simon이 식당 식탁으로 뛰어올라 아이스크림 접시에 내려앉는 모습을 볼 수 있기 때문이다.
(A) 그러고 나서 나는 그 필름을 거꾸로 돌려서 그 고양이가 바닥에 뛰어내리는 것을 지켜보고 모든 아이스크림 방울들이 후루룩 소리를 내며 접시로 돌아가는 것을 볼 수 있다. 필름의 나머지를 보기 전에 나는 Simon이 여러 번 뛰어들었다 뛰어 나오게 하였다.

이종현T의 독해 Point!

이 글은 화자가 부모님이 외출한 첫날 밤, 아버지에게서 필름 영사기를 맡아 과거 가족 영상을 보며 추억에 잠기는 흐름으로 구성되어 있다.
(B)는 글의 pivot 문장으로, 화자가 직접 스크린을 설치하고 조명을 끄고, 'HATTIE-1951'이라고 적힌 필름을 준비해 본격적으로 상영을 시작하는 장면을 묘사하며 이야기의 시작점이자 전환점이다.
(C)는 그 필름 내용 중 한 장면을 회상하며, 자신의 세 번째 생일 파티에서 고양이 Simon이 아이스크림 그릇에 뛰어드는 장면이 나오는 걸 묘사한다. 이는 화자의 정서적 애착이 담긴 추억 장면이다.
(A)는 해당 장면을 반복 재생하거나 되감아 보는 구체적 장난스러운 행동을 묘사하며, 그 장면이 얼마나 재밌고 인상 깊었는지를 강조하면서 글을 마무리한다.
전체 흐름은 (상영 준비 B) → (인상 깊은 추억 장면 C) → (그 장면에 대한 감정과 놀이 A)로, 시간 흐름과 감정 흐름 모두 일관된 구조다.

42.② 우리가 사용하는 대부분의 단어들과 우리가 생각하는 의미들은 더 단순한 개념들의 조합이다.

(B) 의자를 생각해 보라. 여러분이 의자의 개념을 가질 수 있기 전에, 여러분은 기능적인 어떤 물체들이 세상에 존재한다는 것을 이해해야 한다. 이러한 물체들 중 일부는 인간 활동을 지원하는데, 이 경우에는 앉기이다.

(A) 그 중에 어떤 것들은 술집의 의자와 같이 어떤 높은 장소에 앉기 위해 특화되어 있다. 여러분이 어떤 특정한 형태의 의자가 버스를 기다리는 동안에 앉는 목적으로만 사용되는 문화에 대해 알게 된다면, 여러분은 이것을 이상하다고 여길 수는 있으나 그것을 이해하는 데 전혀 어려움을 겪지는 않을 것이다.

(C) '의자'와 '버스 기다리기'란 개념들의 조합은 '버스를 기다리는 동안 사용되는 의자'라는 새롭고 복잡한 개념을 만들게 해준다. 그러나 의자라는 기본적인 개념은 우리가 당연하게 여기는 더 단순한 개념들, 즉 사물, 가구, 앉기라는 개념들로부터 형성된다.

이종현T의 독해 Point!

이 글은 복잡한 개념들이 어떻게 더 단순한 개념들의 조합으로 구성되어 있는지를 'chair(의자)'라는 사례를 통해 설명한다.
(B)는 글의 pivot 문장으로, 우리가 의자라는 개념을 이해하려면 먼저 '기능적 물체', '앉는 행위', '인체를 지탱하는 구조' 등의 단순한 개념들이 먼저 있어야 한다는 점을 설명하며 핵심 논지를 제시한다.
(A)는 (B)의 개념을 확장하여, 문화에 따라 의자의 종류나 사용 목적이 달라도, 그 조합은 여전히 이해 가능하다는 사례적 설명을 덧붙인다.
(C)는 글을 마무리하며, 기본 개념들을 조합하면 새로운 복합 개념이 생기며, 우리가 복잡한 개념을 어떻게 형성하고 이해하는지를 정리한다.
전체 흐름은 (기본 개념 구성 B) → (문화적 다양성 예시 A) → (복합 개념의 원리 정리 C)로 명확하고 일관된 논리 구조를 따른다.

43.③ Ohio 주 Canton에 전에 살았던 사람이 그녀의 학급 친구들에게 그 도시의 이미지에 대해 묘사하려고 노력하고 있었다. 그녀는 그들에게 이 중소도시에 대한 이미지가 없다는 것을 알았다. 그녀는 Canton을 주요 생산시설과 도시 활성화 프로그램을 갖춘 도시로 묘사했다.

(B) 그녀의 설명은 Canton을 아무 이미지가 없는 도시에서 부정적인 이미지로 바꾸었다. 학생들은 Canton을 전형적이고, 지루한 산업화 도시라고 결론지었다.

(C) 그때 그녀는 갑자기 한 경험을 떠올렸다. "저는 선생님으로부터 2차 세계대전 때 Canton이 독일군의 주요 공격 대상이었다고 들었던 것을 기억해요." 시카고, 뉴욕 그리고 로스앤젤레스 바로 다음에 Canton이라는 이름이 등장한다고 상상해 봐라.

(A) 그 사실이 갑자기 Canton의 이미지를 분명하게 했다. 만약 Canton이 파괴된다면, 국가는 쇠락할지도 모른다. 바로 그것이 Canton에 산다는 것이 어떤 것인지에 대해 의미와 충만함을 가져다준 이미지이다.

이종현T의 독해 Point!

이 글은 칸톤(Canton, Ohio)이라는 도시가 처음에는 평범하고 부정적인 이미지로 인식되지만, 개인적인 기억을 통해 그 이미지가 강렬하고 의미 있는 것으로 전환되는 과정을 보여준다.
(B)는 글의 pivot 문장으로, 학생이 설명한 칸톤에 대해 처음에는 "전형적인 산업도시 → 지루하고 부정적인 이미지"라는 인식이 형성되었음을 설명하며 이야기를 출발시킨다.
(C)는 그 이미지에 반전을 가져오는 결정적 기억으로 "2차 세계대전 당시 독일의 공격 목표 중 하나였던 도시"라는 역사적 사실을 떠올리며 칸톤의 의미를 새롭게 정립할 단서를 제공한다.
(A)는 그 기억이 "칸톤이 무너진다면 국가가 위태롭다"는 강력한 상징성을 부여하게 되는 감정적 반전으로 이어졌음을 보여주며, 글을 인상 깊게 마무리한다.
전체 흐름은 (초기 부정적 인식 B) → (개인적 경험에 기반한 이미지 전환 C) → (그 이미지의 정서적 상징 강화 A)로, 한 줄 논리 흐름과 심리적 변화의 순서가 완벽히 정돈된다.

Unit 2. 문장 삽입 유형

1.④ 동전은 사용하기 매우 편리했지만 무거웠습니다. 10세기 중국에서는 철제 동전의 중앙에 사각형 구멍이 있었고 끈으로 100개의 무거운 묶음으로 묶었습니다. 사람들은 영수증을 받는 대가로 이 묶음을 상인들에게 맡기 시작했습니다. 영수증은 시간이 지남에 따라 상인들로부터 상품을 구매하는 데 사용될 수 있습니다. 11세기에 중국 정부는 이 영수증을 발행하기 시작했으며, 이 영수증은 세계 최초의 지폐가 되었습니다. 정부가 그 가치를 보장하지 않으면 돈은 가치가 없을 것입니다. 지폐는 국민들이 그 가치에 대한 신뢰를 갖지 못하면 가치가 없습니다.

이종현T의 독해 Point!

제시문은 "the world's first paper money"라는 새로운 소재(종이화폐의 등장)를 소개하며, 앞의 "receipts" 흐름에서 본격적으로 "money"에 대한 논리가 시작되는 '시작점' 역할을 하므로 정답은 ④번이다. (④ 다음 문장부터는 "money"에 대한 본질적 논의가 이어지므로, 제시문이 그 흐름의 출발점이 됨).

2.④ 예술가들은 이탈리아 르네상스 시대에 누드에서 그림을 그리기 시작한 것으로 여겨집니다. 이 시기에 주니어 워크숍 견습생들은 그들의 임무 중 일부로 행동했습니다. 그림은 보통 교회의 불쾌감을 피하기 위해 남성 누드에서 그려졌습니다. 르네상스 시대 여성 신체의 그림을 자세히 보면 대부분 약간의 조정을 거친 젊은 남성들이라는 것을 알 수 있습니다. 이 시기에 예술가들은 신체의 이상적인 비율을 정의하려고 노력했고, 레오나르도는 원과 정사각형 안에 남성을 그렸고, 두러는 연구를 더 발전시켜 신체의 무한한 측정에 완벽함을 추구하며 네 권의 삽화 설명을 제작했습니다. 해부학을 연구하는 르네상스 예술가들은 의학자들보다 수십 년 앞서 있었습니다. 미켈란젤로는 표면 형태에 대한 이해를 완벽하게 하기 위해 해부학에 참석했고, 레오나르도는 우리의 물리적 메커니즘을 직접 보고 발견하기 위해 몸을 열었습니다. 레오나르도는 심지어 자신이 뇌 아래와 눈 뒤의 뇌하수체 화석에서 영혼을 찾았다고 믿었으며, 눈이 영혼의 창이라는 이론에 물리적 기초를 제공했습니다.

이종현T의 독해 Point!

인물들간의 차이점이 시작되는 부분이고, ④번 뒤에 Leonardo의 두 번째 믿음이 나오고 있으니 먼저 나오는 부분에 찍으면 ④번이다.

3.① 1890년대 후반, 두 명의 독일 심리학자 게오르그 밀러와 알폰스 필체커는 기억이 뇌에서 고정되거나 "기억화"되는 데 한 시간 정도 걸린다는 사실을 발견했습니다. 이후 연구를 통해 단기 및 장기 형태의 기억이 존재한다는 사실을 확인하고 전자가 후자로 전환되는 통합 단계의 중요성에 대한 추가 증거를 제공했습니다. 1960년대 펜실베이니아 대학교의 신경과 전문의 루이 플렉스너는 특히 흥미로운 발견을 했습니다. 그는 쥐에게 세포가 단백질을 생산하지 못하도록 하는 항생제를 주사한 후 동물들이 장기 기억을 형성할 수 없을 뿐만 아니라 단기 기억을 계속 저장할 수 있다는 사실을 발견했습니다. 그 의미는 분명했습니다. 장기 기억은 단기 기억의 더 강한 형태일 뿐만 아니라 단기 기억을 저장하는 것입니다. 두 가지 유형의 기억은 서로 다른 생물학적 과정을 수반합니다. 장기 기억을 저장하려면 새로운 단백질의 합성이 필요합니다. 단기 기억을 저장하는 것은 그렇지 않습니다. 최근 연구에서는 단기 기억과 장기 기억의 물리적 작용 문제로 전환했습니다. 결과는 경험이 반복되는 시간이 많을수록 경험의 기억이 더 오래 지속된다는 것을 보여주었습니다. 반복은 통합을 촉진합니다. 특히 연구자들이 신경 신호에 대한 반복의 생리적 영향을 조사했을 때 놀라운 사실을 발견했습니다. © 시냅스의 신경전달물질 농도가 변화하여 뉴런 간의 기존 연결 강도가 달라졌을 뿐만 아니라 뉴런은 완전히 새로운 시냅스 말단이 성장했습니다. 즉 장기 기억의 형성에는 생화학적 변화뿐만 아니라 해부학적 변화도 수반됩니다. 이것이 기억 통합에 새로운 단백질이 필요한 이유를 설명합니다. 단백질은 세포의 구조적 변화를 생성하는 데 중요한 역할을 합니다.

이종현T의 독해 Point!

두 종류 기억의 차이점에 대한 논리가 시작되는 지점이므로 시작점 역할인 ⓐ에 들어가야 하며, 정답은 ①번이다.

4.⑤ 진정으로 독서를 즐기려면 독서가 제2의 본성이 되어야 합니다. "아이들은 조용히, 소리 내어 모두 읽어야 합니다."라고 주디 치텀은 말합니다. 바로 이때 아이의 유창성, 즉 부드럽고 표현력 있게 읽는 능력이 중요하다고 치텀 박사는 말합니다. 아이들은 익숙한 텍스트를 연습하면서 유창성을 얻으므로, 아이가 같은 책을 반복해서 선택하더라도 걱정하지 마세요. 아이가 소리 내어 읽는 것에 대해 불안해한다면, 아이가 혼자 또는 녹음 장치로 읽게 한 다음 자신이나 동생을 위해 다시 재생하도록

하세요. 또는 그가 더 관대한 청취자를 즐겁게 해주도록 격려하세요. 캘리포니아 대학교 데이비스 캠퍼스의 한 연구에 따르면, 반려견에게 소리 내어 읽어주는 둘째 graders가 10주 동안 읽기 능력이 12% 향상된 것으로 나타났습니다.

이종현T의 독해 Point!

개에게 읽는 사례가 시작되며 '더 관대한 청자'를 처음 제시하는 시작점이므로 정답은 ⑤번이다.

5.④ 모든 것을 바꾼 것은 노르만 프랑스의 침략이었습니다. 1066년 헤이스팅스 전투에서 해롤드 왕이 패배하면서 런던에 프랑스 왕들의 왕조가 세워졌습니다(첫 번째 헤이스팅스의 승리자 윌리엄 1세는 실제로 영국에서 보내는 시간이 매우 적었습니다). 그리고 그 후 300년 동안 프랑스는 영국의 권력, 통치, 문화의 거의 모든 영역에서 영향력을 행사했습니다. 노르만 프랑스어는 영국 행정부의 언어가 되었고, 시간이 지나면서 영국의 정치적인 대화 형태로 자리 잡았습니다. 올드 잉글리시는 잠시 경멸을 받기 시작했고, 농부와 평민의 언어로 거만하게 여겨졌습니다. 그럼에도 불구하고 많은 변화가 있었지만, 고대 영어는 실제로 살아남았습니다. 한 세기 반 동안의 언어적 미스터리 끝에, 아무도 이 언어에 무슨 일이 일어났는지 확신하지 못했던 올드 잉글리시는 기적적으로 살아남아 현재 미들 잉글리시로 불리게 되었고, 프랑스어에서 수천 개의 새로운 외래어를 채택했으며, 그렇게 함으로써 더욱 강해졌습니다. 마침내, 영어 문학의 초기 인물 중 가장 인상적인 제프리 초서의 글에서 역사상 가장 큰 이점을 발휘하게 되었습니다.

이종현T의 독해 Point!

Old English가 살아남는다는 새로운 논리가 처음 등장하는 시작점이므로 정답은 ④번이다.

6.③ 아이스킬로스의 오레스테이아가 끝날 무렵, 등장인물들의 고대 세계에서 두 가지 변화가 일어납니다. 유명한 변화 속에서 아테나는 끝없는 피의 복수의 순환을 대체하고 종식시키기 위해 법적 기관을 소개합니다. 그녀는 아테네 시민단체에서 선발된 독립적인 제3자 판사, 배심원단 등 합리적인 논증 절차와 증거의 무게를 갖춘 법정을 세우며, 이제 피의 죄책감은 고대 복수의 여신인 퓨리들이 아닌 법으로 해결될 것이라고 발표합니다. 그러나 퓨리들은 단순히 무시되지 않습니다. 대신, 아테나는 그들이 같은 법적 기관과 도시의 미래 건강에 얼마나 중요한지를 인정하여 도시에 합류하도록 설득하고, 그들에게 지하의 명예로운 장소를 제공합니다. 일반적으로 아테나의 이러한 움직임은 법체계가 어두운 복수의 열정을 통합하고 이를 존중해야 한다는 인식으로 이해됩니다. 따라서 위대한 헬레니즘자 휴 로이드 존스는 "에린예스의 특권을 폐지하기를 원하지 않고, 아테나는 그 특권을 보존하기 위해 불안해하고 있다"고 결론짓습니다

이종현T의 독해 Point!

앞 문장에서 Furies를 제거하지 않았다는 부정 논리가 제시되므로, "Instead"로 전환해 구체적 조치를 설명하는 시작점인 ⓒ에 들어가야 하며, 정답은 ③번이다.

7.② 많은 미국인이 탄수화물을 너무 많이 섭취하기 때문에 지방이 생긴다는 일반적인 믿음이 있습니다. 고지방, 저지방 식단은 고지방 식단과 칼로리가 같더라도 체중 증가, 인슐린 및 혈당 수치 상승, 당뇨병 증가로 이어진다는 아이디어입니다. 이 연구에서는 그런 일이 일어나지 않았습니다. 다른 사람들은 저지방 식단이 사람들이 자연스럽게 체중을 감량할 수 있게 한다는 반대 의견을 내놓기도 했습니다. 하지만 다시 말하지만, 그 믿음은 연구 데이터에 의해 뒷받침되지 않았습니다. 심장병 위험 요인으로는 심장병 위험을 증가시키는 LDL 콜레스테롤만 영향을 받았습니다. 고지방 식단을 섭취하는 여성의 수치는 약간 높았지만 심장병 위험에 눈에 띄는 차이를 보일 만큼 높지는 않았습니다. 모든 연구 참가자가 여성이었지만 결과는 남성에게도 적용되어야 합니다.

이종현T의 독해 Point!

두 번째 믿음(저지방 식단이 체중 감량을 돕는다는 주장)이 나온 뒤, again이라는 표현을 통해 그 믿음도 부정된다는 구조이므로 두 번째 반박이 시작되는 ⓑ에 들어가야 하며, 정답은 ②번이다.

8.④ 현대의 예측 방법은 단거리 예측에 관해서는 상당히 정확하지만, 예측이 길어질수록 예측이 틀릴 가능성이 더 높아집니다. 현재의 기상 조건을 수학적으로 계산하는 방법은 날씨의 혼란스러운 특성으로 인해 정확한 예측을 약 5일 전으로 제한하고 있습니다. 기상학자들은 계산 데이터 수집 방법의 결과를 현재 발생하는 실제 대기 조건과 결합합니다. 전 세계 곳곳에서 다양한 수준의 온도, 이슬점, 바람에 관한 현재 정보를 수집하여 과거 조건을 기반으로 한 컴퓨터 모델과 비교하여 가능한 기상 패턴을 도출할 수 있는 단서를 제공합니다. 그러나

기상 방법의 과학과 방법론은 개선되었지만 대기 및 기상 관련 활동에 대한 이해에는 여전히 큰 격차가 있습니다. 그 결과, 다양한 기상 조건을 관찰하고 컴퓨터 생성 모델처럼 미래 기상 조건을 정확하게 예측할 수 있는 가능성이 높은 변화와 변화에 대해 잘 알고 있는 숙련된 기상학자가 있습니다.

이종현T의 독해 Point!

컴퓨터 중심의 기술 설명에서 인간 기상학자의 중요성으로 논리가 전환되는 시작점이므로 정답은 ④번이다.

9.④ 연극 무대에서 커튼이 닫히면, 관객은 박수갈채를 보낸다. 머뭇거리면서 스스로 박수를 치는 사람들로 시작해서 다른 사람들이 합류하는 방식이다. 박수갈채는 각각의 사람이 연기자에게 신뢰를 주는 흥미로운 것이다. 그러나 또한 관객들과 섞이려 노력하는 것이기도 한다. 당신은 누군가에 앞서 박수를 치고 싶지는 않을 것이고 모두들 박수를 멈췄을 때 계속 치고 싶어하지 않을 것이다. 사실, 이 현상을 연구해보면, 관객들이 고요에서 완전한 박수갈채로 진행되는 두드러진 패턴이 있다는 것을 발견하게 된다. 세계 곳곳의 연극을 녹화한 영상들은 패턴이 다른 문화적 습관을 초월하고 각기 다른 관객들이 소리가 몇초간 커지는 것을 보여주는 보편적인 하나의 곡선을 따른다는 것을 보여준다.
더 놀랍게도, 이 곡선은 원자 혹은 분자가 빠르고 급격하게 집단적으로 한 종류에서 다른 종류의 행위로 이동하는 물리학에서 알려진 곡선과 정확히 똑같다. 왜냐하면 한 사람이 하는 행동은 주변 다른 사람들이 하는 행동에 매우 강하게 의존하기 때문이다.

이종현T의 독해 Point!

박수의 패턴이 존재한다는 설명(③) 뒤, 그 패턴이 전 세계적으로 동일하다는 보편성을 시작하는 지점이므로 시작점 역할인 (④)에 들어가야 하며, 정답은 ④번이다.

10.③ 1937년 화창한 어느 아침에, 스페인 북부에 있는 Guernica의 한 작은 마을은 장날을 즐기는 사람들로 가득했다. 갑자기, 무언가 끔찍한 일이 일어났다. 독일 군용기가 머리 위에 나타났고 마을 아래로 폭탄을 떨어뜨리기 시작했다. 많은 사람들과 동물들은 즉시 부상당하거나 죽었다. 스페인의 민주주의적으로 선출된 정부는 Francisco Franco라는 군사 지도자를 상대로 시민 전쟁을 하고 있었다. 바로 그 Franco가 독일에게 Guernica를 폭격해달라고 요청한 것이다. 그 당시에, 스페인의 잘 알려진 예술가 Pablo Picasso는 Paris에 살고 있는 중이었다. 폭격이 있고 며칠 후, Picasso는 신문을 보았다. 앞면에는 Guernica의 죽음과 파괴에 관한 큰 흑백사진이 있었다. 그의 조국에 있는 이 사람들의 고통은 Picasso의 심금을 울렸다. Picasso는 스페인 시민 전쟁 동안에 스페인을 위한 정치 활동가가 되었다. 그는 그 해 Paris에서 열리는 세계 박람회에 전시하기 위해 Guernica의 폭격에 대해서 그림을 그리기로 결심했다. 그는 많은 사람들이 박람회에 올 것을 알고 있었다. 그는 그림이 방문객들을 생각하고 말하고 스페인을 돕기 위해 무언가를 해야 될 영감을 줄 것이라 기대했다.

이종현T의 독해 Point!

Picasso가 신문을 봤다는 말(③)을 구체적으로 설명하는 시작점이므로 정답은 ③번이다.

11.④ 디즈니의 작품은 꽤 요정 이야기, 신화, 민간전승에서 많이 이끌어져 나온다. 그것들은 전형적인 요소들이 풍부하다. 피노키오는 어떻게 이러한 요소들이 피상적 현실주의 아래에 잠기는 대신에 강조될 수 있는가에 대한 좋은 예이다. 초기의 영화에서, 소년/인형 피노키오는 "진정한 소년"이 되기 위해서 그는 그가 "용감하고 신뢰적이며, 이타적"이라는 것을 보여주어야 한다고 듣게 된다. 이 영화의 세 가지 중요한 에피소드는 젊은이의 도덕적 용기를 시험하는 의식적인 시험이다. 그는 경악스럽게도 처음 두 가지에 실패하지만, 그가 고래 에피소드를 포함한 진실한 용기, 정식, 이타심을 논증하는 곳에서 스스로를 만회한다. 그것으로서, 대부분의 디즈니 작품들과 같이, 피노키오 에서의 가치들은 전통적이고 보수적이며, 가족 단위의 신성함에 대한 확신, 우리의 운명을 이끄는 더 높은 힘의 중요성과 사회의 규칙에 의한 행동의 필요성이다.

이종현T의 독해 Point!

세 가지 시련의 결과를 정리한 후, 그로부터 보수적 가치를 도출하는 구조이므로 도덕적 메시지가 시작되는 ④가 시작점이며 정답은 ④번이다.

12.③ 다양한 공기 오염원들은 인간의 건강과 환경에 해로운 영향을 끼치는 것을 알려지고 의심되어져 왔다. 유럽 대부분 지역에서, 이러한 오염원들은 주로 난방, 발전소 또는 자동차의 산물이다. 이러한 요소들로부터 온 오염원들은 인접지에서의 문제점들을 증명할 뿐만 아니라 먼 거리로 이동할 수 있다. 일반적으로 만약 당신이 어리고 건강 상태가 양호하다면, 적당한 공해 수준은 단기간에 심각한 결과를 불러일으킬 가능성은 거의

없다. 그러나, 높은 수준의 공해와 장기간 노출되는 것은 인간의 건강을 위협하는 더 심각한 증상과 질환으로 이어질 수 있다. 폐 혹은 심장 질환을 앓고 있는 사람들은 공해의 영향에 더 취약할 것이다.

이종현T의 독해 Point!

건강한 사람에게는 문제가 없다는 전제(②)를 반박하며, 장기 노출 시 심각한 증상이 나타나는 새로운 논리가 시작되는 지점이므로 정답은 ③번이다.

13.④ 가르치는 것으로부터 오는 보상은 무수히 많다. 그 중에 하나는 당신이 학생들과 만드는 정서적 유대관계이다. 당신은 그들이 할 수 있는 최선의 노력을 다하고 문제가 생겼을 때 지원을 해주는 끊임없이 개인적인 수준에서 맞물리고 있다. 당신의 교습과 지도 덕분에 경험을 통해 성장하고 궁극적으로 성공하는 것을 보는 것은 형용할 수 없는 감정을 불러일으킨다. 또한 가르치는 것은 당신 주변 세계에 상당히 긍정적인 영향을 준다고 말할 수 있는 몇 안되는 직업 중 하나이다. 다른 직업이 더 명백한 흔적을 남기더라도 몇몇 사람은 자신의 커리어를 되돌아볼 때 자신들을 통해 수많은 어린 학생들이 그들의 잠재력을 발휘하고 오늘날의 어른이 되었다고 말할 것이다.

이종현T의 독해 Point!

가르침이 세상에 긍정적 영향을 준다는 내용이, 다른 직업과 비교하며 가르침의 가치를 강조하는 ④에서 새로운 논리로 시작되므로 시작점 역할이며 정답은 ④번이다.

14.④ 파충류와 어류는 곤충이나 동물 무리와 물고기 떼에서 발견될 것은 분명하다. 그것들은 대량으로 부화되고 비슷한 환경이 서로 같이 있게끔 만든다. 사회적이고 무리지어 사는 포유류의 경우에는 연관성은 외부 힘의 군집으로 올 뿐만 아니라 내부 자극에 의해 유지된다. 그것들은 단순히 서로를 좋아하고 동시에 같은 장소에서 발견되는 것이 아니다. 그것들은 서로 좋아해서 같이 있는 것이다. 파충류의 세계와 인간 정신의 세계의 차이는 공감능력이 지나칠 수 없는 것이다. 우리는 파충류의 본능적 동기, 식성, 두려움과 증오의 빠르고 단순한 긴급함을 우리 자신내에서 이해할 수 없다. 우리는 단순하게 그것들을 이해할 수 없다. 왜냐하면 우리의 모든 동기는 복잡하기 때문이다. 우리의 것은 단순히 긴급함이 아니라 균형과 그 결과로 생기는 것이다. 그러나 포유류와 조류는 우리 방식과 유사하지만 낮은 단계의 자기억제력과 다른 개인들에 대한 배려심, 사회적 호소, 자제력이 있다. 결론적으로 우리는 거의 모든 종과 관계를 형성할 수 있다. 그들이 고통 받을 때, 그들은 울음소리를 내고 우리의 감정을 불러일으키는 움직임을 한다. 우리는 그것들을 상호 인식을 통해 애완동물로 만들 수 있다. 그들은 우리를 향한 자제력을 갖도록 길들여질 수 있고 키울 수 있고 가르칠 수 있다.

이종현T의 독해 Point!

동물들과의 관계 맺음을 말하며, 앞에서 설명한 포유류·조류의 사회성·교감 가능성에 대한 논리를 정리하는 끝점이므로 정답은 ④번이다.

15.② 세계보건기구(WHO)에 따르면, 2030년에 세계에서 가장 큰 사망 원인은 예방 가능하지만 자발적인 것이다. 오늘날, WHO는 담배가 세계 사망 원인 2위라고 말하였다. 만약에 그 수가 동일한 속도로 증가한다면, 담배와 많은 관련 질병들은 고작 15년 안에 세계에서 가장 높은 사망 원인이 될 것이다. 개발도상국은 가장 영향을 받기 쉽다. 왜냐하면 모든 흡연자의 84%는 1970년 이후로 담배가 증가하고 있는 현재의 중간, 저소득 국가에서 살고 있기 때문이다. 많은 정부가 공공 흡연을 금지하기 위해 조치를 취했고 건강을 위협받는 젊은 잠재적 흡연자들을 교육시킴에도 불구하고, 담배 제품이 완전히 금지될 때까지, 위험을 감수할지 말지는 궁극적으로 개인에게 달려 있다.

이종현T의 독해 Point!

현재 흡연자 대부분이 개발도상국에 있다는 ② 앞에서, 현재 수치가 계속되면 사망률 1위가 될 것이라는 예측을 제시하며 논리의 시작점이 되므로 정답은 ②번이다.

16.③ 공개 연설이라 불리는 보고적 대화는 듣는 청중들에게 전달되는 공식 연설의 문자 그대로 대중적 상황에서만 일어나지는 않는다. 대화를 하는 사람이 더 많을수록, 너가 그들에 대해 덜 알수록, 그리고 그들 사이에 지위적 차이가 더 있을수록, 대화는 더 대중 연설 혹은 보고적 대화가 된다. 사람이 적을수록 너가 그들과 더 친밀할수록 그리고 지위가 더 동등할수록 사적인 대화 혹은 친밀한 대화가 될 가능성이 높다. 더 나아가서, 여성들은 가족 구성원을 제외한 남자가 있을 때 상황이 더 공적이라고 느낀다 - 상냥한 행동을 해야한다는 의미에서 - 그러나 심지어 가족 안에서도, 아버지가 집에 없을 때 어머니와 아이들은 집이 무대 뒤라고 느낄 것이다. 그리고 그가 집에 있을 때는

무대 위처럼 느낄 것이다. 많은 어린이들은 아버지가 집에 있을 때 올바른 행동을 하도록 교육받는다. 이것은 그가 집에 자주 없기 때문이거나 어머니 - 혹은 아버지 - 가 아버지가 집에 있을 때 그를 방해하지 않기를 원하기 때문이다.

이종현T의 독해 Point!

가족이 예외라는 말(②)을 반박하고, 아버지 유무에 따라 달라지는 가족 내 분위기를 보여주는 사례가 시작되는 지점이므로 정답은 ③번이다.

17.④ 어떤 사람은 총명하고 논리 정연한 개개인들은 다른 사람들을 모욕할 필요를 못 느낄 것이라고 생각하지만 그들도 그런 필요를 느낀다. 그들은 그들이 모욕 안에서 사용하는 언어를 조심스럽게 말로 표현하면서 이런 필요성을 가장한다. 예를 들어 학술대회에서 어떤 남성이 Nietzsche의 작품에 관한 논문을 발표한 후에 관객 속 누군가가 발표자의 주장에 치명적인 결함으로 보이는 것을 드러내는 질문을 던진다고 가정해보자. 이런 경우에, 발표자는 질문자를 심한 멍청이라고 부를 가능성이 적다. 그는 아마 대신에 이렇게 응답할 것이다. " 질문하신 분은 Nietzsche의 작품을 자세히 읽어 보지 못하신 것이 분명합니다." 관객 속 그 학자는 발표자가 방금 자신을 품격과 우아함을 갖추어 완전 멍청이로 불렀다는 것을 즉시 알아챌 것이다.

이종현T의 독해 Point!

우회적 표현의 실제 예시를 제시하며, 그것이 결국 청중에게 모욕으로 인식된다는 평가(④)로 이어지는 시작점이므로 정답은 ④번이다.

18.② 학생들이 받아들여지고 안전하고 탐구하기에 자유롭다고 느끼는 환경을 조성하는 것은 학습에 중요하다. 그러나 교내 훈육 문제도 다루어질 필요가 있다. 교사는 학습이 이루어지는 여유롭고 공개적인 환경을 유지하면서 허용되는 행위 장벽을 제거할 필요가 있다. 너그러운 인격을 갖춘 교사는 긍정적인 학습 환경을 만드는 데 일가견이 있다. 그러나, 만약에 그들이 너무 관대하다면, 그들은 주요한 훈육 문제를 겪을 수 있다. 어린 학생들은 얼만큼 교묘히 모면할 수 있는지 항상 점검한다. 그리고 친해지려하고 선뜻 수용하려고 매우 노력하는 교사는 교실이 완전히 통제불능이 되는 것을 발견하게 될 것이다. 엄격한 인성과 수업 방식을 가지고 있는 교사는 교실 훈육이 더 잘되지만 규칙을 너무 엄격하게 적용하면 부정적인 효과를 낳을 수 있다. 학생들이 실수를 할 때, 조문 그대로를 따르는 과도하게 엄격한 반응들은 참가를 저해하고, 특히 만약 교사가 학우들 앞에서 학생을 민망하게 만든다면 긴장된 분위기를 형성할 수 있다.

이종현T의 독해 Point!

느슨한 교사의 장점 → 그러나 문제도 있다(제시문) → 실제 문제 사례(②)라는 흐름이므로, 제시문은 끝점으로서 (②) 앞에 들어가는 것이 가장 적절하다.

19.③ 고객의 요구를 더 잘 이해하는 것은 매출 증가와 더 큰 시장 점유율을 가져올 수 있다. Chris Craft의 부사장이자 총 지배인인 Bob MacNeil은 이 말을 믿는 사람이다. 그는 자신의 회사가 고객의 불만을 들음으로써 그 회사 제품을 향상시키는 것을 지켜보는 직접적인 경험을 했다. 그러나 고객들이 항상 회사에 직접적으로 자신들의 불만을 표하는 것은 아니기 때문에 때때로 그들을 도와서 일을 해 나가야 한다고 MacNeil은 말한다. 어떤 보트 소유주들은 자기들이 무엇을 요청해야 하는지 확신하지 못하거나 보트 중개인에게 성가신 존재로 인식될까 두렵기 때문에 불만을 표현하지 않는다고 말한다. 다른 어떤 보트 소유주들은 그들이 파는 보트에 대한 그들의 지식을 신뢰하지 못하거나 아니면 모든 사람이 이런 문제를 겪고 있다고 생각한다. 그래서 Bob Neil은 보트 소유주들이 보트를 타고 있을 때 적극적으로 불만을 끌어내기 위해 나가서 그들과 소통하라고 자기 회사의 중개인들을 독려한다.

이종현T의 독해 Point!

제시문은 "고객이 불만을 말하지 않는다"는 결과이고, ③은 그 원인을 설명하므로, 제시문은 새로운 논리의 시작점으로서 ③번 앞이 가장 자연스럽다.

20.④ 소비자가 쓰는 돈의 약 48퍼센트를 50세 이상의 사람들이 쓴다고 추정된다. 그들은 전체 고급 승용차의 약 48퍼센트를 구매하고 호화로운 여행의 약 80퍼센트를 책임진다. 그들은 심지어 매년 전체 장난감의 약 25퍼센트를 구매한다. (미국에는 약 5천 5백만 명의 50세 이상의 조부모들이 있다.) 그럼에도 불구하고 마케팅 및 판매 촉진 프로그램은 보통 이러한 소비자들을 훨씬 더 나이가 많은 것처럼 취급한다. 예를 들어, 나이 많은 소비자들은 특정 상품에 고정되어 있고 새로운 선택 가능한 상품을 써 보려고 하지 않는다는 근거 없는 믿음이 있다. 그러니 왜 신상품의 광고가 나이 많은 소비자들은 겨냥해야 한다는 말인가? 사실 쇼핑몰에 있는 500명의 50세가 넘는 사람들

의 설문 조사는 그들의 약 80퍼센트가 신상품을 써 보고자 하는 의지가 꽤 있다는 것을 보여 주었다.

이종현T의 독해 Point!

제시문은 "노인은 새로운 제품을 시도하지 않는다"는 고정관념 예시(시작점)이며, ⑤에서 그 실제와 다른 조사 결과를 보여주므로, 제시문은 ④번 뒤 새로운 논리의 시작점이다.

21.③ 심리학 연구자들은 인간 행동을 설명하는 데 도움이 되며 예측할 수도 있는 연구를 수행할 과학적 방법을 따른다. 이것은 달팽이나 음파를 연구하는 것보다 훨씬 도전적인 일이다. 그것은 종종 자연스런 환경보다는 실험실 내에서 행동 검증하기와 모집단의 진정한 단면에서 추출된 자료를 수집한다기보다는 (심리학 개론 수업의 학생들 같은) 쉽게 쓸 수 있는 사람들에게 참여해 달라고 부탁하기와 같은 타협을 요구한다. 사람들의 생각을 바꾸지(이를 반응성이라 한다) 않고 그들이 생각하는 바에 다가가는 방안을 상상해내는 것은 종종 대단한 영리함을 요구한다. 그들이 관찰되고 있다는 것을 단지 알고 있는 것만으로도 사람들은 다르게 행동하게 될 수 있다. 사람들은 그들의 진정한 감정보다 사회적으로 더 바람직하다고 느끼는 답을 내놓을지도 모른다. 그러나 심리학의 이러한 어려움에도 불구하고, 과학적 기법의 대가는 연구 결과가 반복 가능하다는 것이다. 즉, 같은 절차를 따라서 동일한 실험을 다시 작동시켜 보면, 같은 결과를 얻을 가능성이 매우 클 것이다.

이종현T의 독해 Point!

제시문은 사람의 생각을 건드리지 않고 측정하는 게 어렵다(시작점)는 문제 제기로, ③~④가 그 구체적 예시이므로 ③번 앞이 새로운 논리의 시작점이다.

22.⑤ 월드 와이드 웹과 같은 우리의 21세기 기술은 우리가 우리의 언어로 단어를 정의하는 방식에 깊이 영향을 끼친다. 인터넷 이전 시대에서는 인쇄된 사전이 항상 단어가 의미하는 바와 그것이 사용되는 방식에 대한 최종 권위의 역할을 했다. 사전의 저자들은 전통적으로 특정 단어가 사용되는 방식의 가능한 한 많은 예를 주의 깊게 분석함으로써 그것의 정의에 도달했다. 어떤 표준 탁상용 사전에서 발견되는 몇몇 복잡한 단어들이 9~10개의 가능한 용례를 가지고 있을 순 있지만, 이러한 정의조차도 가능한 모든 용법을 다루지는 못한다. 사전편찬자 Erin Mckean에 따르면, 최근의 연구에서 현대 소설에서 무작위로 고른 여러 구절에서, 명사, 동사, 형용사의 13% 대형 탁상용 사전에서 발견되지 않는 방식으로 사용되었음이 나타났다. 전통적 사전의 주요 단점은 단어가 사용되는 방식의 표본 추출만을 제공하는 데 이용 가능한 제한된 공간만이 있다는 것이다. 다시 말해서, 그 물리적 공간의 제약 때문에 표준 사전에 진입하지 못한 다수의 더 현대적인 용법들이 있다.

이종현T의 독해 Point!

제시문은 전통적 사전은 공간의 제약 때문에 단점이 있다는 새로운 논리의 시작점이므로 정답은 ⑤번이다.

23.⑤ 몇 년 전에 North Carolina 대학교의 학생들이 한 실험에 참여했다. 그 학생들은 20개의 수학문제를 할 수 있는 한 많이 풀도록 5분이 주어졌다. 각각의 학생들은 동일한 작은 방에서 실험을 끝냈지만 그들 중 일부에게는 12개의 전구가 밝게 켜져 있었고 다른 학생들에게는 단지 4개의 전구가 더 어두침침하게 켜져 있었다. 5분이 경과한 후에 학생들은 실험자에게 그들이 얼마나 많은 문제를 맞혔는지 이야기했다. 밝은 방의 학생들은 꽤 솔직했으며 방에서 누군가가 그들을 지켜보고 있음을 느꼈다고 보고했다. 한편 어두침침하게 불이 켜진 방의 학생들은 그들의 점수를 대략 50퍼센트 부풀렸고, 방에서 그들의 신분이 드러나지 않음을 느꼈다고 보고했다. 여하튼 그 방의 학생들은 정직하게 행동해야 한다는 도덕적 제약으로부터 해방되어 있었다. 연구자들은 이러한 결과를 어둠이 그들의 익명성을 보존할 것이라는 착각 때문으로 보았다.

이종현T의 독해 Point!

제시문은 밝기 차이에 따른 부정직한 행동 결과를 요약·해석(끝점)한 것으로, 앞 문장들의 실험 상황과 구체적 행동 묘사를 결론적으로 정리하므로 ⑤번 앞이 논리의 끝점이다.

24.⑤ 일반 서적은 독자에게 주제에 대한 더 풍요로운 이해를 제공하면서 흥미로운 관찰과 세부사항을 가지고 주제에 활력을 불어넣을 공간을 제공할 수 있다. 교과서는 너무나 많은 주제를 다루어야 하기 때문에 하나의 주제를 조금이라도 깊이 있게 발전시킬 수 없다. 그러므로 교과서는 일반 서적에서 유효한 흥미진진한 종류의 제시를 허용하지 않는 주제들에 대한 넓고 결과적으로 더 얕은 견해를 제공한다. 예를 들어, 교과서의 한 단락은 단지 소행성이 지구를 강타할 수 있다고 언급할 뿐이다.

그러나 일반 서적은 소행성의 대기 진입, 그것의 행성과의 충돌, 그리고 25마일 깊이와 100마일의 너비인 분화구의 폭발의 사건을 시간 순으로 기록한다. 그것은 충돌 시점에서의 증발, 지진, 화재와, 암흑과 몹시 낮은 기온이 뒤따르는 강력한 열기의 전 세계적 시기를 유발하는 파편을 매혹적으로 상세히 기술한다. 교과서가 허용하는 한정된 공간 속에 이러한 종류의 세부사항과 통찰력을 독자들에게 제공하기는 어렵다.

이종현T의 독해 Point!

제시문은 trade book이 제공하는 생생한 세부묘사의 결론 요약(끝점)으로, 앞의 예시 설명(③~④)을 종합 · 강조하며 마무리하므로 ⑤번 앞이 논리의 끝점이다.

25.④ 심리학에서 다양성의 한 측면은 심리학자들이 연구하고 다루는 광범위한 사람들에 있다. 이 변화는 중요한데, 그 이유는 대부분의 심리학자가 모든 사람이 매우 비슷하고, 한 집단에 대한 연구나 치료 노력에서 나온 어떤 원칙이든 모든 사람, 모든 곳에 적용될 것이라고 한 때 생각했기 때문이다. 그들은 부분적으로는 옳았는데, 세상 사람들이 여러 면에서 실제로 비슷하기 때문이다. 그들은 집단을 이루어 생활하고, 신앙을 가지고, 규칙, 음악, 춤, 그리고 게임을 만들어 내는 경향이 있다. 신경 세포 활동의 원칙이나 열 또는 신맛에 대한 반응은 미소에 대한 인식과 마찬가지로, 어디서나 남성과 여성에게 있어 똑같다. 하지만 모든 사람의 도덕적 가치관, 성취동기, 또는 의사소통 방식이 똑같은 것은 아니다. 이러한 것과 행동 및 정신 과정의 많은 다른 측면은 사람의 성별, 민족적 배경, 사회적 계급, 그리고 그들이 성장하는 문화를 포함한 사회 문화적 요인에 의해 영향을 받는다. 이 변수들은 특히 문화에 따라 행동과 정신 과정에서 많은 유의미한 차이를 만들어 낸다.

이종현T의 독해 Point!

제시문은 사람마다 도덕성 · 동기 · 소통 방식이 다르다는 새로운 논리의 시작점이며, ④에서 그 차이를 문화 · 성별 등의 요인으로 설명하므로 ④번 앞이 시작점이다.

26.④ 진화는 종이 이동하는 큰 고속도로와 매우 비슷하다. 방향 변화는 상당히 점진적인데, 너무 급회전하면 빠르게 이동하는 차량(즉, 진화 중인 종)이 도로에서 날아가 멸종될 것이기 때문이다. 생물학적 관점에서, 이러한 고속도로 개념은, 특히 유전적 관점에서, 다양한 동물 종 사이의 많은 유사성과 함께, 연속적인 느린 변화의 형태로 나타난다. 일부 사람들은, 현대 생화학의 최근 연구 결과가 인간이 우리가 생각했을 수 있는 것만큼 유전적으로 독특하지 않다는 것을 시사한다는 것을 알게 되면, 놀라거나 심지어 심기가 불편할 수도 있다. DNA 분석은 분자와 유전자 관점에서 인간과 침팬지가 최소한 98퍼센트 같다는 것을 나타낸다. 이 유사성의 정도가 매우 가까우므로 일부 과학자는 이종 교배를 수행하여 잡종을 만드는 것이 가능할 수도 있다는 점을 제시했다. 물론, 아마도 도덕적, 윤리적 고려는 그러한 유전적 실험을 금지하겠지만, 이 가능성은 인간이 다른 영장류와 얼마나 유사한지를 실제로 분명히 보여 준다. 우리의 애완견처럼 인간과 거리가 먼 것처럼 보이는 동물조차도 여전히 우리와 매우 유사하다.

이종현T의 독해 Point!

제시문은 유인원과 인간의 유사성이 너무 커서 교배 가능성까지 제기되었다는 충격적 예시(끝점)로, ③~④의 유사성 설명을 요약 · 강조하므로 ④번 앞이 논리의 끝점이다.

27.③ 소셜 네트워크 사용자들을 폭로나 사생활 위협 또는 침해로부터 보호하기 위해 기술이 사용될 수 있는 방법은 여러 가지가 있다. 더 철저한 기술적 해결책에는 소셜 미디어/소셜 네트워크를 작동하지 않게 하거나 사용을 금지하는 것이 포함된다. 예를 들어, 일부 학교와 직장은 소셜 네트워킹 사이트에 대한 명백한 제한을 두거나, 어떤 경우에는 완전한 금지를 시행하고, 학생 및 직원들이 이러한 사이트에 접근하지 못하도록 소셜 네트워크를 정보통신 기술 차원에서 사용할 수 없게 만든다. 이 해결책의 문제는 이런 사이트를 이용하는 이점 역시 사라진다는 것이다. 게다가, 이렇게 하면 학교에 있는 동안이나 근무 시간 동안에는 이러한 사이트의 사용을 막을 수는 있지만, 수업(근무) 시간 후에 행해지는 일들에는 아무런 영향을 미치지 못한다. 온라인 환경에서 발생하는 맥락의 붕괴는 학교 시간이나 근무 시간 외에 발생한 온라인상의 정보 교환이 사람들의 학교생활이나 직장 생활에 영향을 줄 정도로 사람들의 직장 생활과 사생활 간 경계를 모호하게 한다. 그러므로 이러한 전략을 이용하는 것이 잠재적 위험을 전반적으로 최소화 하는데 반드시 효과적인 것은 아니다.

이종현T의 독해 Point!

제시문은 소셜 미디어 차단의 단점(시작점)을 제시하며, ③에서 그 단점인 "차단의 제한적 효과"를 구체적으로 설명하므로, ③번 앞이 새로운 논리의 시작점이다.

28.④ 인류 집단이 시간을 거치며 진보함에 따라, 수렵 채집인 문화의 발달 역시 그러했다. 언뜻 보기에, 이 문화가 매우 간단해 보이지만, 꽤 복잡했고 여전히 꽤 복잡하다. 전 세계에는 이러한 삶의 방식을 유지하는 토착민 집단이 여전히 존재한다. 다른 무엇보다, 이 문화는 간단한 가족 단위에 기반을 두었는데, 이것이 가족들 간의 친족 유대로 확장되었다. 그러한 친족 관계가 결국 결합되어 씨족으로 불리는 더 크게 연결된 집단을 형성하였다. 씨족은 서로 연결되어 부족으로 발전하였다. 부족은 사냥과 채집을 통해 존재했고 그 과정에서 정치 지도자(족장)와 종교계 인사 (성직자)를 포함하는 정교한 사회적 정치적 조직을 만들었다. 수렵 채집 문화에는 또한 성별 분업이 있었다. 남성은 타고난 상체의 강인함 때문에 사냥, 전쟁, 그리고 힘든 노동을 주도했다. 여성은 채집을 하고 음식을 준비하였으며, 또한 부족의 어린이들을 돌보았다.

이종현T의 독해 Point!

제시문은 수렵채집 사회 내 성별 분업이 있었다는 새로운 논리의 시작점이며, ④와 ⑤가 각각 남녀 역할 구체화이므로, ④번 앞이 시작점이다.

29.⑤ 통상 바다를 통한 통신이 육지를 걸친 통신보다 더 빨랐다. 예를 들어, 멕시코에서 스페인 사람들은 Zacatecas에 있는 광산에서 Mexico City까지 가는 유명한 '실버 로드'처럼 소위 '왕립 도로'를 건설해야 했다. 이 도로들의 명칭은 현대 캘리포니아와 뉴멕시코에서 존속하고 있다. 서유럽보다 인구가 덜 조밀하고 도시들이 더 작고 수가 더 적은 동유럽에서 통신은 이에 상응하게 더 느렸다. 예를 들어, 예카테리나 2세 시기의 제정 러시아에서는 St. Petersburg에서 보내진 칙령이 시베리아에 있는 Kamchatka에 도달하는 데 18개월이 걸렸을 것이고, 그 답신이 수도에 도달하는 데 18개월이 더 걸렸을 것이다. 통신 문제는 러시아를 제외한 초기 현대 유럽 제국들이 왜 해상 제국이었는지를 설명하는 데 도움이 된다. 그것들에는 포르투갈 · 스페인 · 네덜란드 · 프랑스 · 영국의 대륙에 걸친 제국들, 그리고 발트해 주변에 건설된 유럽의 스웨덴 제국도 포함되었다.

이종현T의 독해 Point!

제시문은 왜 대부분 제국들이 해상 제국이었는지를 설명하는 핵심 결론(끝점)으로, ⑤에서 그 구체적 예시(어떤 제국들이 있었는가)가 나오므로 ⑤번 앞이 논리의 끝점이다.

30.④ 지역 수준에서의 사회적, 경제적, 환경적 지속 가능성 증진에 대한 관심이 증가하고 있다. 이 개념은 환경 관련 연구 문헌에서 나온 것이지만 지역 사회 개발의 맥락에서 훨씬 더 넓은 의미를 지닌다. 지역 사회의 지속 가능성을 증진하려는 노력은 지역의 사회, 경제, 환경 기반의 장기적 생존에 기여하는 지역 정책에 초점을 맞춘다. 지속 가능성은 자주 지역 사회 개발의 결과로 여겨지지만, 우리는 그것을 지역 사회 개발 시행 과정 전체에 걸친 지침으로 간주한다. 이 접근법은 우리가 지역의 경제적, 사회적, 환경적 목표 사이의 상호 연결성을 조사하도록 만든다. 이러한 상호 작용은 흔히 3대 핵심 원칙으로 언급된다. 예를 들어, 경제 개발을 증진하는 행위는 환경의 지속 가능성을 보장하고 지역 사회 내 소외된 주민에게 기회를 제공해야 한다.

이종현T의 독해 Point!

제시문은 지역의 경제 · 사회 · 환경 목표가 서로 연결된다는 새로운 논리의 시작점이며, ④는 그 상호작용을 가리키는 용어(Triple Bottom Line)를 소개하므로, ④번 앞이 시작점이다.

31.⑤ 기후는 패턴이 형성될 정도로 충분히 오랜 기간 동안에 걸쳐 일어난 날씨의 총합이다. 전통적으로 '평년 기후'를 결정하는 기간은 30년이다. 따라서, 기후는 특정 기간에 걸친 약간의 변동성을 포함하는 기후 상태의 집합 평균이다. 월별, 계절별, 혹은 연간 시간 척도상의 동일한 종류의 그런 기후 상태 사이의 차이를 평균 또는 변동성의 변화를 포함하여 기후 변동이라고 한다. 하지만, 기후 변화는 알려져 있을지도 모르는 어떤 요인에 따른 평년 기후의 변화인데, 다년간 지속된다. 위에 따르면, 매우 습하거나 매우 건조한 날씨와 같은 계절별 또는 연도별 영향은 만약 그것이 평년 기후의 예상된 변동의 범위 안에 있으면 기후 변동으로 기술될 수 있다. 그러나 온난화의 결과로 해빙이 서서히 녹는 것은 최종적으로 기후 변화로 해석될 수 있다.

이종현T의 독해 Point!

제시문은 기후 변동의 개념을 실제 사례(강우 · 가뭄)에 적용해 설명하는 구체적 정리(끝점)로, 앞의 개념 정의(③)와 기후 변화 구분(④)을 현상으로 마무리하므로 ⑤번 앞이 끝점이다.

32.④ 우주는 그것이 생겨난 처음 순간에 너무 빠르게 식어서 수소, 헬륨, 그리고 (극소량의) 리튬보다 더 무겁거나 더 복잡한 원소를 만들어내는 것이 불가능했다. 초기 우주의 열기와 혼돈 속에서 더 복잡한 것은 아무것도 살아남을 수 없었다. 화학적 관점에서 초기 우주는 매우 단순했는데, 너무나도 단순하여 우리의 지구나 거기에 사는 생물체와 같은 복잡한 물체를 생성할 수 없었다. 최초의 항성들과 은하계들은 거의 수소와 헬륨에 지나지 않는 것으로 구성되었다. 그러나 그것들은 단순한 구성요소로 복잡한 물체를 만드는 우리 우주의 정말 놀라운 능력의 징후였다. 항성들은 일단 생겨난 후, 생물체를 포함한 더욱 복잡한 독립체 를 위한 기반을 다졌는데, 그것들의 불타는 핵에서 수소와 헬륨을 모든 다른 원소로 바꾼 연금술을 행했기 때문이다.

이종현T의 독해 Point!

제시문은 단순한 원소들이 모여 복잡한 존재를 만들어낸다는 새로운 논리의 시작점으로, ④에서 별이 그러한 복잡성의 기초가 되었음을 설명하므로 ④번 앞이 시작점이다.

33.③ 단지 특정 종류의 독창적인 사람이 예술에 대한 노출을 추구하는 것은 아니다. 예술은 또한 결과적으로 창의적인 통찰력의 강력한 원천으로서의 역할을 한다. 갈릴레오가 달 표면에 산이 있다는 정말 놀라운 발견을 했을 때, 사실 그의 망원경은 그 발견을 뒷받침해 줄 만큼 충분한 확대 능력을 갖추고 있지 않았다. 대신, 그는 달의 밝은 지역과 어두운 지역을 구분 짓는 지그재그 패턴을 알아 보았다. 다른 천문학자들도 유사한 망원경을 통해 관찰을 하고 있었지만, 갈릴레오만이 그 어둡고 밝은 지역들이 암시하는 바를 제대로 인식할 수 있었다. 그는 물리학과 천문학에서 필요로 하는 깊이 있는 경험뿐 아니라 회화와 소묘에 폭넓은 경험도 또한 지니고 있었다. 빛과 그림자를 묘사하는 데 집중하는 'chiaroscuro'라 일컬어지는 기법에서의 예술적 훈련 덕분에, 갈릴레오는 다른 이들은 발견하지 못한 (달 표면의) 산을 발견할 수 있었다.

이종현T의 독해 Point!

제시문은 갈릴레오가 달의 명암에서 '지그재그 경계'를 인식했다는 관찰의 구체적 시작점(시작점)이며, ③은 그가 그 명암의 의미를 이해한 유일한 인물이라는 설명이 이어지므로 ③번 앞이 새로운 논리의 시작점이다.

34.② 인류학자 Bronislaw Malinowski가 남태평양의 Trobriand 제도에 사는 원주민들의 일상생활을 관찰했을 때, 그는 그 섬사람들이 주술 의식을 많이 사용하긴 했지만, 특정한 활동들을 위해서만 그것들을 아껴두었던 것에 주목했다. 예를 들면 그들은 보호받고 있는 (환초로 둘러싸인) 초호의 많은 물고기를 잡으러 갈 때는 주술을 사용하지 않았지만, 넓은 바다에서 물고기를 잡을 때는 그렇게 했다(주술을 사용했다). 그것이 그들이 주술을 사용하는지 안 하는지를 결정하는 것은 위험의 존재라는 것을 시사했을지도 모르지만, 그 설명은 다른 관찰에는 맞지 않았다. 예를 들어, 그 섬사람들은 곤충들이 그들의 농작물을 망치지 못하게 하기 위해서는 주술을 사용했지만, 정원 가꾸기에서는 일반적으로 그렇게 하지 않았다. Malinowski는 그 차이를 만들어낸 것이 통제력이라는 것을 깨달았다. 그 섬사람들은 자신의 노력과 기술이 성공이나 실패를 결정할 것이라고 생각할 때는 주술에 의지하지 않았다. 결과가 운이나 그들이 통제할 수 없는 다른 요소들을 포함할 때는 그렇게 했다(주술에 의지했다).

이종현T의 독해 Point!

제시문은 ①에서 제시된 '위험한 환경에서만 마법 사용'이라는 예시를 요약하며 반박을 유도하는 전환부(끝점)로, ②번 앞이 해당 논리의 마무리이자 전환점이므로 끝점이다.

35.② 사람들이 이 나라에서 저 나라로 혹은 이 지역에서 저 지역으로 이동할 때, 그 들의 경제적 지위가 변할지도 모른다. 그들은 새로운 식품과 새로운 음식 풍습에 노출될 것이다. 그들의 원래 음식 풍습이 영양적으로 충분했을지도 모르지만, 그들의 새로운 환경은 그들로 하여금 그들의 식습관을 바꾸도록 유도할지도 모른다. 예를 들어 우유가 이사 전에 그들 식단에서 주식이었는데 새로운 환경에서는 대단히 비싸다면, 탄산음료, 커피, 혹은 차와 같은 더 저렴하고 영양적으로 열등한 음료를 위해 우유는 포기될지도 모른다. 사탕이 그들의 이전 환경에서는 사치였을지도 모르지만 그들의 새로운 환경에서는 비싸지 않고 널리 퍼져있을지도 모른다. 결과적으로 한 가정이 탄산음료나 사탕의 소비를 증가시키고 영양이 더 풍부한 식품의 구매는 제한할지도 모른다. 식품의 영양가를 잘 모르는 사람은 쇼핑을 할 때 그러한 실수들을 쉽게 저지를 수 있다.

이종현T의 독해 Point!

제시문은 새 환경에서 식습관이 바뀔 수 있다는 새로운 논리의 시작점이며, ②는 그 구체적 사례(우유 → 값싼

음료 대체)를 설명하므로 ②번 앞이 시작점이다.

36.③ 좋은 연구 설계를 선택하는 것은 단지 어떤 특정 방법을 선택하는 것 이상을 요구한다. 연구원들은 자신들이 사용하려고 하는 방법이 윤리적인지 알아내야 한다. 즉, 연구를 설계할 때, 조사자들은 참가하는 사람들의 권리를 침해하지 않는 방식으로 그렇게 해야 한다. 모든 연구 프로젝트가 이러한 보호 조치를 가지고 있는지 확실히 하기 위해, 연구자들은 자료가 수집되기 전에 전문가와 지역 사회 대표자들로 구성된 지역 심사원단에 의한 공식 검토를 위한 제안된 연구를 제출해야 한다. 이 심사원단의 찬성이 있어야만 과학자들은 자신들의 연구를 시작할 수 있다. 만약 검토 심사원단이 제안된 연구의 어떤 측면을 찬성하지 않는다면, 그 연구원은 심사원단의 찬성을 얻기 위해 그 측면들을 수정하여 다시 제출해야 한다. 마찬가지로, 연구의 한 구성 요소가 바뀔 때마다, 검토심사원단은 반드시 통지를 받고 찬성을 해야 한다.

이종현T의 독해 Point!

제시문은 연구 윤리를 위한 '사전 심사 절차' 도입에 대한 새로운 설명의 시작점이며, ③은 그 심사 없이는 연구가 시작될 수 없음을 강조하므로 ③번 앞이 시작점이다.

37.① 알다시피 옷은 악천후로부터 보호를 해준다. 그러나 직물과 의복은 단지 몸을 보호해주는 것을 넘어서는 다른 역할도 가지고 있다. 옷과 직물 둘 다 비언어적 소통의 수단으로 사용된다. 명백한 예는 특정한 사회적 역할을 알려 주는 제복과 이러한(결혼이라는) 통과의례를 기념하기 위해 서구 문화가 사용하는 현대의 백색 웨딩드레스일 것이다. 두 가지 유형의 의복 모두 보는 사람에게 비언어적으로 중요한 정보를 전달한다. 백색 드레스를 입고 있는 여성은 곧 결혼을 하고 사회 속에서 자신의 지위와 역할을 바꿀 것이다. 제복을 입은 사람은 경찰, 간호사, 혹은 군인과 같은 사회 속에서 어떤 전문적인 기능을 맡고 있다. 그러므로 의류는 집단 구성원 자격에 관한 정보를 시각적으로 전달해주며 정체성의 표시로서 기능한다고 할 수 있다. 의복 착용자가 (자신을) 보는 사람이 받게 되길 바라는 메시지에 따라 부, 교육 수준, 혹은 사회적 지위를 보여주기 위하여 옷을 간편하게 입을 수도 잘 차려입을 수도 있다.

이종현T의 독해 Point!

제시문은 앞서 언급된 의복의 상징적 기능(신분 · 의례 전달)을 보여주는 구체적 예시 요약(끝점)으로, ①에서 그 예시들이 일반화된 설명으로 이어지므로 ①번 앞이 논리의 끝점이다.

38.④ 현대의 관점에서 보면, 과학과 기술 사이의 중요하고도 필수적인 연관성에 대해 이해하는 것은 당연하다. 그러나 지난 500년 동안, 기술은 특정한 발견, 개념, 수학방정식을 기다릴 필요가 없었다. 실은 그것이 바로 1500년의 중국이 많은 측면에서 유럽이나 중동 국가들보다 더 선진적인 것처럼 보였던 이유이다. 설득력 있는 과학 이론이나 잘 통제된 실험이 없이도 완벽하게 작동하는 (심지어 정교하기까지 한) 시계, 화약, 나침반 혹은 의학적 치료를 탄생시킬 수 있다. 하지만 일단 과학이 급격히 발전하면, 그것(과학)과 기술의 연계는 훨씬 더 강해진다. 우리 시대의 과학이 없이도 핵발전소나 초음속 항공기, 컴퓨터, 레이저 또는 여러 가지의 효과적인 의학적, 외과적 중재를 얻을 수 있을 것이라고는 거의 상상할 수 없다. 과학이 없는 그런 사회는 기술 혁신이 박탈당한 채로 남아있거나 기술 혁신을 이룬 사회로부터 그것을 단지 모방할 것임이 틀림 없다.

이종현T의 독해 Point!

제시문은 과학이 본격적으로 발전한 이후 기술과의 관계가 더욱 밀접해진다는 새로운 논리의 시작점이며, ④는 그 밀접한 연결 사례(현대 기술들)를 구체적으로 보여주므로 ④번 앞이 시작점이다.

39.④ 지난 40년의 사회학적 변화 때문에, 우리는 미국 사회에서 더는 남성의 역할과 여성의 역할에 대한 특정 개념을 고수하지 않는다. 그러나 그것이 모든 고정관념이 제거되었음을 의미하지는 않는다. 그것은 오히려 고정관념의 '수'가 증대되었다는 것을 뜻한다. 널리 퍼진 매체 영향력의 시기가 도래하기 전에, 남편 혹은 아내가 무엇을 해야 하고 어떻게 그 또는 그녀가 행동해야 하는지에 대한 한 사람의 생각은 주로 그 자신의 부모에 의해 영향을 받았다. 그러나 텔레비전의 만연, 증가한 이동성, 증대되는 문화적 다양성, 그리고 한부모 가정의 확산 과 함께 역할 모델은 종종 가정 바깥의 힘으로부터 영향을 받게 되었다. 당신이 어떤 영향에 노출되었든, 아마 당신의 배우자는 부부의 역할을 당신과는 다소 다르게 인식할 것이다. 사랑을 더욱 효과적으로 표현하기 위해 고정관념을 검토하고 바꾸려는 개방적인 마음이 필요하다.

이종현T의 독해 Point!

제시문은 가정 외부 요인이 역할 인식에 영향을 준다는

새로운 논리의 시작점이며, ④는 그로 인해 배우자 간 역할 인식이 다를 수 있음을 설명하므로 ④번 앞이 시작점이다.

40.④ 미국에는 대중교통, 공원, 공공 박물관과 도서관 같은 공공재가 상당히 증가해야 한다. 그리고 그것들은 이용자들에게 무료여야 한다. 그러한 공공재는 그것들에 상응하는 사유재, 예를 들어, 자가용이나 깔끔하게 정돈된 정원, 미술 소장품, 책과 같은 것들을 누릴 형편이 안되는 사람들의 삶의 질을 향상시킨다. 이런 식으로, 공공재는 정체되어 있거나 감소하는 임금의 영향을 어느 정도 상쇄한다. 공공재는 일반적으로, 부족한 자원과 환경에 사적인 재화 보다 영향을 덜 끼치고, 일자리를 창출하며 경제에 전반적인 수요를 증가시킨다. <u>공공재를 무료로 만드는 것은 이러한 사회적 혜택을 극대화한다.</u> 예를 들어, 고속철도를 포함하여 무료 대중교통의 시스템을 확대하면 미국인들로 하여금 일 년에 850억 달러가 넘는 비용을 낭비되는 시간과 기름에 들이게 하는 것으로 추정되는 교통 체증을 상당히 감소시킬 것이고, 탄소 배출도 줄일 것이다. 그 혜택은 비용보다 훨씬 더 크다.

이종현T의 독해 Point!

제시문은 공공재를 무료로 제공하는 것이 사회 전체에 이롭다는 주장(시작점)이며, ④는 그에 대한 구체적 사례(교통)를 설명하므로 ④번 앞이 시작점이다.

41.③ 농업이 일단 시작되면 빨리 확산되는 이유 중 하나는 처음 몇 번의 농작물이 이후의 농작물보다 더 많이 생산되고 더 쉽게 자라며, 따라서 농부들이 경작되지 않은 땅으로 옮겨가는 데 언제나 열성적이기 때문이다. 숲을 태워 없애면, 비옥한 토양이 남는다. 땅에 작은 구멍을 파고, 씨앗을 심고, 그것이 자라기를 기다리기만 하면 된다. <u>그러나 몇 년 후에, 토양은 단단해져서 갈아야 하며, 잡초가 급증해 간다.</u> 이제 그 비옥함을 다시 증가시키고자 그 땅을 쉬게 하면, 좋은 모판을 만들기 위해 억센 풀뿌리를 제거할 필요가 있다. 그리고 그것을 위해서는 쟁기와 쟁기를 끌 소가 필요하다. 그러나 소는 먹이를 먹어야 하므로, 경작할 수 있는 땅뿐만 아니라 목초지도 필요하다. 이동 농업이 숲에 사는 많은 종족에게 오늘날까지 인기가 많은 것은 놀라운 일이 아니다.

이종현T의 독해 Point!

제시문은 시간이 지나며 토양이 압축되고 잡초가 번식한다는 문제 상황의 시작점이며, ③은 그 문제를 해결하기 위한 구체적 작업(뿌리 제거와 쟁기 사용)을 설명하므로 ③번 앞이 시작점이다.

42.④ 독창적인 사람이 되기 위해, 과격한 위험을 감수해야만 한다. 이 믿음이 우리의 문화적 정서 속에 너무 깊이 박혀있어서 우리는 좀처럼 그것에 대해 생각하는 것을 심지어 멈추지조차 않는다. 하지만, 나는 독창성이 극단적인 위험을 감수하는 것을 필요로 한다는 이 근거 없는 믿음이 틀렸음을 입증하고, 당신에게 독창적인 사람들이 우리가 알고 있는 것보다 실제로는 훨씬 더 평범하다는 것을 납득시키고 싶다. 사업과 정치에서 과학과 예술에 이르기까지, 모든 영역에서, 독창적인 아이디어를 가지고 세상을 발전시킨 사람들은 좀처럼 신념과 헌신의 모범이 되는 사람들이 아니다. 그들이 전통들에 이의를 제기하고 현재의 상태에 도전할 때, 그들은 표면적으로는 대담하고 확신에 찬 것처럼 보일 수도 있다. <u>하지만 그 층들을 벗겨내면, 진실은 그들 또한 두려움과 자기 회의로 고심한다는 것이다.</u> 우리는 그들을 자발적으로 행동하는 사람들이라고 여기지만, 그들의 노력은 다른 사람들에 의해 자주 부채질 되고 때로는 강요받는다. 그리고 그들이 위험을 갈망하는 것처럼 보이는 만큼, 그들은 그 갈망을 피하는 것을 정말로 선호한다.

이종현T의 독해 Point!

제시문은 자기주도적으로 보이는 오리지널들도 실제로는 불안과 의심을 가진다는 사실을 드러내는 반전 결론(끝점)으로, ④에서의 겉모습 묘사를 정리 · 반박하므로 ④번 앞이 끝점이다.

43.③ 육류, 가금육, 그리고 생선은 종종 높은 수치의 박테리아를 보유하고 있기 때문에 특별한 취급이 요구된다. 게다가 그것들은 촉촉하고 영양이 풍부한 환경을 제공하는데, 이는 세균 증식에 이상적이다. 교차 오염을 방지하기 위해 그런 음식들과 접촉하게 된 어떤 것이든 씻어라. <u>예를 들어, 하나의 접시에서 날고기를 양념에 재운 후, 그 고기를 조리한 후에 다시 그 동일한 접시에 놓지 마라.</u> 그것을 재사용하기 전에 뜨거운 비눗물에 세척하라. 그렇지 않으면 날고기로부터 불가피하게 접시에 남게 된 박테리아가 조리된 음식 혹은 다른 음식을 오염시키고 그 속에서 증식할 수 있는데, 이는 교차 오염의 전형적인 예이다. 마찬가지로, 예를 들어 도마 위에서 닭고기 껍질을 벗긴 후 도마를 (그리고 당신의 손을) 씻어라. 그렇게 하지 않고 샐러드용 생채소를 썰기 위해 그 오염된 도마를 사용한다면, 그 채소

는 그 가금육으로부터 나온 박테리아에 오염될 수 있다.

이종현T의 독해 Point!

제시문은 익힌 고기를 다시 같은 그릇에 담지 말라는 구체적 예시(시작점)이며, ③에서 그 예시의 원인과 결과(세균 오염)를 설명하므로 ③번 앞이 시작점이다.

Unit 3. 무관한 문장 유형

1.② 다른 시각에서 다른 시각으로 더 깊이 들어가 인과관계를 탐구할 때다. 창조 예술이 역사를 통틀어 모든 곳에서 인간의 마음을 빼앗은 이유는 무엇일까? 우리는 최고의 미술관과 심포니 홀에서도 답을 찾지 못할 것이다. 재즈와 록의 혁신은 인간의 경험에서 더 직접적으로 생겨나는데, 아마도 우리에게 그 답을 더 잘 알려 줄 수 있을 것이다. 그럼에도 불구하고 할리우드 작곡가들은 재즈의 용어와 록의 구조화 모델을 실험하기 시작했다. 창조 예술은 보편적이고 유전적인 특성을 수반하기 때문에 답은 진화 생물학에 있다. 호모 사피엔스는 약 10만년 동안 존재해 왔지만 문맹 문화는 그 중 10분의 1도 되지 않았다. 그래서 왜 보편적인 창조 예술이 있는지에 대한 미스터리는 인간이 존재의 처음 10분의 9동안 무엇을 하고 있었는지에 대한 질문으로 귀결된다.

이종현T의 독해 Point!

②번 선지 다음 문장은 창조 예술에 관한 얘기이고, ②번 앞 문장도 창조 예술에 관한 얘기인데 ②번만 할리우드 작곡가들의 실험에 관한 이야기이므로 정답은 ②번이 된다.

2.③ 유리가 깨지지 않도록 하려면 유리 근처와 유리의 모든 움직임이 평행이어야 하며(긁을 때 유리에 압력을 가하지 않아야 함), 항상 pull-type 스크레이퍼를 사용해야 한다. 그렇게 하면 모든 힘이 유리에서 떨어져서 깨지지 않는다. 유리 고정핀을 제거하려면 Full-type 스크레이퍼의 날카로운 모서리를 부드러운 metal points에 걸고 퍼티와 함께 당겨 빼낸다. 유리 제조사들은 생산 원가를 줄이기 위해 공장을 동아시아 일부 국가로 이전하기 시작했다. 유리 부분이 모두 제거되었는지, 유리 가장자리 옆과 아래에 있는 오래된 퍼티가 느슨한지 다시 확인한다. 그렇지 않다면, 당신은 다시 한 번의 열기가 필요하다.

이종현T의 독해 Point!

③번 다음 문장은 유리 부분 제거에 대한 얘기이고 ③번 앞 문장도 제거에 대한 얘기인데, ③번 문장은 공장 이전에 관한 이야기이므로 정답은 ③번이 된다.

3.② 사물인터넷(IoT)은 디지털과 물질세계를 연결함으로써 기업과 소비자 지형을 혁신할 수 있다. 기존에 인터넷에 연결되지 않았던, 물체를 제작하고, 이동하고, 판매하던 것에 의존하던 산업은 누구나 혜택을 받을 수 있다. 그러나 IoT를 동원할 수

있는 5세대(5G) 광대역통신 기반시설이 없는 산업도 많다. IoT가 기업에 가져올 수 있는 구체적인 혜택은 기술 활용 방법에 따라 달라진다. 일례로 센서 활용으로 사용 수준에 따라 조명이나 난방을 최적화하여 폐기물을 줄이거나, 온도 모니터링으로 운반 중인 제품의 변질을 줄일 수 있다. IoT는 파이프라인을 통해 활동을 분석하여 출력을 극대화하고 새로운 자원 풀의 식별을 돕는 음향 해상 유전 센서 등 수익 창출과 생산성 향상도 가능하다.

이종현T의 독해 Point!

②번 선지 다음 문장은 Iot의 혜택에 관한 것이고 ②번 앞도 혜택에 관한 이야기인데 ②번 문장만 기반 시설이 없는 산업에 관한 이야기이므로 정답은 ②번이 된다.

4.③ 일반 시민뿐만 아니라 범죄학 학생들도 마약의 범죄화가 20세기 미국 창작물이라는 사실을 모르는 경우가 많다. 이전에 우리가 지금 "마약"이라고 해석하는 것은 건강을 해칠(혹은 향상시킬) 가능성이 있는 방대한 양의 다른 물질들과 다르게 다루어지지 않았다. 지금 우리가 생각하는 '중독성 마약'은 한때 의약품으로 식품첨가물로도 쉽게 구할 수 있었다. 코카콜라는 코카인을 자극성 재료로 포함시켜 '진짜'라고 광고에 부응한 적이 있으며, 이후 카페인으로 대체되었다. 지난 40년간 법 집행부가 특정 약물을 적극적으로 제거해야 한다는 생각을 근거로 한 '마약 전쟁'이 목격되어 왔다. 의회가 1914년 해리슨 법을 통과시키면서 약물에 대한 우리의 현대적 관점은 아편제의 판매와 소유를 효과적으로 범죄화하면서 시작되었다. 마리화나를 불법화하는 법률은 1930년까지 16개 주에서, 1937년까지 모든 주에서 시행되었다.

이종현T의 독해 Point!

③번 다음 문장은 1914년 이후의 변화에 대한 얘기이고, ③번 앞 문장은 과거의 약을 활용했던 것에 관한 얘기이고, ③번 문장은 마약 전쟁에 대한 얘기이므로 정답은 ③번이 된다.

5.③ 미국은 서로 다른 배경의 사람들이 어떤 식으로든 모두 똑같아진다는 점에서 사실 '용광로'가 아니다. 미국은 항상 생각, 태도, 행동의 다양성을 내재하고 있다. 예를 들어, 미국의 초기부터 존재한 기본 원칙인 교회와 주(州)의 헌법적 분리는 모든 종교인들이 숭배와 종교 행위에 대해 똑같은 자유와 권리를 갖는다는 것을 보장한다. 다양한 종교적 배경을 가진 사람들이 함께 하나의 종교로 '융합'될 것으로 기대되지 않는다. 갈등은 배경이 같든 다르든 간에, 단순히 사람들 사이에서 일어난다. 다른 법들은 피부색, 성별, 나이에 상관없이 모든 사람들의 동등한 권리를 보장한다. 미국은 심지어 공식적인 국가 언어조차 가지고 있지 않으며, 다양한 지역에서 많은 정부 간행물과 다른 출판물 또한 다양한 언어로 제공된다. 요컨대, 한 국가로서 미국은 다양성의 현실과 이점을 항상 인식해 왔다.

이종현T의 독해 Point!

③번 앞 문장은 법에 관한 얘기이고, ③번 뒷 문장도 법에 관한 얘기인데 ③번 문장만 갈등에 관한 얘기이므로 정답은 ③번이 된다.

6.④ 기계가 특정 직업에서 개별 근로자를 대체하고 단기적으로는 이것이 종종 어려운 문제를 일으킨다는 것에 대해 아무도 의문을 제기하지 않는다. 예를 들어, 철도에 디젤 엔진과 전력의 사용으로 화부(火夫), 즉 기차의 증기기관용 증기를 생산하는 기관차 보일러에 삽으로 석탄을 퍼넣는 직원의 자리는 쓸모없게 되었지만 노조의 지원 때문에 철도회사는 기차에 사용된 증기 동력이 중단된 후 수년 동안 이 자리를 채워야만 했다. 그러나 그러한 문제들은 일시적이다. 궁극적으로, 기계 기술의 발전은 비용과 가격을 낮추거나 그것을 억제하는 경향이 있고, 사람들이 더 많은 상품을 구입할 수 있도록 함으로써 새로운 고용 기회를 창출한다. 기계는 인간 기술의 필요성을 감소시킨다. 만약 어떤 산업에서 더 적은 노동자를 고용한다면, 다른 산업에서 더 많은 노동자를 고용한다. 동시에 신상품이 도입되고 신산업이 구축된다.

이종현T의 독해 Point!

④번 앞 문장은 새로운 고용 기회를 창출하는 것에 관한 얘기이고, ④번 뒷 얘기도 더 많은 노동자를 고용한다는 얘기인데, ④번은 인간 기술이 필요 없어진다는 얘기이므로 정답은 ④번이 된다.

7.③ 많은 동물들은 효과적으로 협력하고, 몇몇 동물들은 심지어 빌려주기도 한다. 자연에서 가장 유명한 대출자는 흡혈박쥐이다. 이 박쥐들은 동굴 내부에 수천 마리가 모여 매일 밤 먹이를 찾아 날아다닌다. 잠자는 새나 부주의한 포유류를 발견하면, 그것의 피부에 작은 상처를 내고 피를 빨아먹는다. 하지만 모든 흡혈박쥐가 매일 밤 먹이를 구하는 것은 아니다. 불확실한

삶에 대처하기 위해, 흡혈귀들은 피를 서로에게 빌려준다. 그러나 흡혈귀들은 진화적 압박을 완화하고자 대출을 하지 않는다. 먹이를 구하는 데 실패한 흡혈귀는 둥지로 돌아와 좀 더 운이 좋은 친구가 훔친 피를 게워내도록 부탁할 것이다. 흡혈귀들은 피를 빌려준 녀석을 아주 잘 기억하여, 그래서 나중에 그 친구가 배가 고파 둥지로 돌아오면, 그 호의를 빚진 녀석에게 다가갈 것이다.

이종현T의 독해 Point!

③번 앞, 뒤 내용은 전부 흡혈박쥐가 서로 피를 빌려준다는 얘기인데 ③번만 대출을 하지 않는다는 이야기이므로 정답은 ③번이 된다.

8.③ 통상적으로 의사들은 환자들의 최선의 이익을 위해 행동할 때 보통 이타주의와 관련된 행동에 선택의 여지가 없기 때문에 이타적으로 여겨져서는 안 된다. 의사들은 환자들에게 선택의 문제로 면할 수 없는 직업적인 의무가 있다. 물론 의사가 되어 환자들과의 직업적인 관계를 시작하는 것은 선택적인 행위이다. 그러나 일단 의사가 이러한 관계를 시작하면, 의무를 선택할 수는 없다. 의사는 만일 치료를 하는 것이 개인적이고 직업적인 고결함을 위태롭게 한다면 특별한 상황에서 특정 환자를 치료하지 않을 선택을 할 수 있다. 따라서 환자를 치료적 처우가 필요한 개인으로 보는 의사에게는 잠재적인 갈등이 발생한다. 그러나 의사는 환자의 치료가 다른 의사에게 전달되도록 보장해야만 한다. 일단 의사가 되면, 그 사람은 자기 환자에 대해 의학적인 최선의 이익을 다하겠다고 약속을 한다. 이것은 선택이 아니라, 의무이다.

이종현T의 독해 Point!

③번을 기준으로 앞 얘기는 특정 환자를 치료하지 않는 선택에 관한 얘기이고, ③번 뒤는 그래도 의사로서 해야 할 의무에 관한 얘기인데 ③번 문장은 의사에게 생기는 갈등에 관한 얘기이므로 정답은 ③번이 된다.

9.② 다른 기후 문제와 달리 해수면 상승에 관한 과학은 매우 간단하다. 해수면은 여러 상황으로 인해 주로 열이 물에 가하는 작용 때문에 상승한다. 해수면 상승을 막기 위해서는 물의 분자 구조를 이해하는 것이 가장 중요하다. 지구의 온도가 상승함에 따라, 약 90%인 대기권에서 초과된 열의 대부분은 바다에 흡수된다. 물이 따뜻해짐에 따라, 물은 온도계의 수은처럼 팽창한다. 이러한 열의 팽창은 해수면 상승의 3분의 1을 차지한다. 나머지 3분의 2는 산악 빙하 그리고 그린랜드와 남극의 빙상이 녹은 것이다.

이종현T의 독해 Point!

②번 앞은 열과 물의 관계에 대한 얘기이고, ②번 뒷 문장도 열과 물의 관계에 대한 얘기인데 ②번 문장은 물의 분자 구조에 관한 얘기이므로 정답은 ②번이 된다.

10.⑤ 파스타의 인종적 뿌리는 오랫동안 논란이 되어 왔다. 많은 학설들이 거론되었고, 일부 학설들은 전혀 설득력이 없었다. 13세기 탐험가 Marco Polo의 작품을 근거로, 파스타가 중국에서 이탈리아로 왔다는 오랜 근거 없는 믿음은 Polo's Travels란 책의 유명한 구절을 잘못 오역한데서 기인했다. 그 책에서 Polo는 파스타처럼 생긴 어떤 것이 열리는 나무를 언급했다. 그것은 아마도 사고 야자로, 파스타와 유사한 녹말이 많은 음식을 만들지만 파스타는 아니다. 이 나무는 아시아가 원산지이며, 파스타가 중국에서 유래했다는 부인일 수 없는 증거를 제시했다.

이종현T의 독해 Point!

⑤번 앞 얘기는 중국에서 이탈리아로 왔다는 것은 근거 없는 믿음이라고 했는데 ⑤번 문장은 파스타가 중국에서 유래했다는 이야기이므로 정답은 ⑤번이 된다.

11.④ 정의란 개념에 있어서 또 다른 차이점은 법이 무엇인가에 대한 사회의 다양한 견해에 있다. 서구에서, 사람들은 '법'과 '관습'을 꽤 다른 것으로 생각한다. 또한 '죄'(종교적 법을 어기는 것)와 '범죄'(정부의 법을 어기는 것) 사이에도 큰 차이가 있다. 그러나 많은 비서구 문화에서 관습, 법, 그리고 종교적 믿음에는 거의 구분이 없다. 다른 문화에서 이 세 가지는 서로 잘 구분될 수도 있지만 여전히 서구의 것들과는 매우 다르다. 이런 이유들로 어떤 행동은 한 국가에서 범죄로 간주될 수 있지만 다른 국가에서는 사회적으로 용인될 수도 있다. 예를 들어, 세계의 대부분이 도둑을 범죄자로 보지만 공동체 생활을 하고 물건들을 공유하고 있는 작은 마을에서 도둑이란 단어는 거의 의미가 없을 수도 있다. 작은 마을에서는 모든 사람이 어떤 의미에서 판사가 된다. 그러한 사회에서 사람들의 행동에 대한 사회적 반감은 강력한 처벌의 역할을 하고 범죄를 강력히 제지하는 역할도 한다. 묻지 않고 어떤 물건을 가져간 사람은 그저 무례한 사람으로 여길 뿐이다.

이종현T의 독해 Point!

④번 앞 문장은 도둑이라는 단어 자체가 없고 그냥 물건은 공유하는 것이다에 관한 얘기이고, ④번 뒷 얘기도 가져간게 범죄는 아니라는 얘기인데 ④번 혼자 처벌에 관한 얘기이므로 정답은 ④번이 된다.

12.③ 겉으로 보기에 산업화된 농업은 변치 않는 세계 기아 문제를 풀 최고의 해결책이 될 것 같았다. 그러나 작가이자 농부인 Wendell Berry씨가 관찰한 결과, 소위 그런 해결책들도 새로운 문제들을 분파했다. 그리고 지난 수십 년 동안 산업화된 농업이 사람과 지구의 건강에 영향을 미치는 많은 문제를 발생시켰다는 사실이 점차 명확해졌다. 그래서 신기술을 기회로 여긴 회사와 정부가 산업화된 농업의 발빠른 확산을 조성했다. 예를 들어 비료와 농약의 사용은 암 발병률을 높이고 토양과 하천 그리고 지하수를 오염시켰다. 단일 재배 농업은 생물 다양성의 손실로 이어져 생태계의 생산성과 안정성을 악화시켰다.

이종현T의 독해 Point!

③번 앞은 문제 발생에 관한 얘기이고, ③번 뒤에 예시도 문제에 관한 얘기인데 ③번 문장이 문제에 관한 얘기가 아니므로 정답은 ③번이 된다.

13.③ 세련된 밥사발과 오래 끓인 사골 국물까지, 그 메시지는 분명하다. 미와 건강 세트가 영양과 함께 집중 관심이 되고 있다. 오늘날 품위 있게 식사하는 것은 그저 장식을 위한 수단이 아니라 점차 건강하고 바쁜 생활을 위해 몸의 기운을 북돋아 주는 중요한 발판이다. 그러나 멀티태스킹 시대에 이메일과 함께 하는 점심은 누구든 제대로 된 식사 외에 너무나 자주 많은 것을 접시 위에 남긴다. 로컬 푸드에서 오는 이런 영양 결핍은 주로 앉아서 지내는 생활방식에 의해서만 악화된다. 전국 각지에서 걸려오는 주문 전화에 응하는 것은 사업 수완이 좋은 젊은 요리사들과 기술력 있는 개척자들이며, 이들은 건강에 좋은 식사와 집집마다 배달해 주는 편리함을 결합하고 있다. 작년에 깨끗한 주스가 대세였다면, 올해는 디자이너 식사 배달의 해가 되어 가고 있다.

이종현T의 독해 Point!

③번 앞 얘기는 이메일로 점심하는 것에 관한 얘기이고, ③번 뒤도 그렇게 변하게 된 음식 문화 무습에 관한 얘기인데 ③번 문장은 로컬푸드의 문제점에 관한 얘기이므로 정답은 ③번이 된다.

14.④ CT 방사선에 관한 새로운 안전 기준을 최종적으로 마련하기 위하여 연구원들은 CT 정밀 검사를 받아오고 있는 사람들 중에서 암 환자 수를 직접 조사할 예정이다. 다른 나라에서 온 약 열두 가지의 관련 연구들은 향후 몇 년 이내에 발표될 것이다. 그 사이에, 몇몇 연구원들은 좋은 영상 기법이 전형적인 CT 정밀 검사에서 발생되는 방사선량보다 더 적은 양을 만들어 낼 수 있는지의 여부를 검사하기 시작했다. 매사추세츠 종합병원(MGH)의 방사선 전문의들은 그러한 연구를 수행하는 특이한 방법을 가지고 있다. 단층 CT 정밀 검사는 150에서 1,100배 사이로 사람의 몸을 전통적인 엑스레이의 방사선에 노출시킨다. 그러한 방법을 가지고 그들은 사람들을 아프게 만드는 것에 대한 걱정 없이 여러 번 몸을 정밀 촬영하고, 그 정밀 검사가 정확히 의학적 문제를 식별했는지의 여부를 확인하기 위하여 부검을 실시한다. 연구를 위하여 살아서 숨을 쉬는 인간 지원자들을 모집하기보다 그들은 시체와 일을 한다.

이종현T의 독해 Point!

④번 뒤의 그러한 방법에 관한 얘기가 ④번 앞 특이한 방법에서 이어지므로 정답은 ④번이 된다.

15.② 외국어 학습자는 동일한 상황에서 모국어 사용자와 다른 발화 행위를 하거나 그 대신에 어떤 발화 행위도 전혀 하지 않는 쪽을 택할 수도 있다. 이것의 가장 좋은 예는 실제 대화와 화자가 무엇을 말하거나 할지를 결정하는 데 있어서 유연성을 지니는 역할극에서 나온다. 학업 상담 기간 동안에 모국어 사용자와 외국어 학습자가 더 좋아하는 발화 행위는 다르다. 모국어 사용자는 상담 기간마다 학습자보다 더 많은 의견을 제시하지만, 외국어 학습자들은 상담 기간마다 모국어 사용자들이 하는 것보다 더 많이 거절하였다. 게다가, 조언에 대한 발화 행위의 부재는 지도 교수에게 가장 중요했다. 제안과 거절의 두 가지 발화 행위는 통제에서 같은 기능을 하는 것으로 보인다. 모국어 화자는 제안을 함으로써 그들의 강의 일정을 통제한다. 그에 반해서, 외국어 학습자들은 지도 교수의 제안을 차단함으로써 거부를 통해 통제한다. 비록 두 그룹의 학생들은 결국 그들이 어떤 강의를 들을지를 결정하는 데에 참여할지라도, 지도 교수가 인터뷰에서 결과적으로 느끼게 되는 감정은 현저히 다르게 인식된다.

이종현T의 독해 Point!

②번 앞 얘기도 제안과 거절에 대한 얘기이고, ②번 뒷 얘기도 제안과 거절에 관한 얘기인데 ②번 문장은 발화 행위의 부재에 관한 얘기이므로 정답은 ②번이 된다.

16.① 세포 배양의 진보 덕택에, 연구자들은 실험실에서 실제로 먹을 수 있는 고기를 기르는 것에 이전보다 더 가까워졌다. 미국에서 매년 음식을 위해 죽임을 당해야 하는 90억 동물들을 기르는 것에 관한 윤리 문제를 넘어서 공장식 축산 농장은 거대한 양의 쓰레기를 만들어 낸다. 과학자들은 이런 쓰레기를 재활용하기 위한 효율적인 방법을 찾으려고 노력한다. 2조 파운드의 동물 쓰레기는 공기와 물을 오염시킨다. 오염 문제 이외에도, 고기의 세계 수요는 2050년까지 60% 증가할 것으로 예상되고, 이러한 닭, 돼지와 소들을 먹이기 위해 필요한 농지와 곡물의 양은 지속 불가능할지도 모른다. 하지만 배양육을 생산하는 것 - 동물 세포에서 배양되어 실험실에서 자라는 근육 조직 - 은 그러한 장애가 전혀 없다. 사실, 그것은 기존의 고기 생산 방법과 비교해서 아주 구미가 당기게 효율적인데, 이는 45% 더 적은 에너지와 99% 더 적은 땅을 사용한다.

이종현T의 독해 Point!

①번 앞 얘기는 거대한 양의 쓰레기에 관한 얘기이고, ①번 뒤도 많은 쓰레기에 관한 얘기인데 ①번 선지는 해결책에 관한 얘기이므로 정답은 ①번이 된다.

17.④ 유아에게 뛰어난 대화가 부족하다는 점은 우리가 모두 의사소통할 수 있는 능력을 가지고 태어난다는 사실을 모호하게 만들지도 모른다. 언어 능력은 우리의 눈, 귀, 팔, 다리, 그리고 생명 유지와 관련된 장기들에 덧붙여 분만실 안의 작고 울부짖는 우리의 몸속에 존재한다. 그 능력은 자극을 받는 것이 틀림없다 - 우리는 단어를 만들기 위해 사람들의 이야기를 들을 필요가 있다 - 하지만 우리는 말하고자 갈망하며 태어난다. 신생아는 다음과 같은 질문들에 대답하려고 참을성 있게 기다리고 있다 : "내가 내 주변에 있는 물체들을 무엇이라고 부를까요? 내가 어떻게 긍정적인 그리고 부정적인 문장을 만들까요? 내가 어떻게 사물과 사람들에 대한 감정을 표현할 수 있을까요?" 아기가 그런 질문들에 명확하게 생각을 표현할 수 있을 때가 되어서야, 부모는 의사소통을 시작한다. 아이의 뇌는 본능적으로 이러한 질문에 대한 대답을 찾고 그런 다음 그것들을 스펀지처럼 흡수한다.

이종현T의 독해 Point!

④번 앞 문장은 아이가 질문하는 것에 관한 얘기이고, ④번 뒤도 아이의 질문에 관한 얘기인데 ④번 문장은 아기의 표현과 부모의 의사소통의 관계에 관한 얘기이므로 정답은 ④번이 된다.

18.② 내 근처에서 작업을 하던 사람들 몇몇은 나를 보고는 웃곤 했다. 나이가 많은 두세 명의 사람들은 나에게 삽질하는 올바른 방법을 가르쳐주느라 애를 썼다. "자네는 지금 잘못하고 있네." 한 사람이 질책했다. 매일 아침 7시쯤 시작하기 때문에 내 몸이 첫 삽을 뜨지 않으려고 저항하는 것 같았다. 그는 "등을 너무 무리해서 사용하지 말게."라고 알려주었다. 나는 참을성 없이 듣고 막연히 지켜보면서 서 있었다. 그러고 나서 일로 두터워진 그의 손가락이 삽을 움켜쥐고 있는 것을 보았다. 나는 짜증이 났고 잘못된 방법으로 삽질하는 것을 좋아한다고 그에게 말하고 싶었다. 막 그러려고 했으나, 결국 나는 아무 말도 하지 않았다. 오히려 나는 바로 그 순간에, 내가 몇 주 동안의 노동으로 노동자의 세계에 들어갈 자격을 얻을 것이라 기대하는 것은 자신을 속이는 일이라는 것을 깨달았다. 나는 부모님들이 '진짜 일'이라는 말을 통해 의미하고자 했던 것을 세 달 뒤에 배우지는 않을 것이다. 나에게 있어서 노력과 피로의 느낌은 음미할 수 있는 것이었다. 나의 부모님이 나와 같은 나이였을 때 비슷한 일을 하셨다면 그러한 느낌은 두려운 것이었을 것이다. 피로는 몸과 마음에 서로 다른 타격을 가했다.

이종현T의 독해 Point!

②번 앞 얘기는 다른 사람의 질책에 관한 얘기이고, ②번 뒷 얘기도 다른 사람의 질책, 충고에 관한 얘기인데 ②번 문장은 내 상태에 관한 얘기이므로 정답은 ②번이 된다.

19.② "당신의 혈액형은 무엇입니까?"라는 질문은 서양의 관점에서는 특이한 질문이다. 한국인과 일본인의 관점에서 볼 때 그러한 질문은 굉장히 일반적인 것이다. 이러한 문화권의 사람들은 특정한 성격상의 특징이 혈액형과 관련되어 있다고 믿는다. 하지만 오늘날, 점점 더 많은 서양인들이 겉보기에는 별개인 두 가지 특징 사이의 관련성에 대해 믿고 있다. 이러한 믿음은 서양의 점성술과 12별자리에 대한 개념과 매우 비슷하다. 대부분의 서양인들은 혈액형과 성격 간의 관계에 대한 개념을 모르고 있기 때문에 그러한 질문에 굉장히 놀라워한다. 사실 많은 서양인들은 그들 자신의 혈액형조차 알지 못한다.

이종현T의 독해 Point!

②번 앞 문장은 동양권 사람의 얘기이고, ②번 뒷 문장도 동양권의 믿음에 관한 얘기인데 ②번 문장은 서양 사람들이 점점 더 믿고 있다는 얘기이므로 정답은 ②번이 된다.

Unit 4. 어휘 유형

1~3. 어느 정책 과정이 이용된다 해도 그리고 그것이 아무리 민감하고 차이를 존중한다 해도 정치는 억압될 수 없다. 다시 말하면, 정치에는 끝이 없다. 적절한 제도나 지식, 협의 방법, 참여 메커니즘이 의견 불일치를 없애줄 수 있다고 생각하는 것은 잘못된 것이다. 온갖 종류의 이론들은 의견 불일치를 사라지게 하기 위해 처리하고 관리할 수 있는 방안들이 존재한다는 견해를 지지한다. 이런 이론들의 기저에 있는 생각은 의견 불일치는 잘못된 것이며, 의견 일치가 바람직한 상태라는 것이다. 사실 의견 일치는 모종의 미묘한 강제 없이는〈종종〉생겨나며, 의견 불일치를 표현하는 데 두려움을 느끼지 않는 것이야말로 진정한 자유의 근원이다. 논쟁을 벌이다 보면 의견 불일치가 종종 더 나은 쪽으로 발전하게 되지만, 긍정적으로 발전하는 논쟁들이 의견 불일치를 줄이는 것과 같아야 할 필요는 없다. 정치적 토의에서 의견 불일치를 억압하는 것이 목표가 되어서는 절대로 안 된다. 정치적 의견 불일치가 정상적인 상태가 아니라는 주장에 맞서는 방어책이 필요하다.

이종현T의 독해 Point!

1.③ ⓒ 문장은 "In fact, consensus ⓒ often comes without some forms of subtle coercion..."인데, 앞뒤 논리상 "consensus는 오히려 강압과 함께 온다"는 반어적 표현이므로, often이 아니라 rarely이어야 자연스러움 → ⓒ가 문맥상 부적절하다.

2.① 빈칸 앞 "a positively evolving debate does not have to equal a reduction in disagreement"에 이어, "→ ( ) of disagreement should never be made a goal" 구조이므로 'disagreement를 없애는 것'을 목표로 삼지 말라는 취지 → ① **suppression(억제)**이 문맥상 가장 정확하다.

3.③ 지문 전반에 걸쳐 "정치에서의 불일치는 사라질 수 없으며, 진정한 자유는 두려움 없이 반대 의견을 표현할 수 있을 때 생긴다"고 강조됨 →③은 핵심 논리와 일치한다.
①, ②, ④는 언급되지 않거나 반대 흐름이다.

4~5. 새로운 살인 추리소설의 가장 중요한 특징 중 하나는 소설이 독자들에게 부여하는 새로운 요구였는데, 그것은 독자들이 이야기를 만들고, 범인을 정하는 데 적극적인 역할을 해달라는 요구였다. 예전의 사형집행 설교문은 독자들이 설교문의 공식적인 확정적 진리(사형수의 죄상이 사실임)를 성직자적 권위에 입각해 받아들이기만을 요구했었지만, 새로운 법정 소설은 사실상 독자들을 유죄판결 쪽이나 무죄판결 쪽에 표를 던져야 하는 〈수령인〉으로 대접해주었다.
유죄 판결을 받은 살인자의 자기변호 진술 옆의 여백에 "이 진술은 보편적으로 처음부터 끝까지 거짓말로 여겨짐"이라고 써넣는 익명의 독자는 독자로서의 그의 역할에 대한 이러한 기대에 잘 부응하고 있는 것이었다. 그러나 살인 추리소설은 독자들이 단순히 투표하는 것 이상을 하도록 요구했다. 살인 추리소설은 독자들로 하여금 증거를 꼼꼼하게 살피고, 사건의 단편들을 종합하고, 추적하고, 탐지하고, 조사하고 "진상을 밝히면서" 적극적으로 이야기를 만들게 했는데, 이는 사실상, 신과 같은 서술자 〈소설가〉가 뒤로 물러난 후 사건의 주요 이야기를 만드는 책임을 독자들 스스로 떠맡게 한 것이었다.
이런 목적을 위해, 살인 추리소설은 독자들을 범죄 수사에 끌어들여, 주요 증거에 대한 시각적인 삽화와 범죄현장에 대한 생생한 삽화를 제공했는데, 범죄현장 삽화에는 독자들이 3차원 공간에서 범죄를 재구성하도록 도와주는 지도인 건물의 정면도와 실내도, 그리고 살인자의 접근 방식(뒷 창문 또는 잠겨 있지 않은 문)에 특별히 주의를 기울이고, 때때로 점선으로 살인자의 경로를 추적하고, 피해자의 시신의 정확한 위치에 더욱 주목한 건물의 평면도가 있었다.

이종현T의 독해 Point!

4.③ 글 전체의 핵심 결과는 "새로운 추리소설은 독자가 단순 수용자가 아니라, 능동적으로 이야기 구조를 재구성해야 한다"는 것이다.
→ 독자들은 단서 수집, 탐색, 조합, 탐정 역할까지 수행해야 하므로 ③ 독자가 민첩하게 서사 구조를 따라가야 한다는 내용이 핵심 주제와 정확히 일치한다.
① "결말을 미리 알고 싶어한다" → 언급 없음 = X
② "인기가 없다" → 내용 없음 = X
④ "서사가 독자 흥미를 방해" → 오히려 흥미를 유도함 = X

5.① Ⓐ 문장은 "readers are recipients" 즉, 수동적으로 받아들이는 존재라고 말하지만
→ 글 전체는 오히려 독자가 능동적으로 재구성하는 주체로 묘사됨 → Ⓐ는 전체 글 흐름과 반대되는 전제이므로 논리상 가장

어색한 문장이다.
Ⓑ "작가 대신 서사를 책임지게 된 배경"
Ⓒ "범죄 수사에 독자가 참여"
Ⓓ "입체적 사건 재구성 역할"
→ 모두 글 흐름상 독자의 능동성 강조와 맞아떨어짐 → 적절

6~7. 그것은 유전자 요법 연구자들이 오랫동안 예감해온 불길한 소식인데, 한 임상시험에서 '치료용 유전자를 지닌 바이러스'를 주입받은 혈우병 환자가 간 종양에 걸렸다는 것이다. 이에 미국 식품의약국은 문제의 임상시험을 중단시켰고, 그 연구를 지원한 네덜란드의 업체 유니큐어는 '바이러스 자체가 암을 초래했는지'의 여부를 조사하고 있다. 유전자요법 전문가들은 그럴 가능성은 낮다고 말한다. 환자에게 간암에 걸릴 위험을 증가시키는 기저질환이 있었다는 것이다. 그럼에도 불구하고, 과학자들은 수백 건의 또 다른 유전자 요법 시험에 사용되는 바이러스 전달 시스템(또는 벡터)인 아데노 부속 바이러스(AAV)의 역할을 배제하는 것이 대단히 중요하다고 말한다. "모든 사람들은 진상을 알고 싶어 합니다."라고 유니큐어의 연구에 관계하지 않는 의사 겸 과학자인 데이비드 릴리크 랩(David Lillicrap)은 말한다.
다양한 형태로 나타나는 혈액응고장애인 혈우병에 대한 유전자 요법은, 최근 유전자 요법 분야에서 발표된 성공작 중 하나였다. 유니큐어의 B형 혈우병 치료법은 가장 최근 실시된 임상시험에서 6개월 후 54명의 환자 중 52명이 제9인자를 더 이상 주입받을 필요가 없게 되어, 잘 듣는 치료법 중 하나인 것 같다. 그러나 최근에 유니큐어는 임상시험 참가자에 대한 현재 진행 중인 안전성 모니터링의 일환으로 행해진 복부초음파검사에서 2019년 10월 치료받은 환자에게서 간 종양이 발견되어, FDA가 자사에 3건의 임상시험들의 보류를 강제하게 되었다고 밝혔다. 그 뉴스가 보도되자, 유니큐어는 물론이거니와 AAV 유전자 요법을 개발하고 있는 다른 업체들의 주가도 폭락했다.
그럼에도 불구하고, 바이러스가 암을〈초래했다〉고 믿을 만한 근거는 있다. 유니큐어의 지적에 따르면, 환자는 고령이었고, 암의 위험을 증가시키는 간질환이 있었던 것이다. 그는 또한 25여 년 전에 B형과 C형 간염 바이러스에 감염된 적이 있었다. 이 바이러스들에의 만성적인 감염은 그 임상시험 참가자에게서 발견된 유형의 간암인 간세포암종 사례의 80%와 연관이 있는 것이다. 그러나 FDA와 또 다른 사람들은 AAV 벡터가 생쥐 연구에서 암을 초래한 적이 있기 때문에 우려하고 있다. AAV가 전달하는 DNA는 통상적으로 세포의 핵 속에서 자유롭게 떠다니는 고리를 형성한다. 그러나 갓 태어난 생쥐를 대상으로 한 연구에서는 AAV가 때때로 자신의 화물(DNA)을 수령자의 염색체 안으로 통합해 넣어 간암을 초래하는 것으로 밝혀졌다. 그리고 연구원들은 지난해, A형 혈우병에 대해 AAV로 치료받은 개 여러 마리가 염색체 영역 안에 신속한 세포증식을 촉발하는 것으로 보이는 외래 DNA를 갖고 있다고 보고했다. 그러나 이것은 그 개들이 유전자요법 치료를 받은지 여러 해가 지난 일이었으며, 그 개들은 종양에 걸리지 않았다. 유니큐어의 그 환자는 비교적 최근에 유전자 요법 치료를 받았으므로, AAV가 암의 주요 원인이었다는 것은 "생각할 수 없는" 일이라고 릴리크랩은 말한다. 그래도 만약 그 환자가 간염바이러스 감염으로 인해 서서히 증식하는 간 종양을 보유하고 있었다면, MV가 환자의 간세포 DNA에 삽입되어 간 종양의 증식을 촉진했을 수 있다고 그는 덧붙여 말한다.

이종현T의 독해 Point!

6.③ 6번은 암을 발생시키지 않을 수도 있다는 부분의 얘기이므로 반의어를 써야 한다. 따라서 정답은 ③번이다.

7.① 지문 전체는 "임상 시험에서 간암이 발생한 사례"로 인해 → 해당 치료에 사용된 바이러스(AAV)에 대한 우려가 증폭되었고 → FDA와 회사 측이 조사 중이며, 연구진도 이 우려를 공유하고 있음을 언급함 → 따라서 ①번은 전체 글의 요지 및 중심 내용과 정확히 일치한다.

8.③ 우울증은 현대 정신과 질환의 교과서입니다: 우울증은 유전적, 신경화학적, 호르몬적 측면이 정신적 "illness"을 일으키는 생물학적 장애이며, 무력감을 유발하는 환경에 민감하게 반응하는 질환입니다. 주요 우울증은 가슴이 아플 정도로 흔하며, 선진국 인구의 약 15%가 일생 동안 한 번 또는 다른 시점에 고통받고 있습니다. 그리고 우울증은 점점 더 흔해지고 있습니다: 서구 국가들의 우울증 비율은 지난 50년 동안 gradually이 하락했습니다. 일부 사람들은 이 결과를 잠재적으로 650년대의 의사보다 우울증을 진단할 가능성이 더 높기 때문에 잠재적으로 의문을 제기할 수도 있지만, 오늘날 우울증 환자들은 과거보다 의료 지원을 받을 가능성이 높고 의료 전문가들은 우울증을 진단할 가능성이 더 높기 때문에 이러한 연구는 정신과에서 수행된 가장 엄격한 역학 연구 중 하나이며, 이러한 혼란을 고려하여 신중하게 통제되었습니다. 우울증의 비율은 실제로 점점 더 증

가하고 있습니다.

이종현T의 독해 Point!

선지들끼리 맞물리는 선지가 있다. ⓒ는 혼자서 반대 내용을 말하고 있다. 따라서 정답은 ③번이 된다.

ⓒ 문장 : "The rates of depression in Western countries have Ⓒ gradually fallen during the last fifty years."
→ 그런데 바로 앞 문장에서 "It is becoming more common."
→ 뒤 문장에서도 "The rate of depression is indeed ever increasing."
→ 즉, 전체 글 흐름은 우울증 유병률은 증가하고 있다인데, Ⓒ에서 "fallen(감소했다)"는 반대 의미가 되어 문맥상 부적절
Ⓐ sensitive : "environment that produces helplessness"에 대한 반응 → 적절
Ⓑ more : "is becoming more common" → 적절
Ⓓ spurious : 의심받는 연구 결과에 대해 "위조된, 가짜의" → 적절
Ⓔ increasing : "ever increasing"과 최종 결론 일치 → 적절

9~10. 이야기를 과장하는 것을 피하는 한 가지 방법은 아무 말도 하지 않는 것입니다. 그러나 강한 책임감을 느끼는 과학자들이 대중과 정책 입안자들에게 알리고/또는 제안을 하는 것은 현실적인 선택이 아닙니다. 미디어 구성원들과 대화하는 것은 메시지를 전달하고 긍정적인 인식을 얻는 데 장점이 있지만, 오해를 불러일으킬 위험이 있고 반복적인 해명이 필요하며 끝없는 논란에 얽힐 위험이 있습니다. 따라서 미디어와 대화할지 여부는 매우 개별화된 경향이 있습니다. 수십 년 전만 해도 지구 과학자들이 미디어에 관심을 끌 만한 결과를 얻는 것은 드문 일이었고, 그 결과 미디어 접촉이 거의 예상되거나 권장되지 않았습니다. 1970년대에는 미디어와 자주 대화하는 소수의 과학자들이 그렇게 했다는 이유로 동료 과학자들로부터 비판을 받기도 했습니다. 현재 상황은 상당히 다릅니다. 지구 온난화와 관련 문제의 중요성 때문에 많은 과학자들이 목소리를 내야 한다는 책임감을 느끼고 있으며, 많은 기자들이 이러한 감정을 공유하고 있습니다. 또한 많은 과학자들이 미디어의 주목과 그에 따른 대중의 인식을 즐긴다는 사실을 발견하고 있습니다. 동시에 다른 과학자들은 기자들과 대화하는 것을 계속 거부하여 과학에 더 많은 시간을 보존하고 (예 오판 및 언론 보도와 관련된) 기타 불쾌감을 유발할 위험이 있습니다.

이종현T의 독해 Point!

9.② 과학자가 대중들에게 결과에 대해 말하는 것의 장점과 단점이 있다. → 그러니 사람마다 말하고 말고에 대한 선호도가 다를 수 있다가 이 글의 핵심 결과이다. 따라서 이게 들어간 선지를 찾으면 정답은 ②번이다.

10.⑤ (e)에 말을 하지 않는 과학자는 위험을 늘리는 것이 아니라 줄이는 것이므로 정답은 ⑤번이 된다.

11~12. 우리가 상식을 신뢰하는 주된 이유는 순진한 현실주의, 즉 세상을 있는 그대로 본다는 믿음 때문입니다. 우리는 '보는 것이 믿음'이라고 가정하고 세상과 우리 자신에 대한 직관적인 인식을 신뢰합니다. 일상 생활에서 순진한 현실주의는 종종 우리에게 도움이 됩니다. 1차선 도로를 운전하다가 트랙터 트레일러가 시속 120킬로미터로 통제할 수 없을 정도로 움직이는 것을 본다면, 길을 비켜주는 것이 현명한 생각입니다. 대부분의 경우 우리는 우리의 인식을 믿어야 합니다. 하지만 외모는 때때로 기만적일 수 있습니다. 지구는 평평해 보입니다. 태양은 지구 주위를 도는 것처럼 보입니다. 하지만 두 경우 모두 우리의 직관은 틀립니다. 때로는 우리 자신과 타인을 평가할 때 명백해 보이는 것이 우리를 오도할 수 있습니다. 우리의 상식은 우리의 기억이 우리가 본 거의 모든 것을 정확하게 포착한다고 말하지만, 과학적 연구는 그렇지 않다는 것을 보여줍니다. 또한 우리의 상식은 정치적 견해를 공유하지 않는 사람들이 편향되어 있지만 우리는 객관적이라는 것을 보장합니다. 그러나 심리학적 연구는 우리 모두가 편향된 방식으로 정치적 이슈를 평가하는 데 취약하다는 것을 보여줍니다. 따라서 외모를 믿는 경향은 인간 본성에 대한 신뢰할 수 있는 결론을 도출할 수 있습니다. 많은 경우 '믿는 것은 보는 것'이 아니라 우리의 신념이 세상에 대한 우리의 인식을 형성한다는 것입니다.

이종현T의 독해 Point!

11.④ 첫 문장의 논리
우리 - naive realism의 영향 받음 → 우리의 상식을 신뢰
중간에 Yet부터 문제점 반박 → 사실은 믿으면 안되는 것일지도 모른다(문제) → 그리고 뒤에는 중간 논리로 그 이유 → 우리가 보는 것을 믿으면 안되는 것일지도 모른다 라는 결과를 가지고 선지를 찾으면 정답은 ④번이다.

12.⑤ (e)에 우리의 믿음 때문에 생기는 결론이므로 잘못된 결론이 되어야 한다. 정답은 ⑤번이다.

13~14. 어떤 사람들은 감사란 좋은 생각을 하고 좋은 일을 기대하는 것일 뿐이며 인생의 부정적, 고통, 고통을 무시하는 것이라고 주장합니다. 글쎄요, 그것은 틀렸습니다. 감사에 대한 우리의 정의는 혜택을 받고 그 혜택을 위해 자신 외의 다른 사람에게 공로를 돌리는 구체적인 사고 방식으로 간주됩니다. 사실 감사는 매우 어려울 수 있는데, 이는 다른 사람에 대한 의존도를 인식해야 하기 때문이며 항상 긍정적인 것은 아닙니다. 다른 사람의 지지와 관대함을 잘 받아들여야 한다는 의미에서 자신을 겸손하게 받아들여야 합니다. 이는 매우 어려울 수 있습니다 — 대부분의 사람들이 수신자보다 더 잘 주는 사람들입니다.

게다가 감사의 감정은 때때로 부채와 의무에 대한 감정을 자극할 수 있는데, 이는 전혀 긍정적인 생각처럼 들리지 않습니다 : 만약 당신이 제공해 준 것에 감사하면, 그 일을 처리해야 합니다 — 심지어 나중에 적절한 시기에 보답해야 할지도 모릅니다. 이러한 종류의 부채나 의무는 매우 부정적으로 인식될 수 있으며, 이는 사람들에게 진정한 위로를 줄 수 있습니다. 질 서티는 그녀의 에세이 "부채감 없이 감사를 표현하는 방법"에서 이를 탐구합니다.

데이터는 이를 입증합니다. 사람들이 감사할 때 반드시 부정적인 감정에서 자유롭지는 않습니다. 우리는 사람들이 반드시 불안감이나 긴장감, 불행감이 적다는 것을 발견하지 못합니다. 감사를 실천한다고 해서 긍정적인 감정이 더 커지는 것은 아닙니다. 부정적인 감정이 줄어듭니다. 예를 들어 감사가 단순히 긍정적인 사고나 부정의 한 형태였다면 감사 일기를 작성할 때 부정적인 생각이나 감정을 경험하지 않았을 것입니다. 하지만 사실 사람들은 그렇게 합니다.

이종현T의 독해 Point!

13.③ Gratitude란 무엇인지에 대해 반박하는 글이고 마지막 단락에 grateful해지면 → 부정적인 감정이 완전히 사라지진 않는다가 결론이 된다. → 이걸 그대로 찾으면 정답은 ③번이 된다.

14.④ 부채감 때문에 불편해지는 것이므로 ④번이 정답이 된다.

15~16. 모든 사회 시스템에서 사람들의 행동은 사회 규칙의 영향을 받으며 매우 적응력이 뛰어나다는 것은 사실입니다. 개코원숭이를 대상으로 한 자연스러운 실험은 유익합니다. 2004년의 한 연구는 크고 공격적인 수컷이 지배하는 개코원숭이 무리가 모든 지배적인 수컷이 질병에 걸려 죽은 후 어떻게 변했는지 조사했습니다. 더 작고 온화한 수컷만 남아 있는 상황에서 그 무리의 문화는 극적인 변화를 겪었고, 광범위한 괴롭힘과 싸움으로 특징지어지는 사회 구조에서 훨씬 더 평화로운 그루밍으로 바뀌었습니다. 물론 갈등은 여전히 존재했지만 평화로운 방법으로 해결되는 경향이 있었고, 싸움은 작은 개코원숭이를 크게 괴롭히는 것이 아니라 똑같이 일치하는 개코원숭이 사이에서 더 많이 벌어졌습니다. 놀랍게도 원래 수컷들이 모두 죽은 후에도 그 무리의 문화는 지속되었고 외부에서 들어오는 다른 수컷들로 대체되었습니다. 새로운 수컷들은 그룹 규범에 익숙해졌고, 덜 행동하는 법을 배웠습니다. 관대하게 배웠습니다.

물론 인간은 개코원숭이가 아닙니다. 하지만 이것이 기본적으로 서로 다른 인간 사회가 훨씬 다른 행동 규범을 가질 수 있는 이유와 유사할 가능성이 높아 보입니다. 조상을 숭배하고 음식을 공유한 전근대 부족, 왕의 신성한 권리를 받아들이고 봉건 영주를 위해 자유로운 노동을 수행한 중세 농민, 그리고 민주주의와 기업 고용 계약을 믿는 오늘날 사람들을 생각해 보세요. 인간 사회는 개코원숭이 사회보다 훨씬 더 복잡하고 선택의 폭이 넓지만, 요점은 행동 규범이 그 반대가 아니라 문화와 학습의 산물이라는 것입니다.

이종현T의 독해 Point!

15.② 첫 문장의 인과관계가 사회적 규칙에 따라 사람의 행동이 달라진다는 얘기가 된다. 더 이상 결과의 결과가 없으므로 이게 들어간 선지를 찾으면 정답은 ②번이 된다.

16.③ (c) 앞에 less가 있으므로 (c)엔 반대말인 과격하게 같은 표현이 들어가야 규칙에 잘 순응한다는 얘기가 된다. 따라서 정답은 ③번이 된다.

17~18. 당연히 안전하지 않게 설계되고 불안정하게 구현된 소프트웨어의 사용은 몇 가지 위험을 초래합니다. 배포된 소프트웨어가 사용자 사이트에 도달한 후, 시스템 및 애플리케이션 소프트웨어의 설치와 관리가 부적절하게 수행되면 이러한 소프트웨어의 성능과 적절한 작동에 악영향을 미칠 수 있습니다. 이러한 시스템의 복잡성과 불충분한 문서화로 인해 사용자들은

이러한 시스템을 "적절하게" 사용하려는 시도의 효과를 거의 이해하지 못합니다. 따라서 사용자들은 새로운 기능을 사용하는 학습에서 어떤 기능이 어떤 효과를 가질 수 있는지, 그리고 원치 않는 부작용을 피하기 위해 어떤 예방 조치를 취해야 하는지를 방법론적으로 이해하려고 노력하기보다는 "시행착오" 방법을 무시합니다. 이러한 다소 "탐구적인" 시스템 사용 방법은 종종 잠재적으로 해로운 영향을 미칠 수 있는 위험한 태도로 이어집니다. 예를 들어, 적절한 주의 없이 알려지지 않은 첨부 파일을 클릭하는 등의 문제가 발생할 수 있습니다.
소프트웨어 제조업체들은 종종 소프트웨어의 실패가 주로 사용자의 부적절한 행동으로 인해 발생한다고 주장합니다. 그러나 대부분은 아니더라도 많은 경우, 인간과 컴퓨터 간의 인터페이스(예 화면에 기능과 작업이 표시되거나 마우스와 키보드와 같은 입력 장치의 취급)가 부적절하게 설계되어 사용자가 도움말 기능의 지원을 제대로 받지 못하는 경우가 많습니다(많은 경우 존재하는 기능이 너무 복잡하여 사용자를 더욱 오도하는 경우가 많습니다). 사용자들은 주로 자신의 작업에 관심이 있지만, 작업 성과가 저하된다고 생각할 때 예방 조치를 잊어버리고 때로는 보안 조치를 우회하는 경향이 있다는 것을 인정해야 합니다.

이종현T의 독해 Point!

17.① 첫 문장의 결과는 software에 risk가 생길 수 있는 것이고 이 뒤에 얘기가 전부 그 원인을 받아주는 중간 논리가 되므로 이 결과가 그대로 들어가 있는 선지를 찾으면 정답은 ①번이 된다.

18.② (b) 다음 문장에 explorative가 있으므로 탐험적 방법을 사용하는 것이고 그렇다면 trial and error를 하는 것이니 disregard는 틀렸다. 정답은 ②번이 된다.

19~20. 1930년대에 영국의 심리학자 프레데릭 바틀렛 경은 우리가 경험하는 사건들을 통해 세상에 대한 지식을 점진적으로 쌓아가고, 이러한 경험들이 조직적인 정신 구조에 모여 "스킴마타"라고 부르도록 제안했습니다. 그 결과, 이러한 스킴마타(또는 "스킴마타")는 새로운 경험을 이해하고 이를 기억할 수 있는 틀을 형성하는 데 도움을 줍니다. 이 배열의 잠재적인 단점 중 하나는 현재의 스킴마타에 맞지 않는 정보와 사건들을 이해하고 기억하는 것이 상대적으로 어렵다는 점입니다. 바틀렛의 고전적인 시연 중 하나는 영국 대학생에게 학습하고 기억할 수 있는 독특한 북미 민담을 제시하는 것이었습니다. 학생의 서면 회상은 원본과 달리 길이가 짧고 여러 세부 사항을 생략했습니다. 첫 번째 학생의 서면 회상은 두 번째 학생에게 주어져 학습하고 회상하게 되었고, 그 결과 더 특이한 세부 사항들이 생략되었지만, 다른 세부 사항들이 추가되어 영어 귀에 더 일관되고 이해하기 쉽게 되었습니다. 이 절차는 열 명의 학생들이 이전의 재현을 배우고 자신만의 버전을 제작할 때까지 반복되었습니다. 시리즈가 끝날 무렵에는 재현이 훨씬 짧아졌고, 원본의 초자연적인 세부 사항들은 사라졌으며, 전체 이야기는 1930년대 영국 대학생들의 경험에 더 가까워졌습니다. 따라서 이 시연은 기억의 구성적 성격과 신념과 태도가 회상과 이해에 미치는 영향을 보여줍니다. 가십은 바틀렛의 발견과 반대되는 일반적인 예로, 이야기가 이야기를 가로지르면서 점진적으로 변화합니다. 잠시 은유로 돌아가자면, 인간의 기억은 녹음기와 같지 않습니다!

이종현T의 독해 Point!

19.① 첫 두 문장이 결과의 결과이고 최종 결과가 기억을 하는 것이다. 그래서 이 글의 핵심 논리는 우리의 경험 → 기억이 된다는 얘기가 된다. 경험이 기억이 되는 것 때문에 생기는 결과가 뒤에 없으므로 정답은 ①번이 된다.

20.⑤ (e) 뒤에 나오는 얘기를 보면 여행하면서 이야기가 바뀌는 것이므로 앞의 논리와 같다. 따라서 정답은 similar로 바꿔야 하는 ⑤번이 답이다.

21~22. 싱가포르에서는 도로 요금 때문에 도로에서 시속 40마일의 속도를 달성할 수 있을 것으로 기대할 수 있습니다. 부유층은 이 속도를 감당할 가능성이 높지만, 버스도 이러한 속도를 달성할 수 있으며, 버스 규모의 경제로 인해 이 속도를 달성하기 위한 1인당 여행 비용을 낮춥니다. 통근 비용에는 휘발유, 주차, 도로 사용료에 대한 본인 부담금 지출분만 아니라 잃어버린 시간의 가치도 포함됩니다. 교통 혼잡으로 인해 통근에 15분이 아닌 30분이 걸린다면 통근자는 15분을 잃은 것입니다. 경제학자들은 이렇게 잃어버린 시간을 시간당 임금의 절반으로 평가하는 경험 법칙을 채택했습니다. 예를 들어, 제가 시간당 80달러를 벌고 교통 체증으로 15분을 잃으면 잃어버린 시간에 10달러(.25 × 80 × .5)의 $을 지불해야 합니다. 혼잡으로 인한 손실된 시간을 절약하기 위해 스톡홀름, 런던, 싱가포르와 같은 도시에서는 도로 요금제를 도입했습니다. 이러한 도시의 운전자들은 더 빠른 속도로 이동하여 시간을 절약하지만, 최대 사용 시간에 이동하려면 더 많은 돈을 지불해야 합니다. 도로 요금제를 도입한 도시가 거의 없는 이유 중 하나는 행동 경제학에 초점을

맞추고 있는데, 사람들은 도로가 무료인 것에 익숙하다는 점입니다. 한 경제학자에게 이는 혼잡한 도로는 귀중한 시간을 낭비하기 때문에 혼란스러운 설명입니다. 이 시간 비용은 무료 도로를 무료로 이용할 수 없다는 것을 의미합니다. 도로 요금제에 대한 합의에 대한 두 번째 설명은 많은 가난한 사람들이 도로 사용료를 지불하기보다는 시간을 이용해 출퇴근 비용을 지불하는 것을 선호한다는 것입니다.

이종현T의 독해 Point!

21.① 이 글은 road pricing을 반대하는 글이고, 그 반대하는 이유에 대한 글이므로 이걸 담은 선지를 찾으면 정답은 ①번이 된다.

22.⑤ (e)에 들어가야 하는 것은 동의/합의가 아니고 의견불일치가 되어야 하므로 정답은 ⑤번이 된다.

23~24. 자신의 삶에서 흔히 발생하는 믿음의 오류에 대해 말하자면, 과학자들은 항상 더 나은 결론에 도달하려고 노력하며, 이는 개인으로서 하지 않는 일이며, 적어도 기본적으로는 그렇지 않으며, 더 나아가 기관들도 그렇게 잘하지 못하는 일이라는 점을 기억하세요. 과학이 귀무 가설이라고 부르는 것을 찾지 않습니다. 즉, 어떤 것을 믿을 때 그것이 자신의 가정과 어떻게 일치하는지 보기 위해 반대의 증거를 찾는 경우는 드뭅니다. 이것이 도시 전설, 민속, 미신 등 모든 것의 근원입니다. 의심을 갖는 것은 자신의 강한 수트가 아닙니다. 기업과 다른 기관들은 기관의 잘못에 주의를 기울이는 임무를 맡은 부서를 따로 두는 경우가 거의 없습니다. 과학과 달리 대부분의 인간 사업에는 운영상 최악의 상황을 찾기 위해 헌신하는 특별 부서가 포함됩니다 - 단순한 불만 부서가 아니라 조직이 올바른 길을 가고 있는지 묻는 부서가 포함됩니다. 모든 인간의 노력은 체계적으로 멈추고 현재 잘못 알고 있는지 물어봐야 합니다. 뇌를 두드리기 위해서는 그 부서가 두개골에서 지속적으로 운영되어야 합니다. 과학적 방법의 교훈을 빌려 개인 생활에 적용하는 것이 좋습니다. 바느질을 하고 골프를 치며 고양이 동영상을 둘러보는 동안 과학은 어리석음과 싸우고 있습니다. 다른 어떤 인간 기업도 그렇게 열심히 싸우지 않거나 적어도 싸우고 승리하지 못하고 있습니다.

이종현T의 독해 Point!

23.⑤ 첫 문장부터 문제점과 해결책이 나온다. 상식의 오류에 빠진 것이 문제, 과학자가 그것을 해결해주는 것이 해결책이 된다. 그리고 더 이상 반박이 없으므로 이게 들어간 선지를 찾으면 정답은 ⑤번이 된다.

24.③ (c) 앞의 결과를 생각하면 잘못된 부분을 포함시키는 것이 아니고 제외시키는 것이므로 정답은 ③번이 된다.

25~26. 스포츠 대회와 운동 경력의 극적인 변화를 따라가면, 우리는 우수성, 승리, 명성, 부를 추구하고 실패와 상실에 대처하기 위한 운동선수들의 노력을 목격할 수 있습니다. 그리고 연극이나 소설의 드라마가 작가의 창작물의 대본 드라마인 반면, 스포츠의 드라마는 그들의 결정에 따른 결과를 감수해야 하는 실제 사람들의 드라마입니다. 이것이 제가 스포츠가 "실제 삶"과 날카롭게 분리되어야 한다는 생각을 지지하는 한 가지 이유입니다. 우리가 스포츠를 볼 때, 우리는 등장인물을 보는 것이 아닙니다. 로미오 역을 맡은 배우는 공연이 끝날 때 죽지 않고, 집에 가면 등장인물의 곤경을 뒤로하고 떠나게 됩니다. 반면에, 선수들이 목표를 추구하면서 겪는 부상은 리허설되지 않으며, 패배한 팀의 쿼터백도 경기 결과를 포기할 수 없습니다. 만약 스포츠의 이러한 특징들이 반드시 스포츠를 윤리적 성찰에 대한 격려로 만들지 않는다면, 적어도 스포츠가 이 점에서 열등하지 않다는 것을 보여준다고 생각합니다. 최소한 셰익스피어의 연극을 좋은 삶의 본질에 대한 우리 자신의 사고의 정당한 출처로 간주하는 것이 합리적이라면, 스포츠가 그러한 성찰 능력을 발휘할 수 있는 능력이 낮다고 생각할 이유가 없다고 주장하고 싶습니다.

이종현T의 독해 Point!

25.② 첫 문장의 논리는 스포츠 덕분에 우리는 좋은 인간의 삶을 살아가는 것을 본다는 얘기가 되므로 즉 스포츠가 우리가 좋은 삶을 알 수 있게 해준다는 것이 핵심 논리가 된다. 이게 들어간 선지를 찾으면 정답은 ②번이 된다.

26.② (b)에 목적어 부분의 that절은 스포츠와 우리의 삶을 분리시킨다는 것인데 그 주장엔 반대하므로 정답은 ②번이 된다.

27~28. 미디어의 소유권은 배포되는 정보의 성격을 통제할 수 있게 합니다. 미디어의 공공 소유를 지지하는 사람들은 정보가 공공재이기 때문에, 즉 일단 일부 소비자에게 제공된 후에는

비용을 지불하지 않은 다른 소비자들로부터 정보를 멀리하기 어렵기 때문에 개인 소유자들이 사회적으로 바람직한 것보다 적은 정보를 제공하는 경향이 있다고 주장합니다. 또한, 개인 소유의 경우 미디어 산업이 사회에서 좁은 집단의 견해만을 대변할 위험이 있으며, 대중에게 바람직한 문화적 또는 교육적 주제나 가치를 노출시키기 위해서는 미디어의 국가 소유가 필요하다고 주장합니다.
공공 소유에 반대하는 사람들은 정부의 미디어 통제가 사람들을 조종하는 데 사용될 수 있으며, 현 정부에 유리하게 제공되는 정보를 왜곡할 수 있다고 주장합니다. 게다가, 경험에 따르면 정부 소유 기업은 소비자 수요에 반응할 가능성이 적습니다. 마지막으로, 정부 소유 미디어는 경쟁의 대상이 아니므로 품질 저하와 비효율성의 위험이 동시에 발생합니다. 최근 영국 방송공사(BBC)에 관한 기사에서는 정부 소유가 다른 미디어 회사들이 성장하는 것보다 더 쉽게 만든다고 주장합니다. 이 기사는 BBC에 주어진 막대한 세수가 민간 기업에 비해 상대적으로 유리하다고 주장합니다. 또한, 민간 기업으로서 BBC가 더 역동적이어서 글로벌 미디어 회사들과 경쟁할 수 있을 것이라고 주장합니다.

이종현T의 독해 Point!

27.④ 미디어의 소유 덕분에 미디어에 대한 통제권이 생긴다는 것이 첫 문장의 인과관계이다. 그 뒤에 public ownership에 대한 proponents와 opponents가 나오므로 이 둘 입장에 대한 반박이 핵심 논리가 된다. 따라서 정답은 ④번이 된다.

28.⑤ 정부의 소유 때문에 성장을 못하는 것이 맞으므로 정답은 ⑤번이 된다.

29.② 우주가 원자와 빈 공간으로 구성되어 있으며 다른 무엇도 없다는 깨달음, 세상이 우리를 위해 창조주의 섭리로 만들어진 것이 아니라는 깨달음, 우리가 우주의 중심이 아니라는 깨달음, 정서적인 삶이 육체적인 삶과 (A) 별개의 것이 아니며 다른 모든 피조물의 육체적인 삶과 다를 바 없다는 깨달음, 우리의 정신은 우리의 몸과 마찬가지로 물질적인 것이며 영원히 살 수 없다는 깨달음 - 이 모든 것들이 (B) 절망의 원인은 아니다. 반대로 상황을 있는 그대로 이해하는 것은 행복의 가능성으로 가는 중요한 단계이다. 인간이 행복한 삶을 사는 것은 가능하지만, 그것은 그들이 우주의 중심이라고 생각하기 때문이 아니다. 만족시킬 수 없는 욕망과 죽음에 대한 두려움은 인간의 행복에 대한 주요한 (C) 장애물이지만, 그것들은 이성의 실행을 통해 극복될 수 있다.

이종현T의 독해 Point!

(A) distinct vs. indistinct
문장 : "our emotional lives are no more (A) _____ than our physical lives…"
→ 정신과 육체가 다르지 않다 = 구분되지 않는다는 의미여야 하므로
→ indistinct (구별되지 않는)가 자연스럽다
→ ①, ②, ③ 탈락 / ④, ⑤ 후보
(B) despair vs. hope
앞 문장은 "세상이 신에 의해 창조되지 않았고, 우리가 중심이 아님"
→ 그 사실이 "절망의 원인이 아니다"
→ 따라서 절망(despair)이 맞음
→ ③, ④ 탈락 / ②, ⑤ 후보
(C) paths vs. obstacles
문장 : "욕망과 죽음에 대한 공포는 인간 행복의 (C) _______이다, 그러나 극복될 수 있다."
→ 욕망과 공포는 장애물이어야 자연스러움
→ obstacles가 적절
→ ②번 정답 확정

30.④ 명백한 의료 행위인 음악 치료는 20세기, 특히 제1차 세계대전 동안 서양에서 처음 발전했는데, 그때의 의사와 간호사들은 음악이 부상자들의 심리적, 생리적, 인지적, 감정적 상태에 미치는 효과를 목격했다. 음악의 (A) 의학적 특성에 관한 최초의 주요 연구는 1948년에 발표되었는데, 제2차 세계대전 동안 일부 군대 병원과 공장에서 계속 이용한 음악 치료 반응이었다. 음악 치료는 이제 정신적 혹은 신체적 장애나 병이 있는 사람들에게 (B) 널리 이용된다. 음악 치료의 가장 중요한 기능들 가운데 하나는, 특히 치과나 화상 그리고 관상동맥 치료에서 수술을 준비하거나, 수술을 하거나, 수술에서 회복중인 환자들의 긴장을 풀어주는 것이다. 지금은 느리고 안정된 템포, 부드러운 음조, 온화한 리듬, 예측 가능한 변화와 단순하게 지속되는 멜로디의 음악이 긴장완화에 (C) 도움이 된다는 사실이 충분히 입증되었다.

이종현T의 독해 Point!

(A) aesthetic vs. medicinal
문장 : "The first major academic study of music's (A) _____ properties..." → 이어지는 맥락에서 "use in hospitals, for wounded soldiers, surgery 등"
→ 치료 목적이므로 → medicinal(치료의)가 적절
→ ①, ② 탈락
(B) rarely vs. widely
문장 : "Music therapy is now (B) _____ used for those with mental and/or physical disabilities"
→ 치료 효과가 "well attested"라고 했으므로 → widely 사용이 적절
→ ①, ⑤ 탈락 / ④ 후보 유지
(C) detrimental vs. conducive
마지막 문장 : "It is well attested that music... is (C) _____ to relaxation" → 문맥상 "relaxation에 도움이 된다"는 뜻
→ conducive(도움이 되는)이 맞음 → ③ 탈락 / ④번 정답 확정

31.① 우리들 대부분은 광대역 인터넷을 당연한 것으로 여기지만, 그러나 거의 미국인 5명 중 1명은 그것에 접속하기가 어렵다고 연방 통신 위원회는 말한다. 교외 지역에서 통신 회사들은 멀리 떨어진 가정에 비용 때문에 설치를 꺼리는 반면에, 저소득 가족은 요금이 (A) 너무 비싸다고 한다. 광대역의 격차를 좁히는 것은 최신의 TV 드라마를 전송하는 것 이상으로 중요하다. 고속 인터넷은 현대 생활의 중요한 도구이며, 아이들이 디지털 방식으로 배우고 어른들이 클라우드 서비스를 통해 일 하는 것을 (B) 가능하게 한다. 연방 통신 위원회는 최근에 소형 광대역 보조금을 승인했지만, 진짜 해결책은 악명 높은 합병 회사의 경쟁을 (C) 고조시키는 데 있다.

이종현T의 독해 Point!

(A) "low-income families can find the fees ( )" → 가난한 가정에게 비싸서 감당 어려운 → prohibitive(부담스러운)
(B) "Closing the broadband gap is about... ( ) kids to learn digitally" → 접근을 가능하게 하는 것이므로 → enabling
(C) "real solution may lie in ( ) competition" → 독점 산업에 대한 해결책은 경쟁 증가 → increased
→ 정답은 ① prohibitive – enabling – increased

32.③ 진화론 학자인 Henry Plotkin이 말하기를, 유기체가 수많은 세대를 거쳐 세상의 지식을 획득하면서, 진화는 필요의 기준에 따라 선택적으로 관련 지식을 보존하고, 그 수집된 지식은 종의 유전자 풀 내에 보관된다. 그렇게 수집된 지식은 개인에게 조금씩 나눠지고, 그 개인들은 특정한 방법으로 어떤 것들을 배우기 위해 (A) 타고난 아이디어와 성향을 가지고 세상에 태어난다. 바꾸어 말하면, 당신이 사바나에서 사냥을 하든 혹은 유튜브에서 수백만의 비디오들 중에서 고르는 간에, 당신의 뇌는 거의 모든 것을 (B) 무시하고 오로지 가장 중요하고 흥미로운 것을 향해 곧장 나아가도록 프로그래밍 되어 있다. 그와 달리, 당신은 마치 귀찮다는 듯이 아무 나무나 바위에 창을 찌르는 것처럼 무한한 비디오 링크들 속에서 길을 잃고 그 중 가치 있는 것을 찾아내기를 헛되이 바란다. 유전자의 (C) 구별해 내는 본성을 이해함으로써, 우리는 기억 속에 남아 관심을 사로잡을 만한 이야기의 토대를 구축하기 시작한다.

이종현T의 독해 Point!

(A) innate vs. acquired
문장 : "individuals... come into the world with (A) ___ ideas and predispositions to learn"
→ "태어날 때부터 특정 방식으로 학습하게 유전적으로 설정돼 있다"는 내용
→ innate(타고난)이 정확히 일치함
(B) adopt vs. ignore
문장 : "your brain is programmed to (B) ___ almost everything and home in on what is most important"
→ 뇌는 대부분을 무시하고(ignore), 중요한 것에 집중하도록 설계됨
→ "adopt everything"은 문맥상 반대이므로 ignore가 적절
(C) discriminating vs. integrating
문장 : "with the (C) ___ nature of our genes, we construct the basis for stories..."
→ 유전자는 중요 정보를 선별(discriminate)하도록 작동
→ 따라서 discriminating(선별적인)이 적절

Unit 5. 빈칸 연결사 유형

1.① 게티즈버그는 대부분의 역사가들에 의해 남북전쟁의 전환점으로 간주되고 있다. 게티즈버그 이전에는 로버트E 리 장군 지휘 하에 있던 남군이 북군을 일련의 주요 전투에서 — 때로는 큰 격차로 — 물리쳤었다. 그러나 이 전투에서는 남군이 패배하여 뒤로 물러났다. 그러나 그들의 물질적 손실보다 훨씬 중요했던 것은 남부 연방이(전쟁) 추진력을 잃었다는 점이었다. 북군은 주도권을 잡았고, 그 후 2년이 못 되어서 마침내 남부 연방을 패배시켰다. 남부 연방의 수뇌부는 북부 연방의 영토에 침입함으로써 전쟁을 계속할 북부 연방의 의지를 흩어놓고 유럽 국가들로 하여금 남부 연방을 독립 국가로 인정하게 하려 했었다. (그렇게 되는) 대신에 기꺼이 싸우려는 북부 연방의 의지는 강해졌고 남북 연방의 의지는 강해졌고, 남부 연방은 외국의 원조를 받을 수 있는 마지막 기회를 날려버렸다.

이종현T의 독해 Point!

A는 앞과 결과가 반대이므로 반박 시작점, B는 앞에서 하지 못한 목표(유럽 설득)를 대신한 결과이므로 'Instead'로 정답은 ①번이다.

2~3. 연구가들은 왕따에 대한 단일한 정의가 존재하지 않기 때문에, 왕따가 얼마나 흔하게 일어나는가를 측정하는 데 어려움을 겪고 있다. 왕따는 언어적인 면에 국한되는가, 아니면 신체적 행위가 있어야 하는가? 만약 당신이 교정에서 조롱을 듣고 그것을 무시하는 법을 알고 있다면, 당신은 괴롭힘을 당한 것인가, 아니면 다지 기분이 나쁜 것인가? 그것이 왕따로 간주되려면 반복적인 행위여야 하는가, 아니면 단 한 번만 발생해도 가능한가? 그것은 전체 학급을 혼란스럽게 하는가, 아니면 단지 한 두 명의 아이에게만 악영향을 미치는가? 이 모든 것들이 왕따를 연구하고 예방법을 만드는 사람들에게 명백하지 않은 것들이다. 대부분의 주의 법은 하나의 괴롭힘과 관련된 행위가 왕따로 간주되기 위해 필요로 되는 정확한 동기와 결과에 대하여 서로 다른 입장을 보인다. 열두 살 먹은 소년이 다른 아이를 조롱한다 해도, 대부분의 주법은 — 피해자가 (적어도 심리적인) 상처를 받았다는 — 명확한 피해와 입증 가능한 의도가 없다면, 그것을 왕따라고 부르지 않는다. 다시 말해서, 다른 아이를 괴롭히는 아이가 (진정으로) 다른 이를 괴롭히는 아이가 되기 위해서는, 그가 단지 남의 기분을 헤아릴 줄 모르는 둔감한 아이였을 수는 없다. 그는 그의 급우를 다치게 하기를 원했어야 한다.

이종현T의 독해 Point!

2.③ 'because' 뒤 원인 자리이고, 다양한 질문이 나오는 결과의 원인이 '정의가 없다'이므로 A는 원인 → 결과 구조로 ③번이 답이다.

3.① B는 그 정의 조건을 풀어쓰는 재진술이므로 ①번이 답이다.

4.③ 20여년의 전쟁을 겪은 아프가니스탄을 똑바로 되돌려 놓기 위해 2001년 이후 진행된 7년간의 전투에서 그 나라의 역사적 유적지들은 방치되어 왔다. 그곳의 고대 유산들은 발흐(Balkh, 아프가니스탄 북부의 도시, 고대 Bactria 왕국의 수도)를 폐허로 만들었던 1220년 칭기스칸의 약탈과 다름없는 만연한 약탈의 희생물이 되었다. 조직범죄 규모로, 공인되지 않은 발굴들이 전문적인 폭력단체들에 의해 자행되고 있는데 국제골동품 암시장과 연계된 지방 반군 지도자들과 심지어는 정부 관료들이 그들을 후원하고 있다. 이런 불법적인 거래 규모에 대한 추정치는 편차가 크지만, 정부 당국에 의하면 40억 달러에 달한다고 하며, 이는 대략 그 나라의 마약거래 규모와 맞먹는 것이다. 이러한 현실은 중앙아시아의 문명의 발달에서 그 나라가 가진 중요한 역할을 이제 막 이해하기 시작한 역사학자들과 고고학자에게 아픔을 준다. 20세기 중반 꽃피기 시작한 아프가니스탄에서의 고고학 연구는 상상조차 할 수 없을 만큼 엄청난 가치를 지닌 보물들을 발굴해냈다. 뿐만 아니라 이러한 발굴들은 그 나라의 금광열을 불러 일으켰으며 자유 계약자로 일하는 수백 명의 '고고학자들'로 하여금 그들 자신의 보물들을 찾아 땅을 파게 만들었는데, (그 보물들의) 암시장에서의 가치가 한 농부의 연간 수입을 훨씬 넘어 섰다. 그러다가, 1797년 시작된 전쟁으로 말미암아 취약했던 정부차원의 보호가 사라지면서, 수천 점에 달하는 돈으로 따질 수 없는 귀중한 문화유물들이 감쪽같이 나라밖으로 사라졌다. 그러나 지금까지 아프가니스탄의 문화유산에 대한 가장 파괴적인 약탈이 걷잡을 수 없게 된 때는 2001년 12월 탈레반 정권의 붕괴와 잇따른 권력의 공백 시기였다. 얄궂게도 빈곤과 전쟁이 유적지들을 안전하게 지켜주었다. 전쟁의 시기에 시민들은 집을 떠나기를 두려워했고 지뢰에 대한 두려움 때문에 많은 유물이 도굴되지 않았다. 전국적으로 벌어진 대대적인 지뢰 제거 활동이 성과를 거두면서, 도굴꾼들은 오랫동안 보존돼 있던 유적지로 돌아오고 있으며, 심지어 새로운 유적지를 발견하고 있기까지 하다.

이종현T의 독해 Point!

전쟁이 유산을 없어지게 했다는 얘기가 앞 얘기이고, 뒤에는 전쟁이 유산을 지켰다는 얘기이므로 역설이 된다. 따라서 정답은 ③번이다.

5.① 은행은 어떻게 이익을 올리는가? 금융 중개기관으로서 은행은 저축하는 사람들에게 지급되는 이자율과 대출에 부과되는 이자율 사이의 차이로 그들이 영업하는 데 충분한 돈을 번다. 고객들이 저축 계좌에 예금을 하면, 고객들은 원금에 대한 이자를 번다. 마찬가지로, 고객들이 대출을 받으면 고객들은 원금에 대한 이자를 지불한다. 예금자에게 주어지는 이자율보다 대출자에게 조금 더 높은 이자율을 부과함으로써 은행은 그 비용을 충당할 수 있다.

이종현T의 독해 Point!

앞 문장은 예금자가 이자를 받고, 뒷 문장은 대출자가 이자를 내는 '같은 구조 반복'이므로 빈칸과 같은 논리의 예시/비교 유지로 정답은 ①번이다.

6.② 청년들은 우리 경제와 사회의 근간을 이루는 자산이다. 유럽 통계청에 따르면, 유럽에 있는 15~29세 청년의 수는 9,400만 명이 넘으며, 그 가운데 15~24세가 6천만 명이 넘고, 25~29세가 3,300만 명이 넘는다. 이것은 사회에 엄청난 자원이 된다. 그러나 만약 국가가 청년들이 가진 잠재력을 완전히 이용하길 원한다면, 그들은 고용하여 생산에 이바지할 수 있게 해야 하고 사회 속으로 통합시켜야 한다. 현재, EU 회원국 대부분에는 청년들을 교육 시스템과 노동시장으로 흡수하고 통합하는 문제가 점점 크게 대두하고 있다. 우리 사회가 청년이라는 배당금으로부터 완전히 이익을 얻고 있는 것은 아니지만, 노동시장으로 부터의 이탈은 청년들 개개인에게도 심각한 영향을 미친다. 이러한 이유로, 특히 인구구성비율이 변하고 인구가 고령화되고 있는 상황에서 지속가능한 경제 · 사회 발전을 위해서는 청년 고용이 대단히 중요하다. 글로벌 경제위기 동안 청년들이 가장 큰 대가를 치렀기 때문에, 그들을 노동시장과 교육 시스템 속으로 통합하는 것이 시급하다는 인식이 새롭게 나타나고 있다. 이 문제를 성공적으로 해결하는 것은 더 나은 삶에 대한 청년들의 열망을 충족시키는 문제일 뿐만 아니라, 전반적으로 사회복지를 향상시키는 데도 반드시 필요하다.
청년들이 노동시장에서 이탈하는 문제는 "베이비 붐 세대"의 핵심이 고용 시장에 합류한 1980년대에 정책토론의 대상이 되었다. 이것은 그 후로 항상 가장 중요한 의제로 다루어져 왔는데, 이는 당시에 청년들에게서 부정적인 성향이 발견되었고, 이것이 오늘날에도 계속되고 있기 때문이다. 이 문제는 설명하기가 쉽지 않다. 더 나이 든 노동자와 비교해서 청년들이 노동시장에서 경쟁력을 갖게 만드는 것은 동기 부여가 높고 일에 신선한 아이디어와 통찰력을 제공할 수 있는 잠재력이다. 반면에, 그들의 경험 부족과 그들의 직업 지향성(적성)을 실험하려는 성향이 그들에게 불리하게 작용할 수 있다.

이종현T의 독해 Point!

문제점과 해결책으로 이어지므로 정답은 ②번이다.

7.⑤ 일반적으로 사람들은 화를 내는 것이 틀림없이 심장에 해로울 것이라 생각한다. 2000년에 노스캐롤라이나대학교에서 실시한 한 연구에서 13,000명의 환자들은 자신들이 화를 내는 경향을 평가하는 설문지를 작성했고, 몇 년 후에 추가 조사를 받았다. 그들의 혈압은 분명 정상이었지만, 자주 화를 낸다고 말했던 사람들은 흡연, 당뇨병, 체중 등의 요인을 참작하더라도 나머지 사람들보다 그 몇 년 동안에 심장마비에 걸릴 확률이 3배 더 높았다. 이와 마찬가지로, 이스트 런던대학교의 마크 맥더모트(Mark McDermott)는 화를 표출하는 사람들이 소리 지르는 것을 참는 사람들보다 심장병에 더 많이 걸린다는 사실을 밝혀냈다.

이종현T의 독해 Point!

앞의 연구 결과와 동일한 결론을 다른 연구자가 반복 제시하므로 '같은 논리 반복' 구조 → 정답은 ⑤번이다.

8.② 침입자가 전산망을 뚫고 나서 침입당한 사실을 그 전산망의 주인이 알아채는 데에는 평균 205일이 걸린다. 사이버 보안 업계가 말하고 있는 대부분의 통계수치, 가령 '9천만 건의 사이버 공격으로 인해 전 세계 경제가 입는 피해규모가 연간 5,750억 달러에 이르는 것으로 추정된다'는 말과 마찬가지로, 그것(205일이라는 것) 또한 어림짐작에 지나지 않는다. 그러나 범죄자들과 사이버상의 장난꾸러기들이 컴퓨터와 전산망을 공격함으로써 많은 이득을 보고 있다는 점과 해결방법을 제공하는 기업들이 고액의 수수료를 청구하고 있다는 점은 분명한 사실이다.

이종현T의 독해 Point!

앞에서 수치를 '추정치에 불과하다'고 깎아내리고, 뒤에서는 실제 해커 활동의 심각성을 보여주므로 반박 구조 → 정답은 ②번이다.

9.① 최근에 기억나는 그 어떤 것보다 이주민 문제가 유럽의 미래에 더 심각한 위협이 되고 있는데, 왜냐하면 그 문제는 중앙은행의 약속이나 다른 누군가의 현금 투입으로 해결될 수 있는 것이 아니기 때문이다. 이것은 유럽의 정체성에 대한 문제이고 그것(유럽의 정체성)이 한 세대 전에 유럽의 유권자들에게 가치 있었던 만큼 현재의 유권자들에게 가치 있는가에 관한 문제이다. 그러는 동안 내내 난민들은 계속 들어올 것이며, 그로 인해 유럽 정부들이 난민들을 받아들이는 희생을 하기는 더 어려워질 것이다.

이종현T의 독해 Point!

앞에서는 유럽이 정체성을 논의하는 동안, 실제로는 난민이 계속 오고 있었다는 동시 진행의 반어적 강조 구조 → 정답은 ①번이다.

10.① 성모 마리아에게 중보기도를 드리는 것과 마리아에게 헌신하는 것은 전 세계적인 현상이다. 고난과 희생뿐만 아니라 어머니의 사랑에 대한 보편적 상징이 된 마리아는 종종 의미를 찾고자 하는 우리의 갈망에 대한 기준이며, 공식적인 교회의 가르침보다 더 초자연적 신에게 가까이하기 쉬운 연결고리이다. 마리아의 두루마기는 안전과 보호를 모두 제공해준다. 언젠가 마리아가 본인에게 어떤 의미인가라는 질문을 받았을 때, 프란치스코(Francis) 교황은 "마리아는 저의 어머니입니다."라고 대답했다.
성모 발현, 즉 외딴 지역이나 분쟁으로 황폐해진 지역에 살고 있는 매우 가난한 어린이들이 종종 경험한 환상들로 인해 마리아는 더 많은 신비와 (영적) 기운을 가지게 되었다. 또한 아이들이 자신들이 한 이야 기에 흔들림이 없는(확신에 차 있는) 경우에는 ― 특히 그 이야기들에 태양들이 돌고 샘물이 솟아오르는 것과 같이 설명할 수 없는 '징후'가 동반되는 경우에는 ― 마리아에 대한 경이로움이 더 커진다.
마리아는 어느 곳에나 있다. 금잔화는 마리아에서 이름을 따온 것이다. 아베마리아 패스는 미식축구에서 패배를 모면하게 한다. 멕시코의 과달 루페(Guadalupe) 성모상은 지금껏 가장 많이 그려진 여성의 초상 가운데 하나이다. 마리아는 포르투갈의 파티마(Fatima)와 아일랜드의 녹크(Knock)와 같은 성지로 매년 수백만 명을 불러 모으고 있으며, 연간 수십억 달러를 벌어들이는 것으로 추정되는 종교관광여행을 지탱 하는 것과 동시에 수천 개의 일자리를 만들어내고 있다. 마리아는 시, 기도서, 음악뿐만 아니라 수많은 위대한 미술 작품과 건축물의 창조에 영감을 주었다. 기독교인들과 마찬가지로 무슬림들도 마리아를 모든 여성들 가운데 가장 성스러운 존재로 간주하고 있고, 마리아가 성경에 나오는 것보다 마리아의 이슬람교 이름인 '마리얌(Maryam)'이 코란에 더 자주 등장한다.
그러나 마리아의 삶에 대한 실마리는 찾기가 어렵다. 마리아를 연구하는 학자들은 얻고자 하는 것을 히브리어 성경, 1세기의 지중해 문서, 신약성경, 고고학 유적 등으로부터 취해야 한다. 밴더빌트(Vanderbilt) 대학교에서 신약성서와 유대교를 연구하고 있는 에이미 질 레빈 (Amy-Jill Levine) 교수는 성서로부터 마리아에 대해 알 수 있는 것이 너무나도 적기 때문에, "어떤 문화적 가치관을 가지고 있든 그것을 마리아에게 투영시킬 수 있습니다."라고 말한다. "마리아는 슬퍼하고 있는 어머니가 될 수도 있고. 젊은 처녀가 될 수도 있고, 여신과 같은 인물이 될 수도 있습니다. 예수가 이상적인 남성인 것과 마찬가지로, 마리아는 이상적인 여성인 것입니다."

이종현T의 독해 Point!

선지에 품사가 섞여 있으므로 품사자리에 맞게 맞춰주면 정답은 ①번이다.

MEMO

이것이 독해다 Part 2 복합유형 총정리

2025년 7월 10일 1판 1쇄 발행

저 자 이 종 현
발행인 남 승 우

발행처 도서출판 상尙학學당堂
주 소 서울특별시 동작구 사당로9가길 6
전 화 02) 595-1692~4
팩 스 02) 595-1394
이메일 shdbooks@naver.com
신 고 2-155호(1968.11.29.)

편 집 엄해숙
표 지 토틀컴

ISBN 978-89-6587-274-0 03740

정가 30,000원